WITHDRAWN

MILTON AND THE ENDS OF TIME

In *Milton and the Ends of Time*, a team of leading international scholars addresses Milton's treatment of millennial and apocalyptic ideas – topics of major importance in the religious and philosophical thought of his day. The subject has wide-ranging ramifications for the interpretation of Milton's poetry and prose, as his speculations on the ends of time played a vital part in shaping the Miltonic quest and vision. This collection revises current critical thinking about his eschatology by arguing that he expressed radical millenarian views after the Restoration and by demonstrating the pervasiveness of apocalyptic ideas in his thought. It provides a broad range of disciplinary and theoretical approaches, including perspectives on Milton's relationship to the visual arts, politics and theology, and science and comparative poetics. This book will be of interest to literary, religious, and political historians of the seventeenth century, as well as Milton specialists.

JULIET CUMMINS is Lecturer in English in the School of Humanities at the University of Western Sydney. She has published essays on literary and legal topics in various journals including *Milton Studies*.

MILTON AND
THE ENDS OF TIME

EDITED BY
JULIET CUMMINS

CAMBRIDGE
UNIVERSITY PRESS

PUBLISHED BY THE PRESS SYNDICATE OF THE UNIVERSITY OF CAMBRIDGE
The Pitt Building, Trumpington Street, Cambridge CB2 1RP, United Kingdom

CAMBRIDGE UNIVERSITY PRESS
The Edinburgh Building, Cambridge, CB2 2RU, UK
40 West 20th Street, New York, NY 10011-4211, USA
477 Williamstown Road, Port Melbourne, VIC 3207, Australia
Ruiz de Alarcón 13, 28014 Madrid, Spain
Dock House, The Waterfront, Cape Town 8001, South Africa

http://www.cambridge.org

© Cambridge University Press 2003

First published 2003

Printed in the United Kingdom at the University Press, Cambridge

Typeface Baskerville Monotype 11/12.5 pt   *System* LATEX 2$_\varepsilon$ [TB]

A catalogue record for this book is available from the British Library

ISBN 0 521 81665 3 hardback

Contents

PART II   APOCALYPSE

Acknowledgments

I would like to thank the contributors for their great cooperation and support in the process of creating this volume. I benefited from the expertise of Stephen Dobranski, who generously advised me in the early stages of constructing the collection. Claude Stulting, who was initially a co-editor of the volume, was a wonderful source of inspiration and ideas throughout; I regret that circumstances required him to withdraw from this role. Beverley Sherry was, as always, an acute critic of my work and a generous adviser, while Donna and Tony Gibbs made incisive comments about the Introduction. I am indebted to David Loewenstein for his scholarly advice and for his help in making the volume cohesive, and to Ray Ryan of Cambridge University Press for his support throughout the editorial process. Finally, I wish to thank my husband, Philip Cummins, who always brings me back from apocalypse into the folds of human history.

Illustrations

Contributors

JULIET CUMMINS, University of Western Sydney

KAREN L. EDWARDS, University of Exeter

WILLIAM B. HUNTER, University of Houston

SARAH HUTTON, Middlesex University

BARBARA K. LEWALSKI, Harvard University

DAVID LOEWENSTEIN, University of Wisconsin-Madison

CATHERINE GIMELLI MARTIN, University of Memphis

STELLA P. REVARD, Southern Illinois University

MALABIKA SARKAR, Jadavpur University

JOHN T. SHAWCROSS, University of Kentucky

BEVERLEY SHERRY, University of Sydney

KEN SIMPSON, University College of the Cariboo

CLAUDE N. STULTING, JR., Furman University

Abbreviations

CP   *Complete Prose Works of John Milton*, gen. ed. Don M. Wolfe,
       8 vols. (New Haven, 1953–82).
CW   *The Works of John Milton*, ed. Frank Allen Patterson, 18 vols.
       (New York, 1931–38).
PL   *Paradise Lost*
PR   *Paradise Regained*
SA   *Samson Agonistes*

References to the prose works are given in the form of a roman numeral
to indicate volume number, followed by arabic numerals to indicate page
numbers. References to *Paradise Lost* and *Paradise Regained* are in the form
of a Book number, followed by line numbers.

Introduction: "Those thoughts that wander through eternity"

Juliet Cummins

John Milton's intellectual and imaginative engagement with eschatological ideas is evident in his work from the beginning to the close of his career. Speculation about the end of time and the arrival of the great moment of the apocalypse was fueled by the momentous political and religious upheavals of his day and reached an extraordinary pitch of intensity in mid seventeenth-century England. In the Puritan parliament of 1654, Oliver Cromwell, having reminded his listeners of St. Paul's warning that "*In the last days perilous times should come,*" went on to say, "and surely it may be well feared these are our times."[1] Cromwell's words reflected a widespread view that the world was in decline, and that human history was in its "perilous" closing phases. Dating of biblical events and prophesies suggested to many that the Second Coming would occur in the 1650s or 1660s. Milton was at one with many others of his age in being intensely interested in the last things. Eschatological themes appear throughout his poetry and prose, from his youthful anticipation in the 1620s of "at last" when "our bliss / Full and perfect is" (Nativity Ode, ll. 165–66) to his assertion that Christ's "Kingdome is now at hand" in the 1640s (*Animadversions, CP* 1: 707) and his politically charged allusion in the early 1670s to that kingdom which "shall to pieces dash / All Monarchies besides throughout the world" (*PR* 4.149–50). The essays in this book provide new insights into Milton's lifelong preoccupation with the ends of time – with the Second Coming, the millennium, Judgment Day, the new heaven and earth, and the eternity which follows.

Milton's eschatology has received little attention in recent years, despite its importance in his work.[2] The Sixth International Milton Symposium, held in York in July 1999, took "Milton and the Millennium" as one of its themes, renewing interest in Milton's apocalypticism. This collection of essays emerges from the vigorous discussion at that Symposium about the significance of the millennium and the apocalypse in Milton's poetry and prose, and forms part of the recent reassessment of his political and religious radicalism.[3] Just over half the essays in this collection began as papers at the Symposium and have since been expanded and revised. Others represent responses to debate generated at the time. The international forum which provided the impetus for this book has stimulated interaction in the volume between scholars of different theoretical persuasions from the United States, the United Kingdom, Canada, India, and Australia. The contributors combine their various interests in theology, history, philosophy, authorship, science, politics, and aesthetics with a shared commitment to Milton studies to produce diverse perspectives upon the poet's vision of the ends of time.

The theme of Milton and the millennium prompts comparison between our own millennial moment at the turn of the twenty-first century and seventeenth-century speculation about a millennium which could begin at any time. The wild celebrations with fireworks and rejoicing around the globe which occurred on New Year's Eve 1999 were a far cry from the anxious expectations of religiously minded people in the seventeenth century. These contrasting approaches to the concept of a millennium convey much about the cultures of the respective eras. Our celebration of the dawn of a new millennium (inaccurate though the timing was), was an international, ostentatious, and technological occasion. Festivities for New Year's Eve in Sydney, Tokyo, Paris, London, New York, and other cities were beamed one by one on to television and computer screens across the world. Each city celebrated the moment differently, but each joined in a common recognition of a particular way of conceiving of and measuring time. The main anxieties surrounding the event concerned computer-systems failure, with surprisingly few predictions of the world's end. Despite the Christian significance of the date, its celebration appeared to be primarily secular. Globalization, multimedia, digitally governed systems, and secularization are defining elements of the contemporary world.

The disparity between our recent experience of the passing of a millennium and the seventeenth century's expectation of *the* millennium reveals the rapidity with which society has changed in the past few centuries. Three to four hundred years ago, the word "millennium" referred almost exclusively to John's vision of saints who "lived and reigned with Christ a thousand years" (Rev. 20:4). The orthodox, Augustinian interpretation of this verse is that the "thousand years" refers to the spiritual reign of Christ and his saints from the time of Christ's resurrection until the rising of Antichrist.[4] In the seventeenth century, however, there was a resurgence of the millenarian view that the verse was to be taken literally. Christ would either reign on earth with his saints for a thousand years, or would reign through them. Millenarianism was often generally associated with radical Puritanism, but beliefs about the imminence of the millennium, the people's role in bringing it about, and the nature of the kingdom which Christ might establish have political implications which provide an index of their precise historical moment. Many Parliamentarians during the Civil War identified themselves with the "saints" who would establish the conditions for Christ's kingdom on earth, Fifth Monarchists in the 1650s used Christ's imminent political utopia to justify revolutionary action against the Protectorate, and after the Restoration millenarianism could imply adherence to the Good Old Cause.[5] For this reason Milton's developing millenarian views over the course of these decades give some indication of his shifting positions in contemporary political contests.

The essays in the first part of the collection, "Millennium," provide a major revision of the traditional assessment of Milton's millenarianism. It has long been recognized that Milton held millenarian ideas in the 1640s and 1650s, but it has generally been thought that these diminished with the failure of the Puritan cause. Michael Fixler thought that Milton "progressively experienced" a reaction "to the millenarian claims of the saints," Austin C. Dobbins maintained that in *Paradise Lost* "Milton rejected the millennial position" and C. A. Patrides agreed.[6] These views are challenged in diverse ways in Part I of the collection.

In the first chapter in this book, Barbara Lewalski demonstrates that Milton appealed to the idea of the millennium throughout his career in order to urge personal, ecclesiastical, social, and political reformation. Examining Milton's prose and major poetry, she shows that Milton used his expectation of the millennium to draw support for "eradicating bishops, idolatry and kingship, disestablishing the church, and promoting religious and intellectual liberty." She argues that even in Milton's last poems, *Paradise Regained* and *Samson Agonistes*, he emphasizes the need to prepare for the millennium, while at the same time accepting that it may not be imminent.

Sarah Hutton's chapter places Milton's millenarian ideas within the context of those of his contemporaries at Christ's College, Joseph Mede and Henry More. Hutton contends that Milton follows Mede in the unusual identification of the Last Judgment with the millennium. She shows that this position is expressed in *De Doctrina Christiana*, and argues that Milton uses it in *Paradise Lost* implicitly to affirm a belief in the millennium.

Stella Revard's chapter offers the first comprehensive examination of Milton's millenarianism in the context of contemporary political, religious, and millenarian thought. Revard argues that Milton's writings express millenarian views throughout his career, and focuses particularly upon his epics *Paradise Lost* and *Paradise Regained*, which have previously been characterized as relatively quietist in this respect. By showing that the epics covertly express millenarian sentiments she demonstrates the poet's continuing engagement with radical politics and religion at the time of his major poems.

The following chapter, by Malabika Sarkar, considers Milton's post-Restoration responses to the defeat of his early expectation that the republican government would usher in the millennium. Sarkar argues that, while Milton may have retained faith in the millennium after the Restoration, astronomical images in *Paradise Lost* reveal him to be questioning and analyzing the reasons for its failure to materialize in the immediate present. She contends that Milton's Satan identifies himself with stars and comets which had been regarded as signs of Christ's imminent return earlier in the seventeenth century. Milton's association of these signs with Satan rather than the Second Coming "is a fierce indictment of the false hopes raised in the century of the immediate advent of the promised millennium and the misreadings of celestial signs that fueled such hopes."

The essays of William Hunter and John Shawcross provide divergent views of the significance of the millennium in *De Doctrina Christiana*, and the implications this has for the authorship of the treatise. Hunter advances his argument that Milton is not the author of *De Doctrina* by contrasting its scant treatment of the millennium with Milton's discussion of it in his political pamphlets. The treatise appears to Hunter to be inconsistent with Milton's authorship because it largely ignores the millennium and collapses it into the Last Judgment in accordance with a Continental tradition. Hunter also challenges the view, advanced by others in Part I, that Milton expressed millenarian views before writing *Lycidas* (1637) or in his epic poetry after *The Readie and Easie Way* (1660).

John Shawcross responds by arguing that there is nothing about the treatment of the millennium in *De Doctrina Christiana* which suggests it is not written by John Milton. He points out that the millennium plays only a small role in the scriptural account of the apocalypse and is inconsistent with other aspects of Revelation, a good reason why it is not a focus of a treatise concerned with Christian doctrine. The treatise, like many of Milton's other works, expresses a belief that Christ will reign for a thousand years. While Hunter sees *De Doctrina*'s lack of overt concern with the political aspects of millenarianism as an indication that it was not written by Milton, Shawcross argues that this lack of concern is a feature of the treatise's genre.

Part II of the collection, "Apocalypse," is concerned generally with the apocalypse and with Milton's conception of the relationship between time and eternity in the later poems. While the two are traditionally conceived of as distinct, Milton's Raphael instructs Adam that time is "in Eternitie" (*PL* 5.581). Milton also conflates different historical periods with each other in his epic, as if time has a unity which is not superficially apparent. In Milton's complex depictions of history, beginnings anticipate endings and endings infiltrate middles: significantly, Eden, the "paradise lost," is a shadow of the last paradise which will obtain when earth becomes heaven and heaven earth.[7] The essays in this part examine Milton's poetic portrayal of time and the apocalypse in the contexts of aesthetics, comparative poetics, philosophy, politics, theology, and science.

Illustrations become a significant component of the study in the first essay in Part II, where Beverley Sherry examines the imagery associated with time and eternity in *Paradise Lost*, and the nineteenth-century artist John Martin's apocalyptic portrayal of such images. Sherry sees light and darkness as, paradoxically, at once temporal and eternal in Milton's epic and maintains that Martin's mezzotints capture this paradox. They show light and darkness operating in time, but the "images of ever receding light and ever deepening darkness" also evoke "dimensions of timelessness which correspond to the apocalyptic perspectives of *Paradise Lost*."

Catherine Gimelli Martin also explores the poetic figuration of time, comparing the enclosed gardens of Milton and Marvell in order to explore their divergent spatial, temporal, and spiritual orientations. Marvell's enclosed gardens tend to be static, remote retreats where "an active God" supplies the wants of "his passive people," while Milton's Eden is active, mutable and profoundly temporal, just as his eternity comprehends time and change. Martin shows that the dualist sense of time which shapes the enclosed gardens in Marvell's poetry gives rise to a rupture between human history and the apocalypse. On the other hand, the monism underlying Milton's portrayal of Eden supports a conception of divine providence as immanent and progressive, and history and the apocalypse as belonging to a continuum.

My chapter then extends Martin's focus on Milton's monistic portrayal of the relationship between time and eternity in *Paradise Lost* by examining apocalyptic transformations in the poem. I argue that Milton indicates that the conversion of this world to the "New Heav'ns, new Earth" (12.549) will occur alchemically, existing matter being transmuted to a more refined state. There are also indications in the poem that human beings will be materially transformed at the apocalypse, intensifying metamorphosis experienced in this world. Challenging the predominant critical view that the damned are either annihilated or reduced to the materials of chaos, I claim that Milton insists on their eternal existence and ongoing material and spiritual degradation.

Claude Stulting contests the view that *Paradise Lost* is consistently monistic, maintaining that there is a radical discontinuity between the prelapsarian and postlapsarian states of humankind. Before the Fall God is immanent in nature and nature is the means by which Adam and Eve achieve communion with God. However, according to Stulting, in the postlapsarian sections of *Paradise Lost* Adam's and Eve's relationship with God is no longer grounded in the materiality of the created order, but becomes interiorized and situated in history. Milton's new heaven and earth are for Stulting "discontinuous with the original," and the material world of nature remains outside the realms of redemption.

The next chapter turns from *Paradise Lost* to *Paradise Regained* and its engagement with contemporary politics and theology. Ken Simpson argues that Milton provides a critique of the English Reformation in the short epic through scriptural and astrological references to Revelation. He refers to a long line of commentary associating Satan's temptations of Jesus with the trials of the church, and maintains that Milton represents the Anglican church's persecution of dissenters (who belong to the "true," spiritual church) in Satan's persecution of Jesus. Complementing Sarkar's discussion of the association between Satan, comets and false prophesies in *Paradise Lost*, Simpson contends that in *Paradise Regained* Milton has Jesus reject "false portents" (4.491) such as comets because they are sent from Satan. He suggests that the description of Satan as a falling "Autumnal Star" (4.619) or comet in *Paradise Regained* anticipates at once his apocalyptic doom and the fall of the Stuart regime.

The final chapter in this part turns to *Samson Agonistes* and its dramatization of the believer's experience of waiting for revelation and release from worldly hardships. Whereas Samson has traditionally been seen as a type of Christ, Karen Edwards shows that he is "the type of those born afterward who wait, in darkness, for judgment, for apocalypse, for the coming of the Lamb." This reading intensifies Samson's moral and spiritual ambivalence because he ultimately eschews the attitude of patient waiting which Milton extols elsewhere as a means of serving God. The powerful, apocalyptic ending of the poem is thus one of "perfect ambiguity." The play leaves unresolved the question of whether the "rouzing motions" which motivate Samson to bring down the "two massie Pillars" (ll. 1382, 1648) stem from despair or have their source in divine inspiration. Interpretive ambiguity is not only critical to Milton's portrayal of Samson; it is also a condition of all those who wait for revelation, for the ends of time.

The wide range of responses to Milton's eschatology in this book reflects the variety of perspectives which the contributors bring to bear on Milton's work, but it also registers the contradictions and indeterminacies in Milton's representations of the last things. David Loewenstein's Afterword concludes the collection by noting connections between a number of the key essays while also making an argument of its own about the "multiple, divergent and indeed sometimes conflicting visions of the apocalypse and the millennium" in Milton's great poems. Loewenstein contrasts the terrifying apocalyptic destruction of *Samson Agonistes* with Milton's endorsement in *Paradise Regained* of a patient stance of waiting for the millennium. These alternative visionary responses, he argues, are not necessarily incompatible: they both provide a means of imagining the destruction of the Restoration church and state, and the substitution of Christ's kingdom in which God's saints will reign.

The eschatologies discussed in this book may seem largely foreign to twenty-first-century experiences – of historical rather than immediate significance. However, the human concern with endings – and so with structures of meaning – has not changed. The relationship between beginnings, middles, and endings affects our sense of time and our interpretation of meaning and remains fascinating, despite the recent philosophical interrogation of such concepts. While postmodernity has substituted *"Telos* [which] is totally open, is opening itself*"* for an expectation of closure,[8] it cannot entirely do away with the conception of structure which it deconstructs. Similarly, contemporary science retains some links with traditional eschatologies, in that it still entertains the possibility that the end will consist in a return to origins. A leading theory conceives of the end of the universe as a "big crunch" which "would be rather like the big bang that began the universe," a bleak and impersonal version of the Christian replacement of an original with an ultimate paradise.[9] In contemporary culture mystical and spiritual explanations of the end of time have greater credibility. It may no longer be common to expect the Word to appear in the clouds on a white horse, but the promise of spiritual restoration lingers.[10] The collective ideas upon which culture is built, like Belial's thoughts, "wander through eternity" (*PL* 2.148). Shadows of early modern apocalypticism inform our thinking, just as our postmodern society emerges from the lost paradise of Milton's.

NOTES

The title of the introduction comes from Belial's speech in *Paradise Lost* 2.148. Citations of Milton's poetry are from *The Riverside Milton*, ed. Roy Flannagan (Boston, 1998) and references appear in parentheses through the text.

1. Speech in the Painted Chamber to the Parliament, 4 September 1654, in Ivan Roots (ed.), *Speeches of Oliver Cromwell* (London, 1989), p. 31, citing 2 Tim. 3:1 (original italics).

2. The main works on Milton and eschatological matters are several decades old and more confined in their focus than that of this book. See Michael Fixler, *Milton and the Kingdoms of God* (London and Evanston, 1964); Leland Ryken, *The Apocalyptic Vision in Paradise Lost* (Ithaca, 1970); and Austin C. Dobbins, *Milton and the Book of Revelation: The Heavenly Cycle* (University, Alabama, 1975). There have been various articles and book chapters in the 1980s and 1990s on Milton's eschatology, but no full-length studies have been published. The most important of these include Paul Rovang's "Milton's War in Heaven as Apocalyptic Drama: 'Thy Foes Justly Hast in Derision,'" *Milton Quarterly* 28 (1994), pp. 28–35; Samuel Smith's "'Christ's Victorie Over the Dragon': The Apocalypse in *Paradise Regained*," *Milton Studies* 29 (1993), pp. 59–82; the first chapter of David Loewenstein's *Milton and the Drama of History: Historical Vision, Iconoclasm, and the Literary Imagination* (Cambridge, 1990), which examines the relation between "radical millennial thought" and Milton's "sense of history in the early polemics" (pp. 8–9); and Thomas Amorose's "Milton the Apocalyptic Historian: Competing Genres in *Paradise Lost*, Books XI–XII," *Milton Studies* 17 (1983), pp. 141–62. For seventeenth-century eschatology generally, see Richard H. Popkin (ed.), *Millenarianism and Messianism in English Literature and Thought: 1650–1800* (Leiden, 1988); Richard W. Cogley, "Seventeenth-Century English Millenarianism," *Religion* (1987), pp. 379–96; Paul Christianson, *Reformers and Babylon: English Apocalyptic Visions From the Reformation to the Eve of the Civil War* (Toronto, 1978); B. S. Capp, *The Fifth Monarchy Men: A Study in Seventeenth-Century English Millenarianism* (London, 1972); and Bryan W. Ball, *A Great Expectation: Eschatological Thought in English Protestantism to 1660* (Leiden, 1975).

3. See, for example, Stephen B. Dobranski and John P. Rumrich, *Milton and Heresy* (Cambridge, 1998), and David Loewenstein, *Representing Revolution in Milton and his Contemporaries: Religion, Politics, and Polemics in Radical Puritanism* (Cambridge, 2001).

4. See Capp, *The Fifth Monarchy Men*, p. 23; Ball, *A Great Expectation*, pp. 161–62; and Stella Revard's chapter in this book, p. 42.

5. See Capp, *The Fifth Monarchy Men*, pp. 35–45, 59; Christopher Hill, *The Experience of Defeat: Milton and Some Contemporaries* (London, 1984), pp. 50–62, 180–81; and Stella Revard's chapter in this book, pp. 56–57.

6. Fixler, *Milton and the Kingdoms of God*, p. 219; Dobbins, *Milton and the Book of Revelation*, p. 70; C. A. Patrides, "'Something like Prophetick strain': apocalyptic configurations in Milton," in C. A. Patrides and Joseph Wittreich (eds.), *The Apocalypse in English Thought and Literature: Patterns, Antecedents, and Repercussions* (Manchester, 1984), pp. 207–37, especially pp. 226–27.

7. See Helen Wilcox, "'Is this the end of this new glorious world?': *Paradise Lost* and the beginning of the end," *Essays and Studies* 48 (1995), pp. 1–15.

8. Jacques Derrida, *Writing and Difference* (Chicago, 1978), p. 167.

9. Stephen Hawking, *Black Holes and Baby Universes and Other Essays* (London, 1993), p. 146.

10. See Paul Boyer, *When Time Shall Be No More: Prophecy Belief in Modern American Culture* (Cambridge, Mass., 1992). Boyer cites the findings of a 1983 Gallup poll that 62 percent of Americans believed that Jesus would come to earth again (p. 2) and argues that at the beginning of the 1990s a "new scenario, supplementing age-old themes with warnings of ecological catastrophe and visions of a globe restored to Edenic purity, appears capable of sustaining prophecy belief far into the twenty-first century" (p. 337).

Millennium

Milton and the millennium

Barbara K. Lewalski

John Milton lived in a milieu rife with calculations about the date and signs of the endtimes, and with speculation that the Second Coming of Christ to rule the world with his saints was on – or just over – the horizon. The apocalyptic events inaugurating that thousand-year reign according to seventeenth-century millenarians were much more awesome than those foreseen (wrongly as it happened) for Y2K. Milton's culture expected rampant wickedness and apostasy, the four horsemen of the Apocalypse – war, pestilence, famine, and death – wreaking universal havoc, fearsome battles between the Saints and Antichrist leading to Armageddon, and Christ coming in terrible majesty to judge the world. But for the saints the millennium would constitute a new Golden Age, with nature restored and the social and political order perfected.

At Christ's College, Cambridge, Milton would have had some contact with the famous exegete of the Apocalypse, Joseph Mede, who was a prominent Fellow of the college, and with Mede's elaborate system of synchronizing contemporary history with the Book of Revelation, as well as with the prophecies in Daniel, Isaiah, Ezekiel, and elsewhere. That system was spelled out in his highly influential treatise, *Clavis Apocalyptica*, first published in 1627 while Milton was in residence at Christ's, later republished in Latin and translated into English as *The Key of the Revelation* in 1643.[1] During the English Revolution the widespread belief that the world was in the last age intensified at certain signal moments of revolutionary change: the casting out of the bishops root and branch, the army of God winning definitive battles against the royalist armies, the execution of a king seen to be in league with Antichrist, and the founding of a republic. Some millenarians undertook precise calculations of the date when Christ would begin his reign on earth. William Burden was one of several who arrived at the date 1666.[2] Nathanael Homes in *Resurrection Revealed* (1654) worked out the complicated mathematical schemes by which various exegetes of the Book of Revelation arrived at their dates: for Elias Reusner the millennium would begin around 1670, for Ephraim Huet around 1662, for Thomas Brightman around 1680.[3] Radical Fifth Monarchists, making much of the prophecies of the four beasts in Daniel (Dan. 7:22, 26) and the image destroyed by a stone "cut out without hands" (Dan. 2:31–35) – both said to represent the four great empires of history – looked to institute the rule of the saints immediately and probably by force. In *A Brief Description of the Fifth Monarchy* (1653), William Aspinwall wrote that the saints' reign began with the execution of Charles I: "It is said, *That judgment was given to the saints, and they executed judgment on the little horne* [of the fourth beast], Dan. 7.22, 26, which was fulfilled 1648."[4]

In 1653 these groups supposed the Barebones Parliament would install the reign of the saints, but when it relinquished power to Cromwell after a session of barely three months many of them substituted Cromwell for Charles I, as the "little horn" of the fourth beast, usurping the place of King Jesus. In 1657 the Fifth Monarchist Thomas Venner planned an aborted uprising against Cromwell and in 1661 he mounted one (with about forty men) against the restored Charles II. After the Restoration millennial fervor receded, but the series of calamities in 1665–66 – the Dutch War, the Great Plague, and the Great Fire – rekindled it, as descriptions of those events invited association of them with the woes expected at the apocalypse. The Quaker D. Roe makes the connection explicit:

O England, England, what Lamentation may be taken up for thee, for the great calamity that is coming upon thee, and which is already begun in thee, which thou canst not escape … yea the viols of the Wrath of God is pouring upon the nations, and the destroying Angel is gone forth, for the Harvest is ripe, and the Lord is sending forth his Angels, saying, *Thrust in your sickles, for wickedness is grown up to full height* … Thus sayeth the Lord, *I will terribly shake the Nations, and I will bring down the mighty from off their Seats, and I will overturn, overturn, all, until he comes to reign whose right it is, and then shall there be rulers as at the first, and Judges as at the beginning*; … yea, the time is near at hand in which the Lord this work to pass will bring.[5]

An anonymous pamphlet published in 1665 predicted "the Downefall of Babylon in [16]66," to be followed immediately by the return of the ten lost tribes to Jerusalem and the conversion of the Jews; the immediate precursor of the millennium, the preaching of the Gospel "throughout the whole World" would be achieved by 1672.[6]

From early to late, the millennium is important for both the argument and the imaginative vision of Milton's poetry and prose. In *De Doctrina*

Christiana, in a section probably written early and later revised, Milton collects the relevant scripture texts and from them outlines a scenario very like Mede's, in which Christ's judgment of the world is coextensive with his thousand-year reign on earth with his saints; then Christ will defeat Satan in a final fierce battle and the rebel angels and all humankind will be judged – each (Milton underscores) "according to the light which he has received" (*CP* vi: 625).[7] But it is instructive to recognize what Milton does *not* do with this narrative. Neither here nor elsewhere does he offer an exegesis of the symbols in the text of Revelation. He proposes no direct historical equivalents for the seven heads and ten horns of the beast, nor for the seven vials and the seven trumpets. He never refers to specific contemporary events – wars, plagues, fires, apostasies, blasphemies – as signs of impending apocalypse. And he makes no mathematical calculations about dates and times. Nor does he ever look to the Book of Revelation for a model of or sanction for government by the saints now. Arminian that he was, Milton did not suppose that the saints could be identified with any certainty, and in any case, he always supposed that it is for Christ to install their rule, not for them to preempt it. When reformation seemed to be going well, he imagined that the millennium might be close at hand, and when it was in difficulties he deduced, as he declared in what is probably a late addition in *De Doctrina*, that Christ "will be slow to come" (*CP* vi: 618). The reason, he explains, is that the Lord gives more time because he is longsuffering, "not willing that any should perish, but that all should come to repentance" (2 Pet. 3:9).[8]

But while changing political circumstances led Milton to adjust his views as to the timing of the millennium, he appealed from beginning to end to the idea of the millennium to urge personal, ecclesiastical, social, and political reformation, and also certain kinds of political action as preparation for that eventuality. The projected downfall of all tyrants at the millennium offered support to his other arguments from scripture and natural law for eradicating bishops, idolatry and kingship, disestablishing the church, and promoting religious and intellectual liberty. And from 1648 on the projected millenarian reign of Christ as the only rightful earthly king regularly served Milton as an argument for republican government. His core belief, sometimes intimated, sometimes stated explicitly, is that the millennium will come when the English (and presumably others) have become virtuous and free, rejecting all the forces that promote servility, be they popes or bishops or kings or any other such idols.

In 1629, two years after Mede's *Clavis Apocalyptica* predicted a millennium shortly to come, Milton's Nativity Ode critiques that mindset. The poet at age twenty-one portrays awestruck Nature responding to Christ's first coming as if it were his second, and depicts himself as similarly misled, as his enraptured imagination evokes the music of the angelic choirs and the music of the spheres and is led by that music to leap forward to the millennial golden age. But then he reproves such readiness to expect the millennium soon, abruptly recalling himself to the nativity moment – "But wisest Fate says no" (l. 154) – to take account of all the history that must transpire before the moment when "our bliss / Full and perfect is" (ll. 165–66).[9] The final section of the poem treats that period, the kingdom of grace inaugurated at the Nativity, when the "old Dragon" is partly restrained in his powers and all the pagan idols begin to flee from all their shrines. Critics used to think this catalogue much too long (it comprises almost a third of the poem) but Milton intends to suggest, by a kind of formal mimesis, the long and difficult process that must precede the millennium: ridding humankind of all its idols, lovely as well as hideous. The passage has contemporary reference to the "popish" idolatry in the English church and its liturgy being promoted by the newly elevated bishop of London, William Laud. It may also comment, as Stella Revard proposes, on the royal birth expected by Queen Henrietta Maria in a few months' time, already being heralded, through allusions to Virgil's Fourth Eclogue, as an event to inaugurate a Stuart golden age.[10] Milton's Nativity poem insists that the divine child, not the royal one, foreshadows the millennial golden age, but that the millennium can arrive only when idols old and new have been cast out.

In *Lycidas* (1637) Milton devises for St. Peter a fierce jeremiad castigating the Laudian church and clergy. His scornful paradox, "Blind mouthes" (l. 119), brilliantly exposes the ignorance, ambition, and greediness of those bad shepherds who seek only to feed their own bellies, leaving the hungry sheep "swoln with wind" (l. 126) produced by Laudian ceremony and conformity, and subject to the ravages of the Roman Catholic "grim Woolf" (l. 128) raging freely in the Caroline court, especially among the queen's ladies. St. Peter's invective, voicing God's wrath, is not explicitly apocalyptic, but that final divine retribution is one reference point for the formidable if ambiguous "two-handed engine" that stands ready "at the door" to smite the guilty and cleanse the church (ll. 130–31).

In 1641 Milton was at times caught up in the widespread expectation that the millennium might soon begin, and indicated as much by occasional bursts of prophetic and poetic fervor. But his emphasis was always on the duty of the English nation and people to prepare for that event by reforming the church. His first antiprelatical tract, *Of Reformation*, ends with a prophecy that constructs the king, in his role as head of church and state, as simply a placeholder for Christ, the "Eternall and shortly-expected" Messiah King (*CP* 1: 616). In that millennium Milton imagines a fierce vengeance on the vaunting prelates and their supporters, upon whom the other damned will exercise a "*Raving* and *Bestiall Tyranny* over them as their *Slaves* and *Negro's*" (*CP* 1: 617). He cries out in prophetic lamentation and prayer as he considers the immense obstacles to the church's reformation, but then he imagines himself in a bardic role, celebrating and helping to create a reformed English society that will herald Christ's millennial kingdom, in which there will be no more earthly kings. On the verge of that millennium, the Miltonic bard will find his highest poetic subject:

Then amidst the *Hymns*, and *Halleluiahs* of *Saints* some one may perhaps bee heard offering at high *strains* in new and lofty *Measures* to sing and celebrate thy *divine Mercies*, and *marvelous Judgements* in this Land throughout all AGES; whereby this great and Warlike Nation instructed and inur'd to the fervent and continuall practice of *Truth* and *Righteousnesse*, and casting farre from her the *rags* of her old *vices* may presse on hard to that *high* and *happy* emulation to be found the *soberest, wisest*, and *most Christian People* at that day when thou the Eternall and shortly-expected King shalt open the Clouds to judge the severall Kingdomes of the World, and distributing *Nationall Honours* and *Rewards* to Religious and just *Common-wealths*, shalt put an end to all Earthly *Tyrannies*, proclaiming thy universal and milde *Monarchy* through Heaven and Earth. (*CP* 1: 616)

In *Animadversions* (also 1641) Milton again assumes a prophetic voice, offering a long, passionate, poetic prayer couched in imagery from Revelation for the full perfection of the church in the millennial kingdom, once more imagined as near at hand:

Who is there that cannot trace thee now in thy beamy walke through the midst of thy Sanctuary, amidst those golden *candlesticks*...O perfect, and accomplish thy glorious acts...When thou hast settl'd peace in the Church, and righteous judgement in the Kingdome, then shall all thy Saints addresse their voyces of joy, and triumph to thee, standing on the shoare of that red Sea into which our enemies had almost driven us. (*CP* 1: 705–06)

Again Milton imagines himself as a prophet-poet singing of and in that millennial kingdom:

And he that now for haste snatches up a plain, ungarnish't present as a thanke-offering to thee . . . may then perhaps take up a Harp, and sing thee an elaborate Song to Generations . . . Thy Kingdom is now at hand, and thou standing at the dore. Come forth out of thy Royall Chambers, O Prince of all the Kings of the earth, put on the visible roabes of thy imperiall Majesty, take up that unlimited Scepter which thy Almighty Father hath bequeath'd thee; for now the voice of thy Bride calls thee, and all creatures sigh to bee renew'd. (*CP* I: 706–07)

In 1644, with *Areopagitica*, Milton no longer speaks of Christ's Second Coming as imminent, but he does refer to an England being prepared by God for some great change: "all concurrence of signs" and "the general instinct of holy and devout men" indicate, he declares, that God is beginning "some new and great period in his Church, ev'n to the reforming of Reformation it self," and he is revealing this "as his manner is, first to his English-men" (*CP* II: 553). Here the emphasis falls on the duty and responsibility of the English to respond rightly to the challenge of this reforming era. Parliament must not hamper by licensing laws those who are busy collecting pieces of the torn body of Truth, which will be wholly reconstituted only at the Second Coming – an event being rightly prepared for by multitudes of prophets in the new English Israel. As is usual with him, Milton associates their prophecy not with sudden supernatural illumination but with painstaking scholarship:

Behold now this vast City; a City of refuge, the mansion-house of liberty . . . there be pens and heads there, sitting by their studious lamps, musing, searching, revolving new notions and ideas wherewith to present, as with their homage and their fealty the approaching Reformation: others as fast reading, trying all things, assenting to the force of reason and convincement . . . What wants there . . . but wise and faithfull labourers, to make a knowing people, a Nation of Prophets, of Sages, and of Worthies. (*CP* II: 553–54)

The next sentence sounds like a prediction of imminent apocalypse: "We reck'n more then five months yet to harvest; there need not be five weeks, had we but eyes to lift up, the fields are white already." But the allusion – to John 4:35 – refers not to apocalypse but to preaching and gathering a harvest of souls.

After the king's execution on 30 January 1649, Milton appeals occasionally to millennial prophecy as reinforcement for natural law and popular sovereignty arguments supporting the regicide and the republic. He finds it especially effective in countering biblical texts which seem to support divine right kingship. In a passage added to the second edition of *The Tenure of Kings and Magistrates* (September 1649), he castigates the

Presbyterians now decrying the regicide by evoking the millennium when there will be no more earthly kings, only Christ

who is our only King, the root of *David*, and whose Kingdom is eternal righteousness, with all those that Warr under him, whose happiness and final hopes are laid up in that only just & rightful kingdom (which we pray uncessantly may com soon, and in so praying wish hasty ruin and destruction to all Tyrants), eev'n he our immortal King, and all that love him, must of necessity have in abomination these blind and lame Defenders of *Jerusalem*; as the soule of *David* hated them, and forbid them entrance into Gods House, and his own. (*CP* III: 256)

The passage suggests that the English tyrannicide began preparations for Christ's arrival – soon, Milton hopes – and that the republic now established is the only political structure that properly recognizes Christ as the only rightful king. Here the millennial ideal serves to reinforce proper attitudes to hold now, toward monarchs, tyrants, and republics.

In the final pages of *Eikonoklastes* (October 1649), Milton makes his most direct application of apocalyptic symbols to contemporary politics, as he links the justice meted out to Charles in the regicide with the honor accorded the saints in Psalm 149:8, commonly applied to the endtimes:

Therefore *To bind thir Kings in Chaines, and thir Nobles with links of Iron*, is an honour belonging to his Saints; not to build *Babel* (which was *Nimrods* work the first King...) but to destroy it, especially that spiritual *Babel* [the Roman Church]; and first to overcome those European Kings, which receive thir power, not from God, but from the beast; and are counted no better then his ten hornes...untill at last, *joyning thir Armies with the Beast*, whose power first rais'd them, they shall perish with him by the *King of Kings* against whom they have rebell'd...This is thir doom writt'n [Rev. 19], and the utmost that we find concerning them in these latter days. (*CP* III: 598–99)

Milton's move here is to answer scripture with scripture: to set this dire prophecy of Christ's apocalyptic destruction of kings against Charles's claims in *Eikon Basilike* of God's special favor to kings as the greatest patrons of law, justice, order, and religion on earth. Milton does not claim that the regicide inaugurated the millennium, but that it accords with, and is a proper preparative to, the millennial "doom" (Rev. 19) to be visited on kings "in these latter days." In the *Defensio* (1651) he flatly denied the royalist analogy which his literary and political adversary Salmasius so often invoked between divine and human kingship, citing in evidence Christ's sole kingship at the millennium: "who, in fact, is worthy of holding on earth power like that of God but some person who far surpasses all others and even resembles God in goodness and wisdom? The only such person, as I believe, is the son of God whose coming we look for" (*CP* IV 1: 427–28).

Milton probably hoped that the Barebones Parliament which assembled on 4 July 1653 would do something about ensuring religious liberty and church disestablishment, but he did not accept the MPs' claims to special political rights as elect saints. In 1654, referring in the *Defensio Secunda* to the dissolution of that parliament, Milton offered a clear-sighted judgment on their ineptitude:

> The elected members came together. They did nothing. When they in turn had at length exhausted themselves with disputes and quarrels, most of them considering themselves inadequate and unfit for executing such great tasks, they of their own accord dissolved the Parliament. (*CP* IV 1: 671)

In 1655, in the sonnet "On the late Massacher in Piemont," Milton calls down God's vengeance for the horrific slaughter of the Waldensians by the Roman Catholic forces of Savoy, echoing prophetic language from Lamentations, Psalms, Isaiah, and especially the Book of Revelation. As with the two-handed engine of *Lycidas*, the lines derive much of their power from ambiguity as to just what that vengeance might be, when it might come, and who might wield it:

> Avenge O Lord thy slaughter'd Saints, whose bones
> Lie scatter'd on the Alpine mountains cold,
> Ev'n them who kept thy truth so pure of old
> When all our Fathers worship't Stocks and Stones,
> Forget not: in thy book record their groanes
> Who were thy Sheep and in their antient Fold
> Slayn by the bloody *Piemontese* that roll'd
> Mother with Infant down the Rocks. Their moans
> The Vales redoubl'd to the Hills, and they
> To Heav'n. Their martyr'd blood and ashes so
> O're all th'*Italian* fields where still doth sway
> The triple Tyrant: that from these may grow
> A hunderd-fold, who having learnt thy way
> Early may fly the *Babylonian* wo.[11]

The first four lines seem to call for immediate divine retribution for these "slaughter'd Saints" who retained their gospel purity of worship while the rest of Europe was sunk in pagan or Roman Catholic idolatry; they echo Rev. 6:9–10, "the souls of them that were slain for the word of God . . . cried out with a loud voice, saying, How long, O Lord, holy and true, dost thou not judge and avenge our blood on them that dwell on the earth?" The second segment (lines 5–10) modulates from the immediacy of "Avenge" to "Forget not," as the speaker calls on God to record the martyrs' "groanes" and the redoubled "moans" in the book by which humankind will be judged on the Last Day.

After the turn within line 10, the resolution refers to some kinds of immediate retribution in all the regions ruled by the papal "triple Tyrant": allusion to the parable of the sower (Matt. 13:3) in which the seed of God's Word "brought forth fruit, some an hundredfold," and to Tertullian's aphorism, "the blood of the martyrs is the seed of the Church," suggests that the Waldensians' slaughter will result in widespread conversions to Protestantism. But allusion to the myth of Cadmus, who sowed dragons' teeth that sprang up as armed warriors, intimates that Protestant armies might execute God's vengeance soon. And the echo of Jeremiah 51:6 in "Babylonian wo" – "Flee out of the midst of Babylon, and deliver every man his soul: be not cut off in her iniquity; for this is the time of the Lord's vengeance" – predicts violent divine retribution in, perhaps, an imminent apocalypse. In this complex resolution vengeance is the Lord's, now or later, but the human responsibility is to flee the Roman Babylon, as well as, perhaps, to inflict some foretaste of the prophesied "wo" now, as part of Cromwell's proposed Protestant military coalition.

In 1660, in the first edition of *The Readie and Easie Way*, Milton voiced his most caustic judgment of Fifth Monarchist aspirations to theocracy, insisting that separation of church and state is the only route to peace and settlement. Parliamentary elections would then be free of the factional strife unleashed when "every one strives to chuse him whom he takes to be of his religion; and everie faction hath the plea of Gods cause." Also, "ambitious leaders of armies would then have no hypocritical pretences so ready at hand to contest with Parlaments, yea to dissolve them and make way to their own tyrannical designs; [and] . . . I verily suppose there would be then no more pretending to a fifth monarchie of the saints" (*CP* VII: 380). This reference may look back to Cromwell, but it targets most obviously the recent machinations of Generals Lambert and Fleetwood. In the second edition of this tract, published on the eve of the Restoration, Milton appeals with special force to Christ's millennial kingship to reinforce his now desperate republican arguments. No man can rightfully hold royal dominion over other men, except for Christ, "our true and rightfull and only to be expected King . . . the only by him [God] anointed and ordaind since the work of our redemption finisht, Universal Lord of all Mankinde" (*CP* VII: 445).

In *Paradise Lost* (1667, 1674) there are brief references to the Last Judgment and the millennium in Michael's prophecy, offered as some counterweight to the tragic history he has recounted: "so shall the world goe on, / To good malignant, to bad men benigne, / Under her own waight groaning, till the day / Appear of respiration to the just / And vengeance to the wicked, at return / Of him so lately promis'd" (12.537–42).[12] This tragic vision of an external paradise irretrievably lost, along with the promise of "A paradise within thee, happier far" (12.587) might seem a recipe for quietism and retreat from the political arena after the Restoration. But Michael's prophecy shows that in every age the just few have the responsibility to oppose, if God calls them to do so, the Nimrods, or the Pharaohs, or the royalist persecutors of Puritans, even though – like the loyal angels in the War in Heaven – they can win no decisive victories until the Son appears. Millennial expectation is offered to encourage Adam's progeny to continue their resistance to these wicked oppressors, and also to console them for the loss of Eden by describing the blighted earth at last transformed all to paradise, "far happier place / Than this of *Eden*, and far happier daics" (12.464–65). In describing the eternity to follow upon the Son's final victory against Satan, Michael focuses less on heavenly bliss than on the material world: "*Satan* with his perverted World" will be destroyed in flames, from which will arise a wholly purged and refined creation, "New Heav'ns, new Earth, Ages of endless date / Founded in righteousness and peace and love / To bring forth fruits Joy and eternal Bliss" (12.547–51). Milton's monism dictates this emphasis on the restored earth, as it does also in *De Doctrina Christiana*, where he again describes the earth recreated as an Edenic paradise, and explains that the happiness of the just will be enhanced by the possession of heaven and earth and "all those creatures in both which may be useful or delightful" (*CP* VI: 630–32).

Milton said nothing directly about the series of catastrophes in the mid 1660s – notably the Great Plague and the Great Fire – or about that target date for the millennium, 1666. But his last works, *Paradise Regained* and *Samson Agonistes*, published together in 1671,[13] emphasize the fallacy of expecting the millennium soon, while at the same time underscoring the continuing necessity to prepare rightly for it by rigorous moral and political analysis and personal reformation, under the harsh conditions that obtained for dissenters after the Restoration. In *Paradise Regained* a central issue for Jesus is the expectation on all sides that he should at once assume the throne of David, liberate Israel, defeat Rome, and begin his reign on earth. Satan expects God to advance him in "the head of Nations . . . / Their King, their leader, and Supream on Earth" (1.98–99). Jesus first thought himself called "To rescue *Israel* from the *Roman* yoke, /

Then to subdue and quell o're all the earth / Brute violence and proud Tyrannick pow'r, / Till truth were freed, and equity restored" (1.217–20). The apostles, anticipating millenarian Puritans, imagine the moment at hand for the Messiah's kingly reign in Israel:

> Now, now, for sure, deliverance is at hand,
> The Kingdom shall to *Israel* be restor'd
> . . . .
>   God of Israel,
> Send thy Messiah forth, the time is come;
> Behold the Kings of the Earth how they oppress
> Thy chosen, to what highth thir pow'r unjust
> They have exalted, and behind them cast
> All fear of thee, arise and vindicate
> Thy Glory, free thy people from thir yoke.
>
>   (2.35–48)

With the line, "but to a Kingdom thou art born, ordain'd / To sit upon thy Father *David's* Throne" (3.152–53) Satan points directly to the kingly role prescribed by Christ's office, typically taking literally the prophecy that Jesus is to reign as King of Israel. Countering these expectations, Jesus in the course of the temptations clarifies the several manifestations of his kingship in history. First, it is the kingdom within "which every wise and virtuous man obtains": by his temperance and ethical knowledge Jesus defines that kingdom and offers a trenchant critique of the values and practices of secular monarchies. Second, it is his own spiritual kingdom, the invisible church, which he comes by stages to understand and explain. Finally, at some uncertain future date, it is the millennial rule he will exercise over all realms and monarchs.

The exchanges between Satan and Jesus over this issue are fraught with contemporary political implications. Holding up Judas Maccabaeus as a model, Satan goads Jesus to seize his kingdom at once, and so free his country from Roman rulers who have violated God's Temple and God's Law. Jesus' answer applies to his historical situation but also to that of the defeated Puritans; its terms reprove expectation of an imminent millennium and repudiate Fifth Monarchist uprisings – such as Venner's rebellion of 1661. But they also urge continued expectation of and right preparation for that millennial kingdom by waiting on God's time and learning from present trials:

> What if he hath decreed that I shall first
> Be try'd in humble state, and things adverse,
> By tribulations, injuries, insults,

> Contempts, and scorns, and snares, and violence,
> Suffering, abstaining, quietly expecting
> Without distrust or doubt, that he may know
> What I can suffer, how obey?   (3.188–94)

Then Satan shows Jesus the massive display of Parthian armaments and troops, insisting that he can only gain and maintain the throne of Israel and deliver the Ten Lost Tribes enslaved in Parthian territory by conquest of, or league with, Parthia and its military might (3.354–70). This offer of the wrong means to establish Christ's kingdom alludes to that constant target of Milton's polemic, the use of civil power by Protestant magistrates to establish, defend, or maintain the church. Jesus insists that his spiritual kingdom, the invisible church, has no need whatever "Of fleshly arm, / And fragile arms... / Plausible to the world, to me worth naught" (3.387–93). He describes the Ten Lost Tribes in terms applicable to their expected return and conversion just prior to the millennium, but also applicable to the English who, as Milton put it in *The Readie and Easie Way*, chose them a Captain back for Egypt when they supported the Restoration of the monarchy and the Anglican church. Jesus cannot liberate those who enslave themselves by deliberate participation in idolatry, but he holds out hope that God will – in his own good time – call Israelites and Englishmen to repentance and freedom:

> Should I of these the liberty regard,
> Who freed, as to their antient Patrimony,
> Unhumbl'd, unrepentant, unreform'd,
> Headlong would follow; and to thir Gods perhaps
> Of *Bethel* and of *Dan*? no, let them serve
> Thir enemies, who serve Idols with God.
> Yet he at length, time to himself best known,
> Rememb'ring *Abraham*, by some wond'rous call
> May bring them back repentant and sincere,
> And at their passing cleave th' *Assyrian* flood,
> When to their native land with joy they haste.
>   (3.427–37)

Imperial Rome, with its splendid architecture, sumptuous banquets, and every manifestation of dominion and glory is the great kingdom of "all the world," described in terms appropriate to the reign of the degenerate emperor Tiberius but also inviting the usual Protestant associations of Rome with the Roman Catholic church, and that church with the great Antichrist depicted in the Book of Revelation, whose defeat will begin the millennium. Satan urges Jesus to expel the "monster" Tiberius from his throne and so free the Romans (and Israel as part of the Empire) from their "servile yoke" – thereby inaugurating his earthly reign. However, Jesus refuses to free Romans who abandoned republican virtue and so are "Deservedly made vassel" – a refusal which extends to Roman Catholics enslaved to the pope and to English Anglicans and Puritans who invited that danger by restoring the Stuarts. But he then prophesies, in metaphor, how his millennial kingdom will – at last – subdue all others:

> What wise and valiant man would seek to free
> These thus degenerate, by themselves enslav'd,
> Or could of inward slaves make outward free?
> Know therefor when my season comes to sit
> On *David's* Throne, it shall be like a tree
> Spreading and over-shadowing all the Earth,
> Or as a stone that shall to pieces dash
> All Monarchies besides throughout the world,
> And of my Kingdom there shall be no end:
> Means there shall be to this, but what the means,
> Is not for thee to know, nor me to tell. (4.143–53)

The tree seems to refer to the power of his kingdom to transform the earth, and the stone to its power to crush all earthly monarchies and their evils, according to the usual exegesis of the prophecy in Daniel 2.31–45. But Jesus refuses to say when or how his millennial kingdom will come, intimating that it will come when people are ready for it.

The storm and the tower episodes carry adumbrations of Jesus's passion and resurrection, and of his final victory over Satan, with relevance for Puritan dissidents subjected to the storms and tempests of royalist oppression and continually invited, as Jesus was by Satan, to read their plight as a portent of God's displeasure and their coming destruction.[14] But the bright day which follows the storm reminds readers that the resurrection followed the passion, and Christ's victory over Satan on the Tower foreshadows his victory at the Last Day. So may the Puritan dissenters expect a better day – and in due time a victory – if they endure their trials patiently, avoid precipitous action, analyze moral and political issues accurately, and develop their spiritual strength. Jesus' victory is celebrated with an angelic banquet and a long hymn of praise which carries some adumbrations of the millennium through its shifts in tense and perspective. The angels proclaim that Jesus has "Now...aveng'd / Supplanted Adam" and "Regain'd lost Paradise," but also that he is about to "begin to save mankind" (4.606–608, 634–35). Because he now understands himself and has been exercised in all the "rudiments" of his great warfare, he has already won the essential victory. But that victory must be worked out in history as others respond to his teaching and are thereby enabled to become virtuous and free. Then the millennium will come.

There is nothing of millennial renewal in *Samson Agonistes*, but there are adumbrations of apocalypse in Samson's cataclysmic act of pulling down the Philistine temple, evoking the final destruction of Antichrist's forces as well as stories of divine vengeance in the Book of Judges, which, as David Loewenstein notes, radical Puritans readily applied to their own times.[15] After Samson's act Manoa imagines a new future in which Samson's story might inspire other valiant youth to "matchless valor and adventures high," and in which Israel might recognize Samson's act as providing a political *occasione* in Machiavelli's sense: "To *Israel* / Honor hath left, and freedom, let but them / Find courage to lay hold on this occasion" (ll. 1714–16). Milton's dramatic poem is, however, a tragedy: Samson cannot stand in for Christ at the apocalypse and his victory in death is very partial. Also, as we know from the biblical record, Israel continued in corruption and servitude and the Danites became open idolaters. The Samson paradigm shows that all human heroes are flawed, and that Israelites and Englishmen are more disposed to choose "Bondage with ease than strenuous liberty" (l. 271), so that when God raises up his Samsons, or Gideons, or Cromwells their political gains soon collapse under the weight of sin and weakness in themselves and the people. Yet in the drama's historical moment that future is not yet fixed and proper choices are still possible: if the Israelites, or the English, could truly value liberty, could reform themselves, could benefit from the "new acquist / Of true experience" (ll. 1755–56), moral and political, which Samson's story offers the Danites and Milton's dramatization of it offers his countrymen, liberation might just be possible.

As first published, the poem has a coda, ten added lines designed for insertion into the dialogue between Manoa and the Chorus speculating about the fearsome noise heard as the Philistine temple is destroyed. But these lines appear at the end under a bar, with the label, "Omissa." As Stephen Dobranski observes,[16] we cannot know whether Milton hoped the printer could add them in their right place (as lines 1527–35 and 1537) or wanted this presentation, which allows a glimpse of an alternative, apocalyptic ending. The Chorus imagines Samson with his vision miraculously restored, "dealing dole among his foes" and walking over "heaps of slaughter'd." God, they argue, has done as much for Israel of old and to him "nothing is hard." This coda allows Milton to have it both ways. In their proper place within his text these lines are a fantasy, a false hope of Samson fully restored to himself and victorious. As published, they intimate an alternative scenario, if God should again raise up champions for his English Israel, and if a reformed people could lay hold on a new occasion. *Samson Agonistes* ends with an apocalyptic moment of destroying oppressors, but its potential for liberating those enslaved can be realized only if a virtuous citizenry understands the political stakes and values liberty. This drama makes a fit poetic climax to Milton's lifelong effort to help create such citizens.

NOTES

A version of this chapter was originally presented as a paper at the annual dinner meeting of the Milton Society of America on 28 December 1999, in Chicago.

1. Joseph Mede, *Clavis Apocalyptica, ex innatis et insitis visionum characteribus eruta et demonstrata* (Cambridge, 1627); trans. *The Key of the Revelation* (London, 1643); rptd. in *Works*, 2 vols. (London, 1664). For Mede's system, see Sarah Hutton's chapter in this book.

2. William Burden, *Christs Personal Reign on Earth, One Thousand Yeers with his Saints* (London, 1654).

3. Nathanael Homes, *Resurrection Revealed: or The Dawning of the Day-Star, About to rise, and radiate a visible Incomparable Glory . . . For a Thousand yeers Yet to come, before the ultimate Day, of the General Judgement . . .* (London, 1654).

4. William Aspinwall, *A Brief Description of the Fifth Monarchy* (London, 1653), p. 14.

5. D. Roe, *Gods Judgments Still Threatned against thee O England* (London, 1666), pp. 4, 7, 16.

6. *The Last Letters to the London-Merchants and Faithful Ministers concerning the Further Procedings of the Conversion and Restauration of the Jews; with most strange and wonderful Miracles performed . . . A Prophecie touching the Downefall of Babylon in 66, and the time of the Gospel to be Preach'd throughout the whole World* (London, 1665).

7. Milton's scenario for the last days is described in *De Doctrina Christiana*, Book I, Chapter 33.

8. For the debate about the millenarianism of *De Doctrina Christiana*, see the chapters by William Hunter and John Shawcross in this book.

9. Unless otherwise indicated, Milton's early poems are quoted from *Poems of Mr. John Milton* (London, 1645).

10. Stella P. Revard, *Milton and the Tangles of Neaera's Hair* (Columbia, Mo., and London, 1997), p. 81.

11. This sonnet was first published in *Poems, &c. Upon Several Occasions. By Mr. John Milton* (London, 1673), and I quote from that edition.

12. Cited from *Paradise Lost. A Poem in Twelve Books* (London, 1674).

13. I quote these two poems from *Paradise Regain'd. A Poem in IV Books. To which is added Samson Agonistes* (London, 1671).

14. See, for example, [George Starkey], *Royal and other Innocent Bloud crying . . . for due Vengeance* (London, 1660); David Lloyd, *The Picture of the Good Old Cause* (London, 1660); and Roger L'Estrange, *Toleration Discussed* (London, 1663, 1670).

15. David Loewenstein, "The Revenge of the Saint: Radical Religion and Politics in *Samson Agonistes*," *Milton Studies* 33 (1997), pp. 159–80. See also Barbara K. Lewalski, "*Samson Agonistes* and the 'Tragedy' of the Apocalypse," *PMLA* 85 (1970), pp. 1050–62.

16. Stephen Dobranski, *Milton, Authorship, and the Book Trade* (Cambridge, 1999), pp. 41–61.

2

Mede, Milton, and More: Christ's College millenarians

Sarah Hutton

Then amidst the *Hymns*, and *Halleluiahs* of *Saints* some one may perhaps bee heard offering at high *strains* in new and lofty *Measures* to sing and celebrate thy *divine Mercies*, and *marvelous Judgements* in this Land throughout all AGES; whereby this great and Warlike Nation...may presse on hard to that *high* and *happy* emulation to be found the *soberest*, *wisest*, and *most Christian People* at that day when thou the Eternall and shortly-expected King shalt open the Clouds to judge the severall Kingdomes of the World, and distributing *Nationall Honours* and *Rewards* to Religious and just *Common-wealths*, shalt put an end to all Earthly *Tyrannies*, proclaiming thy universal and milde *Monarchy* through Heaven and Earth.

John Milton, *Of Reformation* (*CP* 1:616)

Anticipating thus the monarchy of Christ foretold in the Book of Revelation, Milton rounds off *Of Reformation* (1641). The passage does not refer specifically to the fact that Christ's kingdom was expected to last a thousand years, before the ushering in of "the *datelesse* and *irrevoluble* Circle of *Eternity*" (*CP* 1: 616) which closes time itself, but it does make clear that Milton believed Christ's monarchy to be imminent. Milton's adoption of the language of millenarian expectation is far from unusual in this period. That he should be conversant with such apocalyptic language is hardly surprising, since he was raised in a culture of which apocalyptic belief was a constituent part. Nor was apocalypticism confined to any particular areas of Protestantism: it was characteristic of early modern Protestantism generally – of the Church of England as much as of its Puritan critics and the sects which emerged in the seventeenth century. While events of the 1640s lent a special fervor to apocalyptic speculation, we perhaps need to remind ourselves that Christianity always entailed the promise of the Second Coming of the Messiah. Furthermore, fulfillment of prophetic prediction had always been understood as unshakable confirmation of the truth of the Christian message. In the wake of the

Reformation, Protestants of all persuasions directed their interpretation
of biblical prophecy to the specific end of confirming the truth of reformed Christianity as distinct from the claims of the Church of Rome. It
was during this period that the interpretation of the Book of Revelation
as anti-Catholic became standard in reformed Christendom, the rule
rather than the exception in theological analysis.[1]

The apocalyptic elements in Milton's writing must be understood
within the broad context of seventeenth-century English apocalypticism.
But, as I shall show in this chapter, they can be linked to specific strands
in English millenarian thinking. Not only did Milton live at a time when
millenarianism was integral to religious culture, he was also educated at a
college which made a distinctive contribution to apocalyptic theory. For
Christ's College, Cambridge, was the *alma mater* of the biblical scholar
Joseph Mede (or Mead, 1586–1638) who brought to the study of biblical
prophecy an interpretative method which was hugely influential during
the English Revolution and has left its mark right up to modern times.[2]
The mantle of Joseph Mede was assumed by a younger contemporary of
Milton at Christ's, the Cambridge Platonist Henry More (1614–87), who
did his best to ensure that millenarianism retained a respectable place in
the changed religious and political circumstances of the Restoration. In
all likelihood it was More who encouraged his friend John Worthington
to undertake producing the collected edition of Mede's works, which he
published in 1664. In Joseph Mede, Milton had a Protestant authority
on the Apocalypse whose speculations struck a chord with him and his
contemporaries as they attempted to make sense of history and their
own spiritual commitments. In Henry More we have a figure who is an
important part of the postrevolutionary phase of English apocalypticism
and who, like Milton, drew on Jospeh Mede. In this paper I shall eval-
uate Milton's relationship with both figures: his debt to Mede and his
divergence from More.

The key to Mede's seminal work on the Book of Revelation, his *Clavis
Apocalyptica* of 1627 (and "key" is what the *Clavis* of the title means),
lay not in the meanings ascribed to particular visions or symbols in the
Book of Revelation, but in his organization of them. For Mede detected
patterns of equivalence which enabled him to apply the principle of reading scripture through scripture so as to demonstrate the self-confirming
nature of the prophecies of St. John. Instead of reading the Book of
Revelation as a disordered collection of visions, or as, at best, a dis-
jointed linear narrative, Mede understood it as a series of synchronic
visionary statements, to be grouped according to their coincidence

in time. These groupings he called "synchronisms," explaining to the reader:

By a *Synchronism* of prophecies I meane, when the things therein designed to run along in the same time; as if thou shouldst call it an agreement in time or age: because prophecies of things fall out in the same time run on in time together or Synchronize.[3]

Mede conceived of two main sequences of the prophecies of St. John: the prophecies of the "Closed Book" and those of the "Opened Book," the former foretelling events parallel to, or, rather, synchronic with, those of the latter. The former included the seven seals (Rev. 5) and the seven trumpets (Rev. 8). Mede grouped the prophecies of the "Opened Book" into three successive phases, each of which contained two or more synchronic prophecies – for example, the second group comprised seven prophecies, among them that of the two witnesses (Rev. 11:1), the woman clothed with the sun (Rev. 12), and the seven-horned beast (Rev. 13). The first group coincided with the first six of the seven seals, the second with the first six of the seven trumpets, and the third with the seventh trumpet. This last phase, the sounding of the seventh trumpet (in the "Closed Book" prophecies), is also the period of the millennium, the thousand-year reign of Christ and the saints (Rev. 20) in the "Opened Book" prophecies. The termini of this last period are the binding of Satan and his subsequent release after a thousand years (followed by his final perdition). The millennial period is ushered in by the outpouring of the seven vials of wrath, the first six of which coincide with the sounding of the sixth trumpet, and the seventh of which occurs at the beginning of the sounding of the seventh trumpet.

In 1632 Mede republished *Clavis Apocalyptica* with a corroborating commentary which makes plain that he upheld the Protestant identification of Antichrist with the Roman Catholic church. In a second, posthumously published work, his *The Apostasy of these Latter Times* (first published 1641), Mede set out in detail the evidence, as he saw it, for the corruption of the Roman Catholic church by idolatrous practices (chiefly the demon-worship of the cult of saints) during the Christian era, thereby giving credence to the thesis that the beast of the Apocalypse was the papacy itself. Of course, by this time this view had become standard in the literature of Protestant apocalypticism. But Mede's scheme made it possible to make a consistent and therefore more plausible reading of the Apocalypse in terms of Protestant history, culminating in the overthrow of Antichrist, or the Church of Rome. In this scheme of things, the outpouring of the seven vials of wrath (Rev. 16) constitutes "the Seven several and successive degrees of the Fall of the Apostatical or Pseudo prophetical Beast." Mede insisted, however, that the sounding of the seventh trumpet and the overthrow of the "Romish beast" lay in the future (it was "yet to come").[4] The attraction of his scheme to many of his sectarian readers was that it suggested that the Second Coming was imminent. However, conscious of the dangers of chiliasm, Mede held back from specific dating. He insisted, moreover, that the prophecies of the "Opened Book" were spiritual in import, that they referred to the state of the church and the battle between Christ and the devil.

Mede's synchronic scheme set the mold for seventeenth- and eighteenth-century English readings of the Book of Revelation, both sober and fervent. By an irony of history, his scheme, or variants of it, enjoyed huge popularity among those he would have regarded as his theological nemeses, had he lived to witness the turbulent events of the Civil War and its aftermath.[5] For during this period Mede's ideas attracted a following among a wide cross-section of the opposition to the Laudian church, from the prolocutor of the Westminster Assembly of Divines, William Twisse, to Fifth Monarchists such as Vavasour Powell.[6] The posthumous popular dissemination of his apocalyptic scheme was made possible by the translation of his *Clavis Apocalyptica* into English in 1641, at the behest of Parliament. Thereafter, during the 1640s and 1650s, his was the most frequently reprinted English millenarian treatise, far outnumbering the works of Thomas Brightman (1562–1607) and those of his predecessor at Christ's College, Hugh Broughton (1549–1612), satirized so mercilessly by Ben Jonson in *The Alchemist*. In 1664 Mede's entire oeuvre was collected together and published for Restoration consumption in a suitably scholarly edition by John Worthington. Mede's later admirers numbered none other than Isaac Newton and William Whiston (Newton's successor as Lucasian Professor of Mathematics at Cambridge).[7]

Newton and Whiston also drew on another Cambridge disciple of Mede, Henry More, who had studied at Christ's College after Milton, overlapping with him by one year, and who was subsequently elected to a fellowship there. More shared with Milton a deep love of the poetry of Edmund Spenser. His first publication was a set of long poems written in Spenserian stanzas and neo-Spenserian diction.[8] These poems celebrate More's recent and enthusiastic encounter with "Platonick Philosophy," chiefly Plato, Plotinus, Ficino, and "the mystical divines." More subsequently published works of religious philosophy and entered into correspondence with Descartes. The memorial plaque to him in the church of his home town, Grantham, Lincolnshire, pays tribute to him as one who "by his learned writings in divinity and philosophy [was] one of the greatest glories of our church and nation." In theology More was an opponent of predestinarian Calvinism, an admirer of the heterodox Father, Origen, and a proponent of religious toleration.[9] In the 1640s he was regarded as sufficiently sound to retain his fellowship when others were purged by the Earl of Manchester; he conformed at the Restoration and retained his fellowship in the teeth of concerted attempts to have him ejected as a latitudinarian.[10] The new ecclesiastical hierarchy regarded his Origenism with suspicion, notwithstanding his publicly stated opposition to sectarian extremists.[11]

More's interest in millenarianism is first evident in a work in which he sets out his latitudinarian position, his *An Explanation of the Grand Mystery of Godliness* of 1660. Most of More's writings on the interpretation of the Book of Revelation were published after *Paradise Lost*.[12] His later writings elaborate views that he set out earlier, in *An Explanation of the Grand Mystery of Godliness* and *Synopsis Propheticon* (appended to his *Mystery of Iniquity*, 1664). In 1668 the broad outlines of his position are the subject of the last dialogue of his *Divine Dialogues*. And in 1669 his *Exposition of the Seven Epistles to the Seven Churches* defends his opinion that the account of the seven churches in the first six chapters of the Book of Revelation should be regarded as prophetic of the future state of the Christian church.

One of More's major departures from Mede was to place these prophecies among those of the "Opened Book" and arrange them to run concurrently with events from the prophecy of the first seal to the end of the seventh trumpet. More's arrangement of the span of the seventh trumpet is more complicated than Mede's. The period of the seventh trumpet is subdivided into the seven thunders. Each of these corresponds to an important phase in the millennial scheme set out in the "Opened Book" prophecy. At the first thunder the seven vials are poured out. The second thunder corresponds to the descent of the New Jerusalem and the binding of Satan (Rev. 20), the third thunder to the thousand years of Christ's reign. Satan's release coincides with the fourth thunder, followed by the siege of the holy city (fifth thunder), Christ's coming to judgment (sixth thunder) and conflagration of the earth (seventh thunder). The importance for More of these further subdivisions of the eschatological sequence was that they showed the erroneousness of a purely political interpretation of the millennium. In More's scheme the timespan of the first six trumpets overlaps with that of the last three of the seven churches (Sardis, Philadelphia, and Laodicea). The millennial reign of Christ falls within the second of these, the Philadelphian church.

In addition to differences from Mede in the way he arranged the prophecies, and his inclusion of the account of the seven churches within the scheme, More emphasized the importance of prophetic language and attempted to codify prophetic symbols. In general terms he accepted Mede's synchronic scheme, while stressing the poetic language of St. John. He subscribed to Mede's view of the apostasy of the Church of Rome, and believed the destruction of the papacy would be effected by the outpouring of the vials of wrath. And he remained faithful to Mede in giving emphasis to a spiritual interpretation of the millennium. Although he believed the seventh trumpet was already sounding, he also believed a precondition of the millennium would be spiritual regeneration among the faithful. Like Mede he declined to set a date for the beginning of the millennium. Indeed he was emphatic that no such date could be computed, "no fit time being defined for the future."

Whether Milton was fully conversant with the millenarian studies of Mede and More is hard to say with certainty. But as members of Christ's College, Mede, Milton, and More are likely to have known of one another's existence.[13] It has even been suggested that Mede is "Old Damaetas" of *Lycidas*.[14] Mede's posthumous fame among Parliamentarians must have meant that he was known to Milton as an authority on millenarianism, whether or not Milton was inclined to share the millenarian expectations of many others in the parliamentary party. In the 1640s Milton may well have known of More as a Spenserian poet. More's *Philosophical Poems* (1647) brought him both fame and notoriety when they were pilloried by the alchemist Thomas Vaughan during his brief and unseemly squabble with More.[15] It has been argued that Milton knew More's *Conjectura Cabbalistica* (1653).[16] Whatever Milton's direct knowledge of Mede and More, there is no doubt that during the 1640s and 1650s Milton moved among millenarians: the Hartlib circle, with which he was closely associated, numbered many. Of these, some of his closest associates, including Henry Oldenburg and Lady Ranelagh, wove millennial piety into their very greetings. More, too, was connected with the Hartlib circle, as was his friend John Worthington, Mede's editor.[17]

The importance of the Second Coming of Christ to Milton's major poems needs no demonstration, as the essays in this book testify. Likewise, his incorporation of the language and images of the Book of

Revelation is well attested. In *Paradise Lost* the importance of the Second Coming for providential history is underlined by repeated allusions to it. The momentousness of the event is underlined, first, by the way in which references to it in Books 3 and 12 frame the epic narrative, and then, by a double mention of it in the second of these (12.460–61 and 12.540–46). Here Milton evokes the imagery of the apocalypse, but he does not tie his account to the Book of Revelation in detail. As in *De Doctrina Christiana* 1.33, the events of the Second Coming complete the glorification of Christ of which "the fulfilment and consummation will begin with Christ's second coming to judge the world" (*CP* vi: 614). In Book 3 God's prediction to the Son of the time "When thou attended gloriously in heaven / Shalt in the sky appear" (3.323–24) is repeated to Adam in Book 12, where Michael tells him of the day of "vengeance to the wicked," when Christ will be "in the clouds from heaven to be revealed / In glory of the Father" (12.541, 545–46).

While it is not immediately obvious that Milton drew on any particular interpreter for his reading of Revelation 20, close textual analysis of *De Doctrina* and *Paradise Lost* reveals the influence of Joseph Mede. Milton does not attempt to organize the narrative of events into a synchronic scheme in either work, but Milton, like Mede, saw the postapostolic period of Christianity as one of the corruption of the church:

> Wolves shall succeed for teachers, grievous wolves,
> Who all the sacred mysteries of heaven
> To their own vile advantages shall turn
> Of lucre and ambition, and the truth
> With superstitions and traditions taint.   (12.508–12)

Other Protestant commentators besides Mede subscribed to the apostasy thesis. However, there are details which suggest that Milton's account of the end of time is directly indebted to Mede.[18] This seems to be the case in his account of the Last Judgment. There is no explicit mention of the thousand-year rule of Christ in *Paradise Lost*, but we are told that at "this world's dissolution" Christ will come to judge the faithful and "unfaithful dead" (12.459–61). This is the day "of respiration to the just / And vengeance to the wicked" (12.540–41), "the dread tribunal" graphically described in Book 3:

> forthwith from all the winds
> The living, and forthwith the cited dead
> Of all past ages to the general doom
> Shall hasten, such a peal shall rouse their sleep.

> Then all thy saints assembled, thou shalt judge
> Bad men and angels, they arraigned shall sink
> Beneath thy sentence.   (3.326–32)

In *De Doctrina* Milton mentions two judgments: one which ushers in the thousand years of Christ's reign on earth, and one which follows the final destruction of Satan. The former is conceived as enduring for almost the timespan of the reign of Christ. And Milton pauses to explain that the "day" in question is not to be interpreted literally, but stands for a period of some duration:

I say *at the time of*, rather than *on the day of*, because the word *day* is often used to mean some indefinite period of time, and because it does not seem likely that so many millions of angels and men could be assembled and judged within the space of a single day. Christ's reign, then, will extend from the beginning to the end of this time of judgement, and will continue for some time after the judgement has finished, until all his enemies are subdued. (*CP* vi: 623–24)

Milton adds, further, that the length of period of judgment means that it is appropriately called a reign: "This judgement it seems will not last for one day only but for a considerable length of time, and will really be a reign, rather than a judicial session" (*CP* vi: 625). Thereafter Christ's kingdom is everlasting in the sense that it will last "while the ages of the world endure" or "until time will be no more" (*CP* vi: 627). At that point Christ hands over his kingdom to God.

Joseph Mede, too, describes two resurrections and two judgments. The first of the latter he regarded as being equivalent to the millennial rule of Christ. In so stating, he too explains that the term day is not to be interpreted literally, but symbolically. And he indicates that his interpretation goes against the general view. The thousand years, he writes:

does signifie that *great Day of Judgement* . . . much spoken of by the ancient Church of the Jewes, and by Christ and his Apostles, not some short space of houres (as is commonly beleeved) but (after the manner of the *Hebrews* taking a *day* for time) a confirmed space for many yeeres, and circumscribed with in two resurrections, as it were bounds.[19]

Mede goes on to outline his view that after the resurrection and Last Judgment, Christ will cede his kingdom to God. Thereafter, technically speaking, there will be no kingdom of Christ.

Neither yet . . . shall this Kingdome be after the last resurrection: since the Sonne of man is not to enter upon a Kingdome then; but as Paul witnesseth, to lay it downe and deliver it to his Father.

Mede also supposed that Christ would destroy his enemies by fire, and that his glory would be manifest in "the brightnesse of his coming."[20]

The echoes of Mede are stronger in *De Doctrina* than in *Paradise Lost*, where there is no explicit mention of the thousand years of Christ's reign on earth. However, one telling detail suggests that Milton did not abandon his earlier position in respect of the millennium. In *Paradise Lost* Book 3, God tells Christ about the final Judgment that will be followed by a "New heaven and earth" with "golden days, fruitful of golden deeds" (3.335–37). At this point, God tells him:

> Then thou thy regal sceptre shalt lay by,
> For regal sceptre then no more shall need.
>
> (3.339–40)

The words "regal sceptre" suggest that the Son has been reigning, although at this point in the poem no reference has yet been made to his reign, only to the "dread tribunal" (3.326) of Christ's Judgment. This may be explained if we recall Milton's and Mede's synchronizing of the Last Judgment with the millennial kingdom of Christ. According to both Milton in *De Doctrina* and Mede in *Clavis Apocalyptica*, the rule and Judgment of Christ are one and the same event. And, according to both, the kingdom of Christ will give way to a paradisiacal state of the new heaven and earth once time comes to an end. As Michael reminds us in Book 12, the founding of the new heaven and earth which follows the final conflagration is the transition point between time and eternity, which ushers in "ages of endless date" (12.549). Milton's own comment that the noun "reign" is equivalent to "judicial session" in *De Doctrina* may be applied to the adjective "regal" here in *Paradise Lost*. The immediately preceding "dread tribunal" may be inferred to be a synecdochic reference to Christ's millennial reign. In Joseph Mede, therefore, Milton would have found not merely a Protestant interpretation of the Apocalypse suited to his own sense of providential history, but clues to the sequencing of the last days. It was most likely from Mede that he took the idea that the millennium and the Last Judgment were the same event.

It is unlikely that Henry More exerted a formative influence upon Milton, since most of Milton's ideas about the apocalypse appear to have been formed before More had published extensively on this topic. However, we cannot exclude the possibility that More was conversant with Milton's prose writings. Additionally, More was an important part of the millenarian landscape in which Milton wrote: he shows that apocalyptic speculation continued to generate lively debate in the second half of the seventeenth century. Together Milton and More testify to Mede's general influence on apocalypticism in this period. Neither Milton nor More was a slavish acolyte of Mede, and both were faced with having to adjust to the changed ecclesiastical circumstances of the Restoration. These included, among many other things, the fact that apocalypticism was tainted, in the eyes of the new establishment, with the chiliastic excesses of the English Revolution. Unlike Milton, More conformed to the Church of England, but he attempted to keep the flame of millenarianism alive within the Church. He therefore placed it in an overtly anti-Fifth Monarchist context and played down its political application.[21] More proposed a more quietist view of the overthrow of Antichrist than Mede: the Second Coming would be brought about by increased love, holiness, and charity among the faithful, with the result that the "Papacy would melt away like a bank of snow in the summer sun."[22] The sword is the sword of the spirit, that is, the word of God. The period of the millennial rule of Christ is the last period of the Philadelphian church, characterized by true Christian love and charity. According to More the kingdom of God was to be understood as both an external kingdom (the power of God in nature) and an internal kingdom, an "empire of Divine love," "established in the Love, Peace and Patience of the Lord Jesus."[23]

Arguably, the covert chiliasm discernible in *Paradise Lost* may also be a response to the unfavorable climate in the 1660s, a new caution on the part of an old radical. However, More's emphasis on internal spirituality should not obscure radical differences in religious doctrine between the two men. Unlike Milton, More interpreted biblical prophecy to support Trinitarianism.[24] Ironically, perhaps, in view of his caution regarding political applications of apocalypticism, More chose a political metaphor to describe Christ's gathering of the faithful into the new heaven:

leading Captivity captive rescuing us from the Power of Hell, Death and Hell, does resettle us again in our own land, and re-establish us into the ancient Liberties of the Sons of God, making us Fellow-citizens with the pure and unpolluted Angels, and free Partakers of all the Rights and Immunities of the celestial Kingdom.[25]

The examples of Milton, Mede, and More give us a measure of how deeply apocalypticism was embedded in seventeenth-century culture. Of the three, Mede stands out as the most powerful shaping influence on millenarian thinking in Milton's time. Both Milton and More register the formative influence of Mede, and also the fact that apocalyptic interpretation was not static in this period. Even as we recognize the impact of

Mede in their writings, the contrast between them highlights the fact that the language of apocalypticism resonated with powerful contemporary significance which largely eludes us now. The usefulness of comparative study of Milton and his millenarian contemporaries is that it offers us a starting point for searching for some of the least accessible facets of Milton's cultural formation. It is an open question whether Milton abandoned his millenarianism in later life. But the example of More is instructive to the extent that it shows that it would have been consistent for Milton to continue to maintain his millennialism, albeit adopting a more muted expression of it which focused on the interior millennium of the spirit.

As I noted at the beginning of the chapter, Mede's apocalyptical writings appealed to an extraordinarily broad spectrum of religious opinion, and a wide range of millenarians. Although his *Key* was amenable to being interpreted to predict an imminent millennium, he himself refrained from speculating about a precise date, and expressed preference for a spiritual, rather than political, character of the millennium. After the Restoration put paid to the chiliastic hopes of many of Mede's sectarian interpreters, it was this milder form of millenarianism which must have seemed more applicable to the times. This aspect predominates with More, whose adjustments to Mede's scheme entailed not the abandonment of millenarian beliefs but a deemphasis on the political and a renewed emphasis on the spiritual core of the apocalypse. In like manner Milton's conflation of Christ's rule and judgment as the prelude to the "golden days" of the new Jerusalem in *Paradise Lost* entailed an equivalent adjustment, and one which, like More's, was entirely consistent with his reading of Joseph Mede.

NOTES

1. For the identification of the papacy with Antichrist, see Bryan W. Ball, *A Great Expectation: Eschatological Thought in English Protestantism to 1660* (Leiden, 1975); C. Hill, *Antichrist in Seventeenth-Century England* (London, 1971); and C. A. Patrides and Joseph Wittreich (eds.), *The Apocalypse in English Renaissance Thought and Literature: Patterns, Antecedents and Repercussions* (Manchester, 1984), pp. 125–46.
2. L. Froom, *The Prophetic Faith of our Fathers* (Washington, 1948).
3. Joseph Mede, *The Key of the Revelation* (London, 1643), p. 1.
4. Joseph Mede, *Fragmenta Sacra, or Miscellanies of Divinity*, in Mede, *Works*, ed. John Worthington (London, 1677; first published 1664), Book 5, p. 923.
5. See my "The Appropriation of Joseph Mede: Millenarianism in the 1640s," in James E. Force and Richard H. Popkin (eds.), *The Millenarian*

Turn: Millenarian Contexts of Science, Politics, and Everyday Anglo-American Life in the Seventeenth and Eighteenth Centuries (Dordrecht, 2001).

6. Ibid. As I argue in this chapter, Mede did not share the theological prefer-
    ences of his radical admirers. Christopher Hill's view of Mede as a timid
    anti-Laudian does not, therefore, stand scrutiny.

7. See S. Hutton, "More, Newton and the language of biblical prophecy," and
    R. Iliffe, " 'Making a Shew': Apocalyptic hermeneutics and the sociology of
    Christian idolatry in the work of Isaac Newton and Henry More," in James
    E. Force and Richard H. Popkin, *The Books of Nature and Scripture* (Dordrecht,
    1994), pp. 39–53, 55–88.

8. More's *Psychodia Platonica* (Cambridge, 1642) and *Democritus Platonissans*
    (Cambridge, 1646) were both republished with further poems in his
    Philosophical Poems (Cambridge, 1647).

9. See S. Hutton (ed.), *Henry More (1614–1687). Tercentenary Studies* (Dordrecht,
    1990).

10. Marjorie Nicolson, "Christ's College and the Latitude Men," *Modern Philol-
    ogy* 27 (1929–30), pp. 356–74.

11. For More's reception after the Restoration, see Robert Crocker's biograph-
    ical account in Richard Ward, *The Life of Henry More*, ed. S. Hutton et al.
    (Dordrecht, 2000), pp. xiii–xvi.

12. *Apocalypsis Apocalypseos* (London, 1680); *An Illustration of those Two Ab-
    struse Books Daniel and Revelation* (London, 1685); *Answer to Several Remarks
    upon . . . the Apocalypse and Daniel* (London, 1684); and *Paralipomena Prophetica*
    (London, 1685). More also published *A Plain and Continued Exposition of the
    Several Prophecies or Divine Visions of the Prophet Daniel* (London, 1681).

13. John Rumrich argues that Milton would have known of Mede, and that
    Mede is a "likely source" of certain themes in Milton's works, in "Mead
    and Milton," *Milton Quarterly* 20 (1986), pp. 136–41, on p. 139.

14. Marjorie Nicolson, "Milton's 'Old Damaetas'," *Modern Language Notes* 61
    (1926), pp. 293–300.

15. More attacked under the pseudonym Alazonomastix Philalethes. Vaughan
    responded under the name Eugenius Philalethes. See F. B. Burnham,
    "The More-Vaughan controversy: the revolt against philosophical en-
    thusiasm," *JHI* 35 (1975), pp. 33–49; N. L. Brann, "The conflict be-
    tween reason and magic in seventeenth-century England. A Case Study
    on the Vaughan-More Debate," *Huntington Library Quarterly* 43 (1980), pp.
    103–26; A. Miller-Guinsberg, "Henry More, Thomas Vaughan and the Late
    Renaissance Magical Tradition," *Ambix* 27 (1980), pp. 36–58; and Lotte
    Mulligan, " 'Reason', 'right reason' and 'revelation' in mid-seventeenth-
    century England," in B. Vickers (ed.), *Occult and Scientific Mentalities in the
    Renaissance* (Cambridge 1984), pp. 375–401.

16. Marjorie Nicolson, "Milton and the *Conjectura Cabbalistica*," *Philological Quar-
    terly* 27 (1929–30), pp. 356–74, and R. J. Z. Werblowsky, "Milton and the
    Conjectura Cabbalistica," *Journal of the Warburg and Courtauld Institutes* 18 (1955),
    pp. 90–113.

17. For millenarianism and the Hartlib circle, see M. Greengrass, M. Leslie, and T. Raylor (eds.), *Samuel Hartlib and Universal Reformation* (Cambridge, 1994).

18. Michael Murrin makes a claim for Mede's influence on *Paradise Lost*, but he does not support his claim in any detail. See his "The Revelation and two seventeenth-century commentators," in Patrides and Wittreich (eds.), *The Apocalypse*, pp. 125–46.

19. Mede, *Key*, p. 122.

20. Ibid., p. 124.

21. See my "Henry More and the Book of Revelation," *Studies in Church History*, 10 (1994).

22. More, *Apocalypsis Apocalypseos*, p. xvxi.

23. Henry More, *Divine Dialogues* (London 1668), vol. II, p. 29.

24. Another doctrine on which they diverged was mortalism, accepted by Milton but attacked by More in his poem "Antipsychopannychia," in *Psychodia Platonica*.

25. *An Explanation of the Grand Mystery of Godliness*, in More, *Theological Works* (London 1708), pp. 313–14.

3

Milton and millenarianism: from the Nativity Ode to Paradise Regained

Stella P. Revard

In 1642 *The Personall Reigne of Christ upon Earth*, a posthumously published tract by an exiled Puritan minister, caused a sensation, sparking a debate that was to rage for the remainder of the century. Taking as his text the controversial verses of Revelation 20:1–7, Henry Archer maintained that Jesus Christ was shortly to arrive on earth to set up his thousand-year kingdom with his saints and to crush the tyranny of earthly kings.[1] At the same time English Protestants were looking on the establishment of the Long Parliament and the fall of the prelates as signs that they were living in the times when they could expect the prophecies of Revelation to be fulfilled. In the pamphlets that he wrote during the 1640s and 1650s, John Milton also seems to refer to Christ's personal reign. In *Of Reformation* (1641) he announces the day when "the Eternall and shortly-expected King [shall] open the Clouds to judge the severall Kingdomes of the World, and...put an end to all Earthly *Tyrannies*, proclaiming [his] universal and milde *Monarchy* through Heaven and Earth" (*CP* 1: 616). He pronounces in *Areopagitica* (1644) that "God is decreeing to begin some new and great period in his Church" (*CP* 11: 553). In *Animadversions* (1641) he prays in language touched with apocalyptic fervor for "peace in the Church, and righteous judgement in the Kingdome" (*CP* 1: 706), such as would occur at the millennium when Jesus assumed his throne.

Yet we must take care to assess Milton's references to Christ's kingdom from the perspective of the revolutionary times in which he wrote. Although many Christians believed literally in the prophecies of Revelation 20, just as many denied that these verses in any way predicted Christ's personal kingship. Moreover, Puritans often used the prophetic language of Revelation merely to lend biblical authority to political hopes. When their political hopes dimmed after 1660, millenarianism often seemed part of a past era and a lost cause. Therefore, when we consider the poetical works of Milton's maturity, we must determine whether *Paradise Lost* (1667) and *Paradise Regained* (1671) fulfill or turn aside from the millenarianism that he and other Puritans expressed in the preceding decades.

I

Although Puritans of the 1640s based their millenarianism on the writings of Protestant commentators of the sixteenth century, they defined the millennium from a perspective of their own era. Many, like Archer, resurrected the view of the early church Fathers and a radical sect called the Chiliasts, which, led by the millenary Cerinthus, looked on the millennium described in Revelation 20 as fulfilling Jewish prophecy and predicting the coming of the Messiah as an earthly king.[2] The vantage point of the sixteenth century had been different. Following Wycliffe, Luther, and Calvin, most sixteenth-century Protestants viewed Revelation as describing the last days before the Judgment. Identifying the pope as the Antichrist of Revelation and Rome as Babylon, they expected Christ at his Second Coming to judge a corrupt papacy, not to set up a kingdom on earth.[3] In England James I, in a commentary on Revelation first printed in Edinburgh in that apocalyptic year 1588 and reprinted in London in 1603, declared that Antichrist was raging in the person of the pope:

> Now whether the Pope beareth these markes or not, let any indifferent man iudge: I thinke surely it expoundes it selfe. Doeth hee not usurpe Christ his office, calling himselfe uniuersall Bishoppe and head of the Church? Playeth hee not the parte of *Apollyon*, and *Abaddon* the King of the Locusts.[4]

Yet for James the pope's usurpation of Christ's office did not imply that Christ himself would come to wrest the kingship from him. He adopted the so-called orthodox view, enunciated by Augustine, passed down to later church Fathers, and held by Catholics and most Protestants, that the millennium described in Revelation 20 was a past not a future condition of the church: "the happy estate of the Church, from Christes dayes to the dayes of the defection or falling away of the Antichrist." Augustine had defined the millennium indefinitely as the thousand years from the time of Christ's death until the rise of Antichrist, a view not disputed by Protestant reformers. James held that during the millennium the devil was bound by the preaching of the gospel, but now he was loosed out of hell and was raising many new errors.[5] The Scottish commentator John Napier also took this view, dedicating his commentary (1593) to James and describing the millennium as a spiritual period of the evangelical church that had lasted only until Pope Boniface VIII proclaimed his jubilee in 1300. He warned against the errors of the Chiliasts in expecting a temporal reign of Christ on earth. For him the first trumpet of Revelation had sounded with the destruction of the temple in Jerusalem in 71, the seventh in 1541 with the true profession against Antichrist; the last trumpet would sound in 1786 at the Last Judgment.[6]

Many Protestants would have agreed with James I and Napier that Christ's thousand-year reign was over. When it began and when it ended, however, were in some sense movable dates – some commentators dated its commencement at Christ's birth or resurrection, others at the fall of Jerusalem, still others at Constantine's victory over the pagans in AD 331.[7] David Pareus (1548–1622), the German theologian from Heidelberg, believed the millennium began with Christ's victory over paganism: "Thus therefore the Angell hath bound the *Dragon*, Christ by his coming overthrew Paganisme, delivered the Gentiles from the seduction of Satan, and brought them to the light of the Gospell and faith of the Church." Arthur Dent in *The Ruine of Rome* (1603) summed up a common view: that the millennium lasted from the preaching of Christ and the apostles until the time of Pope Gregory the VII.[8]

The Elizabethan theologian Thomas Brightman (1562–1607) was of a different opinion, however. He divided Satan's thousand-year binding from Christ's thousand-year reign. Satan was bound from the early days of the church until 1300. Immediately after Satan's loosing Christ's reign began, its continuance promised for a thousand years.[9] Pareus, like most other commentators, disputed Brightman's double-dating, maintaining that the thousand years of Christ's reign and Satan's binding had to be the same. He also cautioned against viewing Satan's binding during the millennium as absolute, it being rather a conditional "restraint that he could not rage freely among the Nations."[10] Although Milton respected Pareus, he declined to place the millennium in the years up to 1300. These had hardly been a halcyon period for the church. In *Of Reformation* (1641) he remarks that Constantine's era brought in the institution of bishops, the quarrels over orthodoxies, and the beginning of corrupt clergy: "through *Constantines* lavish Superstition they forsook their *first love*, and set themselvs up two Gods instead, *Mammon* and their Belly" (*CP* 1: 576–77). "At this time," he states, using the language of Daniel, "*Antichrist* began first to put forth his horne" (*CP* 1: 557).

Brightman was especially popular with the Puritans in England who opposed the Laudian regime, and he was dubbed by them "[our] faithfull Watchman or our English Prophet...persecuted and banished by the

Bishops."[11] His Latin commentary on Revelation, *Apocalypsis Apocalypseos*, had been suppressed during his lifetime and was printed posthumously in Frankfurt in 1609. Translated into English, it was first published in Amsterdam and Leiden in 1615 and 1616, but not in England until 1644 by order of Parliament. Although written from a late Elizabethan perspective, the commentary seemed to Puritans to describe the events of the past forty years. To those sympathetic with the struggles of the church in Scotland against Laudianism, Brightman's praise of the Calvinistic Church of Scotland as the Philadelphian church described in chapter 3 of Revelation and his condemnation of the English church as the lukewarm Laodicean congregation seemed amazingly apt. Furthermore, many approved of Brightman's identification of Germany as the stricken Church of Sardis and believed that he had thereby predicted the great war of religion on the Continent when Lutherans took up arms against Catholics. Several tracts published in the early 1640s immediately before the first issue of the commentary in England asserted that Brightman's prophesies had been fulfilled in their times.[12] Brightman's exposition of Daniel, together with his commentary on Revelation, predicted events yet to come – that before the year 1650 the Jews would be called repentant to Jerusalem and the pope run out of Rome, and after 1690 the great Turk destroyed. Thereafter Brightman projected a happy tranquility and perpetual peace in the Reformed church, but denied that Christ himself would reign: his rule on earth, Brightman asserted, was "by ministery of his Servants."[13]

In a different way David Pareus was important to English Puritans for both his political and his theological views. Pareus had early incurred royalist disapproval, his treatises having been publicly burnt at Cambridge and Oxford during James I's reign as anti-royalist. In a tract first published in 1622 then reissued in 1642, David Owen denounced Pareus's view that the tyranny of kings and magistrates could be lawfully restrained by the people.[14] Pareus's commentary on Revelation was readily adopted by the anti-Laudians and was translated into English by parliamentary order in 1644. Milton cited Pareus more than once with approval.[15] Although Pareus believed, as Brightman did, that Revelation in part described the times in which they were now living, he was not a millenarian. He believed the millennium was past, and thought the ancient Chiliasts had operated according to a false chronology.[16] In fact, the title page of the 1644 translation of his commentary announces its antimillenarian stance: "And specially some things upon the 20th Chapter are observed by the same Authour against the Millenaries." He particularly takes issue with the view that the saints would be resurrected and would reign with Christ on earth. What John saw, he insists, was the souls of the martyrs, not their bodies, the first resurrection being understood spiritually and not corporally. Of their reign with Christ, he maintains: "They *reigned* also *with Christ*, not in the Kingdome of Grace, which is in this Life, but in the Kingdome of Glory, which is in Heaven."[17]

In the 1640s Pareus and Brightman were read alongside commentators who took more radical views. The most important of these were Joseph Mede, the learned doctor from Milton's own college, Christ's College, Cambridge, and the German theologian Johann Heinrich Alsted, both of whom died in 1638. Mede and Alsted harkened back to the view of the millennium held by many of the early church Fathers – Justin Martyr, Irenaeus, Hippolytos among them – who thought that Christ himself would rule on earth with the resurrected martyrs for a thousand years, at the end of which the last days of the world and the Last Judgment would follow. Mede's Latin treatise *Clavis Apocalyptica*, published in Cambridge in 1627, described the millennium as a future event and projected, as the Chiliasts had, an earthly reign of Christ. His commentary further explicated his millenarian views.

In the 1620s and 1630s Mede had maintained a correspondence with William Twisse, the future prolocutor of the Westminster Assembly, and with Samuel Hartlib and John Dury, whose views on Revelation 20 agreed with his.[18] He endeavored, however, to maintain a low profile during the religious conflicts of the 1630s, trying his best to keep out of disputes such as those about bowing to the altar.[19] Posthumously, though, Mede was summoned to bear witness by the Long Parliament, the *Clavis* translated in 1643 by Richard More as *The Key of the Revelation* appearing by order of the Committee for Printing with a preface by William Twisse.[20]

Also translated in 1643 by order of Parliament was the Latin treatise of Johann Heinrich Alsted (1588–1638): *Diatribe de mille annis apocalypticis* (literally *The Diatribe Concerning the Thousand Years of the Apocalypse*), which had been first published in Frankfurt in 1627.[21] Its English title emphasized its controversial nature, the Latin being rendered as: *The Beloved City, or The Saints Reign on Earth a Thousand Yeares*. Alsted divides the history of the church into four ages, the third of which he projects will begin in 1694 with Christ's return to earth and will last for a thousand years. Christ's reign will be inaugurated with the fall of Antichrist and the conversion of the Jews.[22] Supporting Mede and Alsted was the English theologian

Nathanael Homes, who in *The Resurrection Revealed* (London, 1654) firmly separated the views of modern millenarians from those of the heretical Chiliast Cerinthus.[23]

A distinctive feature of commentaries such as Mede's, Brightman's, and Alsted's was their coordination of the prophecies of Daniel with those of Revelation. Conservative interpreters believed that Daniel predicted events already past – the persecution of the Jews by Antiochus, the revolt of the Maccabees, and the destruction of the Temple in Jerusalem in AD 70.[24] The millenarians thought that Daniel, like Revelation, foretold events yet to come. For them the kingdom of the saints described in Daniel was one with that predicted in Revelation 20.[25] Daniel identified, moreover, the events that would precede Christ's advent to rule, namely the persecutions of the Christians under Antichrist, the conversion of the Jews and their return to Jerusalem, and the fall of Antichrist. With Antichrist's fall the power of Rome would crumble and the saints would triumph, inaugurating their reign on earth with Christ. Certain chapters of Daniel supplied the numbers that permitted millenarians to date these crucial events.[26] Many commentators dated these events in the 1650s or 1660s. Archer placed the conversion of the Jews before 1556, the breaking of Rome's tyranny before 1666, and Christ's coming before 1700.[27]

In the 1640s millenarianism became an issue that defined and separated Puritans, Presbyterians, and the orthodox oldliners of the Church of England. In the 1630s little divided those who were proclaiming that Christ's earthly kingdom was at hand and those who believed the Last Judgment was imminent. Both groups were anti-Catholic and anti-Laudian and would have agreed that Satan was unbound and raging, persecuting the saints, whom many identified with the martyrs of the church named in Revelation.[28] With the advent of the Long Parliament, the cries that Babylon was falling were heard everywhere. In the sermon *Babylons Downfall*, preached before the House of Commons in 1641, William Bridge announced: "How else shall *Sion* rise, if *Babylon* doe not fall? ... God is making way to such a Jubilee, therefore *Babylon* must fall, and that assuredly."[29] Indeed, in a practical sense, the prophecies of Revelation proved invaluable propaganda in opposing the so-called papist predilections of the English bishops and in advancing the so-called rule of the saints. The commentaries by Mede, Alsted, Brightman, Napier, and Pareus, which were Englished by order of the Long Parliament, stood alongside controversial millenarian tracts, such as Thomas Goodwin's *A Glimpse of Sions Glory* (1641) and Archer's *The Personall Reigne of Christ upon Earth* (1642). But while the publication of radical commentaries on Revelation and tracts on millenarianism called forth strong support from some, it provoked heated rebuttals from others.

Principal among the opponents of millenarianism were the Presbyterians and the dispossessed clergy of the Church of England. In *A Dissvasive from the Errours of the Time* (1645), Robert Baillie, a Presbyterian member of the Westminster Assembly, coupled his denunciation of the Chiliasts with a fierce attack on the Independents, whose rise to political prominence he opposed.[30] He branded them as heretics, maintaining that the views of noted Independents – Archer, Goodwin, Burrowes – were outside orthodox belief. In *Errours and Induration, are the Great Sins and Great Judgments of the Time* (1645), Baillie denounces Archer as "a famous Independent," who "printed the worst and grossest of the Blasphemies," which had been "justly burnt."[31] The final chapter of *A Dissvasive* combines a refutation of millenarianism with an attack on the Independents who espoused it.[32] Of Milton, whose views on divorce he condemned, Baillie wrote: "I doe not know certainely whither [*sic*] this man professeth *Independency* (albeit all the Hereticks here, whereof ever I heard, avow themselves Independents)."[33]

In *Gangraena* (1646) the Presbyterian divine Thomas Edwards also attempts to discredit the Independents as heretics by naming millenarianism as one of their errors. Independency, he asserts, "opens the gate to all kinde of Singularities and Extravagancies," among which he lists "believing those opinions of the personal visible reign of Christ that outward glorious Kingdom which shall be on earth."[34] In his "Epistle Dedicatory" to part 3, he urges Parliament not to pass the Act of Toleration, freely confessing his aim to hinder sectaries from "all places of power and trust in the Kingdome, and from spreading their Errors and Opinions to the hurting of others, keep the unsound from the sound… *Babell* must come down as well as Babylon."[35] In the part 2 of *Gangraena* (1646), Edwards attacked Milton's *Doctrine and Discipline of Divorce*.[36] Milton struck back in his "tailed" sonnet, "On the New Forcers of Conscience under the Long Parliament" (c. 1646), excoriating "Shallow *Edwards*" and Baillie, the "Scotch what d'ye call" (l. 12), as those who would force "our Consciences that Christ set free" (l. 6). While he inveighs against the "*New Presbyter*[s]" who have replaced the "old *Priest*[s]" (l. 14), he also defends the Independents: "Men whose Life, Learning, Faith, and pure intent / Would have been held in high esteem with *Paul* / Must now be nam'd and printed Heretics" (ll. 9–11). In defending the free-thinking Independents, Milton expresses his libertarian principles at the same time as he throws in his lot with men who were looking forward to Christ's earthly rule.

With the rise of the Fifth Monarchists and the dissolution of monarchy and the institutions associated with it, millenarianism took on a yet more threatening aspect for conservative Anglicans and Presbyterians. The Fifth Monarchists were not merely predicting the millennium but urging that military and political action be taken to bring it about.[37] Two very different men followed Baillie and Edwards as opponents both of the Independents and of the Fifth Monarchists: Joseph Hall, Milton's old adversary from the days of the Smectymnuan tracts, and Christopher Love, a Presbyterian preacher, who, like Milton, had opposed Hall and the prelates in the early 1640s but now, like Baillie and Edwards, regarded the sectaries as more dangerous enemies than the bishops. In rejecting the millenarian claims of the Independents and the Fifth Monarchists, Love and Hall were attempting to stem the radical changes that had overtaken English society.

In a sermon on John 14:3, Christopher Love begins his critique of the Chiliasts by querying "whether Christ Jesus in promising to his Disciples to come again, did meane to come to Reigne upon the Earth here a thousand years, or whether it bee to bee meant of Christs last coming to judge the world." Supporting his fellow Presbyterians, Baillie and Edwards, as well as Bishop Hall, his former adversary, Love ridicules both the ancient sect of the "pestilent Heretick" Cerinthus and the foolish contradictions of the modern millenaries who follow the Chiliasts in expecting the "vain and carnall corruptions of a temporall Kingdome." He reserves his fiercest scorn for the Fifth Monarchists, the "Saints of these times," who live in sensuality and commit such wickedness that it would be a scandal for Christ to reign with them. He asserts that they "do make but a bad preparative for Christs reigne, that doe impale Saint-ship, and monopolize Saint-ship unto themselves."[38] Love's opposition to the Fifth Monarchists at a time when they were among Cromwell's strongest allies could not escape having political implications. Love swore in his trial that he had not assisted Charles Stuart, but he was executed in 1651 on the very day that Cromwell won the battle of Worcester.[39]

That antimillenarianism was politically motivated is all too clear when Bishop Joseph Hall reemerges upon the scene, coming out of retirement to publish anonymously in 1650 a tract entitled *The Revelation Unrevealed*, designed to refute the treatises of Archer, Alsted, and Mede.[40] Hall reveals himself on the title page only as "an unfained Lover of *Truth, Peace, Order,* and just *Moderation,*" who is "Laying forth the weak Grounds, and strange

Consequences of that plausible, and too much received *Opinion*." His aim, he says, is only to expose errors in order to protect the credulous and well-minded. However, Hall was in fact far from a disinterested opponent. He aimed to bring modern millenarians into disrepute by linking their views with Chiliastic opinion, "which was so many hundred years ago hooted out of the Christian Church."[41] Throughout his tract he promotes the so-called orthodox position that the millennium referred to in Revelation 20 is a spiritual state in the church and historically long past:

All Christian Authors, till the fag-end of this last Century, understood [the millennium] of the spirituall beauty, and the glory of the Evangelicall Church, under the happy times of the Gospell: Whosoever shall bee pleased to take a strict view of these severall Scriptures, shall finde them onely to import the calling of the *Gentiles*, the conversions of the *Jewes* ... abundance of rich graces poured out upon beleevers, Gods gracious protection, and enlargement of his Christian Church, the subjugation, and overthrow of the publique enemies thereof; all which may well stand without any relation to this pretended domination of the raised Martyrs, or changed Saints.[42]

Where Baillie and Edwards used invective to discredit the millenarians, Hall used ridicule. It is ludicrous to think, maintains Hall, that Christ would descend to earth personally, resurrect the saints – who were already ruling with him in heaven – and reign for a thousand years, only to reascend to heaven to await the Last Judgment. Hall takes great care to explicate the prophesies in Daniel, stating emphatically that these were fulfilled long ago with the destruction of Jerusalem under Titus and do not relate to the so-called persecutions of the Reformed church in the present day.[43] It is a basic error, he maintains, to put a "literall construction upon the prophesies and promises of Scripture, which the holy Ghost intended onely to be spiritually understood." Concerning the so-called conversion of the Jews and their return to the Holy Land, he wonders at those who humor the Jews with the prediction of the "restauration of that pompous and secular glory, which they have hitherto fondly dreamed of." Among these, of course, was Cromwell who readmitted the Jews into England. Hall advises Christians to "keepe close to their old Tenets; and to beware of all either new-devised, or re-divised errours of opinion: whereof this last age of ours is deplorably fruitfull." Like Love, Hall had a special animus for the Fifth Monarchists, warning that "some vainly imagining this Reign of the Saints already begun, cast off Scriptures, and Ordinances as utterly use-lesse, and please themselves in a conceited fruition of their happy Kingdom, and an immediate conversation with the King of Glory."[44]

At first Cromwell may have viewed the Fifth Monarchists' projections of Christ's rule on earth as compatible with his own political ambitions. But once he had set up the Protectorate in 1653, he began to find Christopher Feake, John Rogers, and their group troublesome. A broadsheet put out in the 1650s, *A True Emblem of Antichrist: or Schism Display'd*, called Cromwell Antichrist, naming him as the head of heretical sects such as the Fifth Monarchists. In a speech to Parliament on 4 September 1654, the Protector cautiously dissociates himself from the Fifth Monarchists without ever denying a belief in Christ's future kingdom:

We may reckon among these our spiritual evils, an evil that hath more refinednesse in it, and more colour for it; and hath deceived more people of integrity then the rest have done: for few have been catched with the former mistakes, but such as have Apostatized from their holy profession; such as being corrupt in their Consciences, have been forsaken by God, and left to noysome opinions. But I say, there are others more refined: many honest people, whose hearts are sincere; many of them belonging to God: and that is the mistaken Notion of the fifth Monarchy. A thing pretending more spirituality, then any thing else: A Notion I hope we all honour, wait, and hope for; that Jesus Christ will have a time to set up his Reigne *in our hearts* [my italics], by subduing those Corruptions, and lusts, and evils that are there, which reigne now more in the world, then I hope in due time they shall do; And when more fulnesse of the Spirit is poured forth to subdue iniquity, and bring everlasting righteousness, then will the approach of that Glory be.

Wishing to keep order, Cromwell denies that disruptions in the state are signs of Christ's imminent coming, as the Fifth Monarchists urged: "The Carnal Divisions, and Contentions amongst Christians, so common, are not the symptoms of that Kingdome."[45]

Views very like Cromwell's had already been voiced by a clergyman close to him – John Owen. Himself a millenarian, Owen cited Daniel 2:44 in his sermon of thanksgiving for Cromwell's victory at Worcester, affirming that God even now was advancing Christ's kingdom in preparation for his coming.[46] While he takes Daniel 7:15–16 as his text in a sermon delivered the next year (*Concerning the Kingdome of Christ, And the Power of the Civile Magistrate about the things of the Worship of God*), he seeks to check the invective of the Fifth Monarchists, cautioning against expecting the immediate fulfillment of millenarian prophecies.[47] He warns that those who depart from the spirituality of Christ's rule have degenerated into "carnall Apprehensions" and are dazzled with "gazing after temporall glory." While never directly naming the Fifth Monarchists, Owen maintains:

The comming in of the kingdome of Christ, shall not be by the Arme of flesh, nor shall it be the product of the strifes and contests of men which are in the world . . . It shall be by the glorious manifestation of his own power, and that by his spirit subduing the soules of men unto it; not by the sword of man setting up a few to rule over others.[48]

More to the point, he urges support of those magistrates and rulers who themselves uphold the interest of the Church and the people.[49]

Like Owen, Cromwell demanded civil obedience, calling upon the Fifth Monarchists to submit themselves to magistrates if they "do but pretend for Justice, and righteousness; and be of peaceable spirits." He was especially critical of the way in which they should "entitle themselves, upon this Principle, that they are the only men to rule Kingdomes."[50] Ultimately he felt compelled to deal harshly with them, imprisoning the leaders Christopher Feake and John Rogers when they continued to agitate rebellion. Yet he hesitated to crush them absolutely when, on their release, they continued to denounce London with Rome as anti-Christian and to identify Cromwell as the beast: "London! thou City! and Seat of the second Beast! next to Rome mayst thou look for the Wrath upon thee! for thy bowing down unto the Beast! persecuting the Saints!"[51] The final blow struck against the Fifth Monarchists did not come until after the Restoration, when Charles II executed Thomas Venner and his associates, virtually wiping out the sect, after they led an uprising that had earlier been planned against Cromwell.[52]

Although wary of the Fifth Monarchists, Cromwell retained close to him several clergymen who were proponents of millenarianism – principally Thomas Goodwin, who attended Cromwell on his deathbed. Goodwin had written more than one millenarian tract. In *A Glimpse of Sions Glory* (1641), he interpreted the coming of the Long Parliament as a clear sign that Christ's kingdom on earth was near. In its prefatory epistle W. K. announced, "the day is now dawning, wherein *Sions* Peace and Comforts shall bee fulfilled, *Iesus Christ* set up, the sole and great King of his Church."[53] Some thirteen years later, in the very year that Cromwell moderated his millenarian views, Goodwin is still proclaiming his in *A Sermon of the Fifth Monarchy. Proving by Invincible Arguments, That the Saints shall have a Kingdom here on Earth, Which is yet to come, after the Fourth Monarchy is destroy'd by the Sword of the Saints, the followers of the Lamb* (London, 1654). Goodwin himself promises that Christ the King will make the saints partakers of power in his kingdom on earth, urging patience for those who have lost faith in the millennium. In the preface a so-called "servant of the saints" defends the term Fifth Monarchy Men from being made the butt of scoffers and "a mark of Ignominy and Reproach" ("To the Reader," sig. A2): "Then how cautious ought we to be, of CENSURING those of Gods people who go beyond us in their prayers and desires, lest we prove Opposers of the Spirit of God in them" ("To the Reader," sig. A).

Milton gives short shrift to the Fifth Monarchists in the first edition of *The Readie and Easie Way* (1660), warning against those "ambitious leaders of armies" and their "hypocritical pretences so ready at hand to contest with Parlaments." Were they put down, he remarks, "ther would be then no more pretending to a fifth monarchie of the saints; but much peace and tranquillitee would follow" (*CP* VII: 380–81). Like Owen and Cromwell, he was concerned about the civil disruptions the Fifth Monarchists were inciting. Urging liberty of conscience, he remarks that in the Netherlands civil disquiet ceased when persecution of the Arminians ceased. To criticize the actions of the Fifth Monarchists, however, is not the same as dismissing their millenarian views. Moreover, Milton removed his attack on the Fifth Monarchists from the second edition of *The Readie and Easie Way* (1660).[54]

In a treatise on the Fifth Monarchy published in 1659 and appended to his commentary on Revelation, William Hicks takes a position similar to Milton's. He deplores the Fifth Monarchists' resistance to magistrate rule at the same time as he expresses support for their millenarian views.[55] Some twenty years later Henry More (1614–87) addresses the question of the Fifth Monarchists in *Apocalypsis Apocalypseos* (1680), supporting millenarianism without countenancing revolution brought on by the sword.[56] These views are consonant with those expressed by Milton in *A Treatise of Civil Power* (1659). Although the *Treatise* cites Jesus' refusal to defend himself by military force or to set up a temporal kingdom (John 18:36), its principal concern is not the question of Christ's future kingship but the government of church and state. Milton recognizes that commonwealths must sometimes use "outward force" (*CP* VII: 256–58). Moreover, the citing of Jesus' denial of a temporal kingdom at his first coming is not proof that Milton had given up expectation of his earthly kingship at the second.

Milton affirms his faith in the millennium in *The Readie and Easie Way*. A strong and free commonwealth would ensure such "peace, justice, plentifull trade and all prosperitie" throughout the whole land that would lead:

even to the coming of our true and rightfull and only to be expected King, only worthie as he is our only Saviour, the Messiah, the Christ, the only heir of his eternal father, the only by him anointed and ordaind since the work of our redemption finishd, Universal Lord of all mankinde. (*CP* vii:444–45)

Some editors urge us to view the millenarianism expressed here as mere rhetorical flourish. Milton has, of course, a special agenda in invoking Christ's kingship at this moment. Having mounted an argument against kingship, he uses Christ the King as foil to Charles the king, contrasting Christ's return to earth as true king with Charles II's return to England as spurious king. Until King Messiah comes, Milton argues, a commonwealth, not a restored monarchy, will guarantee the peace, justice, and prosperity that the English have every right to expect. Yet, even if Milton has a political message to get across, we should not dismiss his millenarianism out of hand. From his very first tract in 1641 to this tract written on the eve of the Restoration, millenarianism undergirds Milton's political expectations. The passage just quoted from *The Readie and Easie Way* with its passionate statement concerning Christ's expected kingdom resembles an earlier passage from *Of Reformation*, where Milton encourages the English people to persevere in truth and righteousness, to cast off old vices, and to:

presse on hard to that *high* and *happy* emulation to be found the *soberest*, *wisest*, and *most Christian People* at that day when thou the Eternall and shortly-expected King shalt open the Clouds to judge the severall Kingdomes of the World, and distributing *Nationall Honours* and *Rewards* to Religious and just *Common-wealths*, shalt put an end to all Earthly *Tyrannies*, proclaiming thy universal and milde *Monarchy* through Heaven and Earth. (*CP* i: 616)

It would be a mistake to gloss over the apocalyptic content of these passages and to focus only on their political message.[57]

Furthermore, the apocalyptic views expressed in *Of Reformation* and *The Readie and Easie Way* – tracts written with political ends in mind – closely resemble those expressed in theological treatises such as *De Doctrina Christiana* and Mede's *The Key of the Revelation*. In his commentary to *Key*, Mede described belief in the millennium as the "pillar of the Evangelicall faith," which, if undermined or neglected, would much damage the faith.[58] Both *De Doctrina* and Mede's commentary assign the thousand-year reign of Christ to the time of Christ's coming in judgment, asserting that Christ's reign would be during the day of judgment, which would itself continue a thousand years.[59] Mede compares the Last Judgment to a long symbolic day that begins with the judgment against Antichrist and the appearance of our Lord in flaming fire. At noon of this day occurs the thousand-year reign and the granting of the New Jerusalem to the spouse. Toward evening comes the loosing of Satan, and the day concludes with the judgment of all the dead and the universal resurrection.[60]

The thirty-third chapter of *De Doctrina Christiana* also looks on the millennium as commencing with the Last Judgment and extending for the period of a symbolic day: "Christ's reign, then, will extend from the beginning to the end of this time of judgment, and will continue for some time after the judgment has finished, until all the enemies are subdued." Like Mede's commentary, *De Doctrina* divides Christ's reign of grace from his reign of glory: the reign of grace "also called *the kingdom of heaven*, began with his first advent . . . But his reign of glory will not begin until his second coming, Dan. vii. 13, 14." *De Doctrina* interprets Daniel as referring to Christ's Second Coming, which "is always described as coming *with the clouds*, so it is certainly his second coming which is referred to in the Daniel passage, not his birth, as Junius claims, but his coming to judge the world." *De Doctrina* cites Psalms as well as Revelation to prove that Christ's reign will take place on the earth, Psalms 2:8, 9, compared with Rev. 2:25–27 (*CP* vi:623–24). What is particularly of interest is that *De Doctrina* cites the very texts from Daniel, Psalms, and Isaiah, as well as Matthew, Luke, 1 Corinthians, and Revelation that Mede and Alsted and other millenarians cite to prove the expectation of Christ's earthly reign.[61]

Although the dating of *De Doctrina Christiana* and its status in Milton's canon are problematical, demonstration of Milton's millenarianism does not rest solely on the theological treatise and its likeness to Mede's *Clavis* and other millenarian works.[62] *De Doctrina* merely spells out in theological language what Milton had said elsewhere in *Of Reformation*, *Animadversions* and *The Readie and Easie Way*: that Christ's coming in judgment would occur at the same time as his coming to set up his future reign on earth.

II

How early did Milton the poet become a millenarian, and how are his apocalyptic views reflected in his poetry – early and late? An apocalyptic fervor characterizes *In Quintum Novembris* and the gunpowder epigrams (1625–26), which, like James I's and Napier's commentaries, revile the pope as Antichrist and denounce Catholic attempts to suppress Protestantism. Also, Milton may be alluding indirectly to the millennium in "On the Morning of Christ's Nativity" when he envisions the establishment of a classical Golden Age with Astraea's return to earth. Yet he declines to predict its imminent accomplishment: "wisest Fate says no, / This must not yet be so" (ll. 149–50). The "wakeful trump of doom" has not yet sounded to wake the dead (l. 156).[63] At the same time he appears to share Pareus's view that Satan was partially bound at Christ's birth, pronouncing: "Th'old Dragon under ground, / In straiter limits bound, / Not half so far casts his usurped sway" (ll. 168–70). Others of Milton's early poems – "On Time" and "At a Solemn Music" – also take time or the end of time as themes, and *Lycidas*, too, has its apocalyptic moment. Yet, even though the young Milton probably knew Mede's *Clavis Apocalyptica* (1627), the early poetry does not speak unequivocally of Christ's coming to rule on earth. It apparently took the events of the 1640s to awaken Milton's millenarian expectations fully.

Crucial to our understanding of Milton's millenarianism are the major poems, *Paradise Lost* and *Paradise Regained*, works completed after the Restoration, when the millenarian hopes of the 1640s and 1650s had dimmed for Milton as for others. With royalist censorship once more imposed, moreover, what could have been directly expressed before Charles II's return no longer could be. For example, when Mede's works were issued in a folio edition in 1664, the editor included a special caveat concerning Mede's millenarianism.[64] The *Clavis* was included in Latin only; the English translation of 1643, perhaps viewed as politically dangerous, was suppressed. More and more the millennium was described as a spiritual phenomenon. Conservative theologians such as James Durham proposed that "there is no absolute temporall Kingdom promised . . . there is no ground to expect our Lords presence personally and visibly to converse on earth with His people, though we will not say, but there is in this time an eminent measure of His presence by His Spirit and Power in His Ordinances, and manifestations in His dispensations more than ordinary; that is not controverted."[65] Mede's Cambridge successor, Henry More, also took a conservative view, dissociating himself from political controversy and expressing in *Apocalypsis Apocalypseos* (1680) and in his several treatises on Daniel his belief in Christ's spiritual rather than fleshly reign.[66]

Even modified expressions of millenarianism risked being taken to signal political dissent. Replying to a critique of Henry More's *Exposition on Daniel*, an Answerer asserts that millenarianism promotes seditious and rebellious behavior which is incompatible with monarchy and magistrate rule: "Sound understanding of Daniel and the Apocalypse does not belong to Fanatical Enthusiasts, but to men of a more rational Genius, serene mind, and sober judgment."[67] Others continued to believe in the literal appearance of Christ. Archer's *Personall Reigne of Christ* was reissued in 1661. A pamphlet on Revelation and Daniel, published in 1671, asserted:

> The good new World to come will then begin; for upon the ruine of Satans Kingdom, Christs is set up in the world for 1000 years: for which time Satan is bound, and Christ reigneth personally with his Saints. All which time the Wife of the Lamb, the New *Jerusalem* that came down from God out of Heaven (after whose light the Nations that are saved, shall walk) will be the Mother Citie of Christs said Kingdom.[68]

With millenarianism seen as signaling dissent, Milton had to be circumspect in expressing views he had formerly espoused openly. Although he alludes to Christ's kingship in *Paradise Lost* and *Paradise Regained*, he does so in general terms. It is true that in Book 3 of *Paradise Lost* God refers to the Son's assumption of a regal scepter when he judges mankind with his saints. Also, in Book 12 Michael prophesies Christ's kingship: "he shall ascend / The Throne hereditary, and bound his Reign / With earth's wide bounds, his glory with the Heav'ns" (12.369–71). However, Michael's account of the last days includes only the assurance that the Lord will come in the clouds from heaven "to dissolve / Satan with his perverted World" and raise "New Heav'ns, new Earth, Ages of endless date" (12.546–47, 549). Milton assigns neither dates nor times to Christ's reign, nor does he employ the words millennium or thousand-year. Such an absence of specificity might make one conclude that by the time he wrote *Paradise Lost* he no longer ranked himself among those expecting Christ's return to earth as king. But to do so, I think, would be mistaken. Milton rarely relinquished opinions – especially those dear to him – simply because history seemed to have voted against them. He was no less a believer in a free commonwealth after the Restoration than before. So with the millennium. However, since belief in Christ's earthly kingship was associated with radical sects, to promote millenarianism openly – even in the prophetic sections of *Paradise Lost* – might appear to be resurrecting the Good Old Cause with the resurrected saints.

Yet there are hints everywhere. In Book 3 of *Paradise Lost* Milton specifically describes the Son laying by his regal scepter at the end of time: "For regal Sceptre then no more shall need, / God shall be All in All" (3.340–41). The allusion is to 1 Corinthians 15:28: "And when all things shall be subdued unto him, then shall the Son also himself be subject unto him that put all things under him, that God may be all in all."

Milton undoubtedly knew that most millenarians believed that this text referred to Christ's surrendering of his rule to God at the conclusion of the thousand years. Brightman cites it as evidence that Christ would cease to reign on earth before the Last Judgment: "For Christ shall deliver up the Kingdom to his Father at that time, and God shall be all in all."[69] Moreover, 1 Corinthians 15:28 continued to inspire millenarian debate until the end of the century.[70] For Milton to assign this text to God in Book 3 would certainly have signaled to knowledgeable readers the presence of a millenarian subtext at a significant point in *Paradise Lost*.

Other covert references to the millennium occur throughout *Paradise Lost*. The descriptions of Satan's chaining, which occur in *Paradise Lost* from several different temporal perspectives – now present, now past, now future – surely allude to the thousand-year chaining in Revelation 20:2. In Book 1 Satan lies chained on the burning lake, then breaks his chains (by God's permission) in order to pursue his revenge against God and ultimately against Man. In describing Satan in chains immediately after his fall, Milton seems to look forward to his chaining at the beginning of Christ's thousand-year reign. What is more, when Satan breaks his chains in Book 1, Milton reminds us that he must be loosed from his chains at the end of the millennium. Mede, in his "A Coniecture Concerning Gog and Magog in the Revelation," comments that just as Satan had been set loose by God to tempt our first parents in Eden, he is again loosed (after his thousand-year binding) by God's permission to stir up Gog and Magog to afflict humankind once more.[71]

In Book 4 Gabriel threatens to chain the defiant Satan: "Back to th' infernal pit I drag thee chain'd, / And Seal thee so, as henceforth not to scorn / The facile gates of hell too slightly barr'd" (4.965–67). "Seal" is a significant word. In Revelation the angel with the key to the bottomless pit binds Satan, casts him into the pit, and also sets "a seal on him" (20:3). The mere mention of chaining and sealing recalls the prophecy. In Book 6 another angel – Michael – threatens to drag Satan to hell "Captive . . . in Chains" (6.260), as though to predict that an angel from heaven will ultimately accomplish this task. In Book 6, however, it is the Son who casts Satan out of heaven to "Adamantine Chains and penal Fire" (1.48), returning us at mid-epic to the temporal point with which the epic began.[72] These repeated allusions to chains cannot help having reverberations of Revelation 20:1–3.

Many critics agree that the narrative of Satan's rebellion in Books 5 and 6 is apocalyptic, recounting not merely Satan's first challenge to God's authority but also his final battle against the saints at the end of time.[73] However, critical discussion of the war in heaven rarely takes into account the prophecies of Revelation 20 – Satan's binding in hell and Christ's thousand-year reign – even though both these events are subtly alluded to in Raphael's narrative. Raphael begins with God's decree of the Son's kingship and concludes with Satan cast into hell and the Son's establishment as king.

The initial event in Raphael's narrative – God's setting his king upon the holy hill of Sion – is based on Psalm 2, the very text that millenarians interpreted as a prophecy of Christ's future kingdom. Archer maintains that Psalm 2 applies both to the eternal generation of Christ's person and to the establishment of his earthly kingship. The psalmist, he observes, uses the present to predict future things: "its said, *he reigneth*, because its a sure prophecie, and so speakes as if it were in present, as is usuall in the Prophets, to speak as in present of a future thing."[74] George Hughes and Mary Cary cite Psalm 2 both to celebrate Parliament's victories and to announce Christ's imminent kingdom.[75]

Not only does Milton's God use the prophetic mode in Book 5 to proclaim the Son's kingship, but Satan also reacts by raising the war in response to a predicted kingship rather than one already in place. The Son's reign in heaven, like his future reign on earth, cannot effectively commence until Satan is chained. Renaissance commentators generally agreed that the war in heaven described in Revelation 12 was a future, not a past event. Pareus even comments that the events of chapter 12 are parallel in time with those described in chapter 20.[76]

Together with key passages from Revelation (2:27, 12:5, and 19:15), Psalm 2 predicts Christ's victory over his enemies. Those who have revolted are told: "Kiss the Son, lest he be angry, and ye perish from the way, when his wrath is kindled." Also, it is predicted that Christ will "break them with a rod of iron" (Psalm 2:12, 9).[77] The prophecy of Psalm 2 underlies Abdiel's encounter with Satan at the end of Book 5. Echoing the words of the psalm, Abdiel warns Satan to placate the angry Son:

>   hast'n to appease
> Th' incensed Father, and th' incensed Son
> . . . .
> That Golden Sceptre which thou didst reject
> Is now an Iron Rod to bruise and break
> Thy disobedience.   (5.846–7, 886–88)

Milton's translation of Psalm 2, composed in August 1653, looks forward to this passage. Perhaps in response to the agitations of the early

1650s, Milton endowed the translation with millenarian anticipation. According to millenarians the rod of iron described in Psalm 2 is the means whereby Christ will effect his thousand-year rule on earth. Revelation 2:27 echoes Psalm 2: "he shall rule them with a rod of iron"; Revelation 12:5 alludes to Christ Jesus: "The man child is to rule all nations with a rod of iron." Alsted observes in *The Beloved City*: "You may gather out of these two places, that Christ shall be Lord and King of all people, Jews and Gentiles, when he shall gather them into his Church." Revelation 19:15 is yet more important in this context. The man on the white horse, who leads his armies against the beast and the kings, is the returned Christ who "will rule them with a rod of iron."[78] George Hughes in his sermon *VAE-EUGE-TUBA* remarks that God vindicates a double right: Christ "shall use his Iron Rod as well as his Golden Scepter," and the kingdoms the pope has usurped God now takes "as a spoyle for Christ," subdued as Revelation 19 promises, by the power of the Lord.[79] By making Abdiel refer to both scepter and rod, Milton alludes to the promise of Christ's kingship in Psalm 2 and its realization in Revelation 19 with the defeat of Antichrist, whom Satan here symbolically represents.

The description of the throne of the Son's chariot in Book 6 is drawn from both Revelation and Ezekiel. In Revelation (4:2–5) the throne is ringed with a rainbow and out of it proceed lightning and thunders. In Ezekiel (1:26) the likeness of a throne appears in the midst of the chariot, on which sat a man, readily identified by commentators as Christ. Several sermons celebrating the victories of parliamentary forces allude to Christ appearing enthroned in Ezekiel's chariot. In a sermon preached in 1647 John Carter declares: "The man sitting above upon the throne, is *Lord Jesus Christ*." He connects Christ's appearance in the chariot of Ezekiel with the events stirring the nation: "The living creatures, or Cherubins, they are Angels, good Angels, which are immediatly under the command of Christ."[80] In a thanksgiving sermon for Parliament's victories (1649), Peter Sterry proclaims that the current events demonstrate that "Iesus Christ is now comming forth with his Garment dyed Red in the blood of his Enemies." Citing the numbers of Daniel, he predicts the calling of the Jews and Christ's Second Coming: "The *Outward Calling*, though not the *Inner Conversion* of the *Iewes* is expected neare this time... it is now that *Iesus Christ* shall begin to appear for his People." On the throne of Ezekiel's chariot he sees "the Likeness of a *Man*, which is the *Glorified Person* of our Saviour."[81] In another sermon he takes Revelation 1:7 as his text, describing Christ's appearance in a chariot: "The second Coming of Christ is not on Foot, as a Servant...'Tis as of a Prince in his chariot."[82] When Milton alludes to Christ mounting Ezekiel's chariot, he looks back on sermons such as these which interpret Ezekiel's chariot as a symbol of Christ's coming kingship. In *Paradise Lost* the chariot is both the symbol and the effective means by which the Son claims the kingship ordained for him.

Yet another aspect of Book 6 establishes it as millenarian: throughout it Milton designates the Son's angelic supporters as saints. The word "saint" can signify either an angel or a human being. The Puritans in England, the soldiers of Cromwell's army, and other radical Christians identified themselves with the saints described in Daniel and Revelation. The earliest reference to saints in *Paradise Lost* alludes to the resurrected martyrs assembled with Christ, as in Revelation 20:4, 11, to judge bad men and angels (3.330–31). The saints of Book 6, however, are the warring angels whom God dispatches with Michael and Gabriel: "lead forth to Battle these my Sons / Invincible, lead forth my armed Saints" (6.46–47). The Son goes forth in his chariot, attended by "ten thousand thousand saints" (6.767). Before engaging Satan's army Christ promises them, as in Revelation 14:13, "rest" from battle: "Yea … they may rest from their labors; and their works do follow them":

> Stand still in bright array ye Saints, here stand
> Ye Angels arm'd, this day from Battle rest.
> (6.801–02)

After Satan's expulsion, moreover, the Messiah turns to meet his saints, "who silent stood / Eye-witnesses of his Almighty Acts" (6.882–83). Yet, even before he went forth to conquer Satan, the Son had predicted that his saints would on his return circle God's "holy Mount," singing "unfeign'd *Halleluiahs*" to God (6.743–44). And so they do.

This repeated use of the word "saints" to designate the angels of God's heavenly army would have struck Milton's early readers as particularly meaningful. They must have been reminded, of necessity, of the warring saints of Cromwell's army who went forth to engage Charles I and his cavaliers.[83] But by the time Milton published *Paradise Lost*, such a reminder would have been defeatist: a nostalgic look backward at those who battled for a cause now lost. The "saints" were once more subject to the kings of the earth and no Christ had appeared to rescue them. Yet, although the Civil War had failed to effect Christ's kingdom on earth, the predictions from Revelation remained resonant for the faithful. When Milton at the end of Book 6 describes the Messiah riding triumphant into the "Courts / And Temple of his mighty Father" (6.889–90), he is not looking backward, but ahead. Some critics have taken the Son's triumphant process as the prophecy of Jesus' entry into Jerusalem. Rather, it should be taken as the triumph of Revelation 19, where Christ riding the white horse defeats the earthly armies before commencing his earthly rule. Milton is affirming the prophecies of Daniel and Revelation. The description in *Paradise Lost* of saints "with Jubilee advanc'd," singing the triumph of the "Victorious King" (6.884, 886), echoes the passage from *Of Reformation* where he first expressed his millenarian hopes:

Then amidst the *Hymns* and *Halleluiahs* of *Saints* some one may perhaps bee heard offering at high *strains* in new and lofty *Measures* to sing and celebrate thy *divine Mercies*, and *marvelous Judgements* . . . (*CP* 1:616)

Such echoing suggests that Milton in the 1660s was less pessimistic about England's future than some critics have urged. In *Paradise Lost* he makes Christ's assumption of a heavenly kingship the centerpiece of his epic; in *Paradise Regained* he focuses his attention on the question of Christ's earthly kingship.

James H. Sims has observed that "the reading and interpretation of biblical texts is central to *Paradise Regained*."[84] Both Jesus and Satan quote scripture, but the way they interpret texts – often the same texts – is radically different, especially when the texts are from the prophetic books of the Hebrew Bible and concern the coming of the Messiah and his predicted kingdom. From the moment when Jesus is proclaimed son at his baptism – an event recounted from his, God's, and Satan's perspective – until his victory on the pinnacle, the question of his status as son and of his role as Israel's future king is central to Milton's brief epic. The proclamation of sonship in *Paradise Regained* is in many ways parallel to the proclamation of kingship in *Paradise Lost*. In both epics God affirms the Son as son; both epics use the text of Psalm 2 – the metaphorical begetting of the Son – as a touchstone. Moreover, in both Satan reacts forcefully to a proclamation of sonship.

Milton's view of Christ's kingship in *Paradise Regained* reverberates with echoes of both Revelation and Daniel, the books that millenarians cite most often when they wish to describe Christ's reign on earth. In recreating the historical context of *Paradise Regained*, Milton makes use of the gospels to tell the story of Satan's temptation of the Son. But he employs Revelation only sparingly, mindful that its prophecies were available neither to the Son nor to Satan. Hence Daniel often takes its place as the Son and Satan attempt to decipher prophetic scripture. Daniel refers not only to the coming of the Messiah but also to his setting up of a kingdom with the saints. Millenarians looked on Daniel as the sealed book, Revelation as the open book.[85] Written before the coming of Christ, Daniel could speak only cryptically of events that Revelation could address directly. Hence when Milton turns in *Paradise Regained* to Daniel to undergird the prophecy of Christ's kingdom, he also chooses the cryptic mode.

The prophecy of the Son's kingdom comes from Luke: "the Lord shall give unto him the throne of his father *David* . . . and of his kingdom there shall be no end" (Luke 1:32–33). But supporting Luke are Daniel 2:44, which speaks of a kingdom without end, and Daniel 7:14: "And there was given him dominion . . . his dominion is an everlasting dominion, which shall not pass away, and his kingdom that which shall not be destroyed." Isaiah 9:7 also predicts that the Messiah will occupy the throne of David. To these biblical verses Jesus and his disciples Andrew and Simon turn to validate the Messiah's future kingship. The disciples rejoice, believing that their eyes have now "beheld Messiah . . . so long / Expected of our Fathers"; they hope that "deliverance is at hand," that "The Kingdom shall to *Israel* be restor'd" (2.31–33, 35–36). The verses from Psalm 2 also fuel their expectations: "God of *Israel*, / Send thy *Messiah* forth, the time is come; / Behold the kings of th' Earth how they oppress / Thy chosen" (2.42–45). Jesus has read the same prophecies and ponders if it is his destiny to rescue Israel from the Roman yoke, to subdue and quell "proud Tyrannic pow'r" (1.219). Reading further, however, he learns that he must submit to death, "Ere I the promis'd Kingdom can attain" (1.265). But for him, as for Satan, the nature of that kingdom and the time of its commencement still remain in doubt.

Not until the end of Book 2 does the Son first allude to the Jews' recovery of the kingdom of Israel: "Whose offspring on the Throne of *Judah* sat / So many Ages, and shall yet regain / That seat, and reign in *Israel* without end" (2.440–42). Although he confidently predicts the future Jewish kingdom, Jesus declines to say whether he will assume his place as king. He remarks cryptically: "Besides to give a Kingdom hath been thought / Greater and nobler done, and to lay down / Far more magnanimous than to assume" (2.481–83). Satan, however, insists on the literal nature of the prophecy: "But to a Kingdom thou art born, ordain'd / To sit upon thy Father *David's* Throne" (3.152–53). Reminding Jesus that Judaea is oppressed under Roman yoke, he exhorts him to verify the prophecy of "thy endless reign" (3.178), to act like Judas Maccabeus, and to free his father's house from heathen servitude. It is an interesting challenge, for Satan has coupled an allusion to Maccabeus with one to Antiochus, the ruler who polluted the Temple with abominations. Contemporary interpreters of Daniel took Antiochus as a type of Antichrist and said that the predictions that foretold his fall

spoke not of him but of the Roman Antichrist, who had to fall before
the monarchy of Christ could be established. At this point Satan offers
Jesus the first of the kingdoms – Parthia – describing it as the means
whereby he might gain Israel's throne.

Parthia is a composite of three kingdoms (the Assyrian, the Persian or
Babylonian, and the Greek), the respective nations that previously ruled
the area that Parthia controls. As he describes it, Satan offers the Son a
geography and history lesson:

> here thou behold'st
> *Assyria* and her Empire's ancient bounds,
> ....
> Here *Nineveh*, ...
> There *Babylon* the wonder of all tongues,
> .... *Persepolis*,
> His [Cyrus'] city there thou seest.
> (3.269–70, 275, 280, 284–85)

Assyria was superseded by Persia, which Cyrus as conqueror ruled, and,
as Milton's Satan and Jesus well know, Alexander conquered Cyrus.
Assyria, Persia, and Greece are the first three kingdoms alluded to in
Daniel, kingdoms that the millenarians believed had to fall before the
fourth – Rome – would yield to Christ's fifth monarchy. In the second
chapter of Daniel, Nebuchadnezzar dreamed of an image of gold, silver,
brass, and iron; Daniel interpreted the image as four monarchies which
would perish before God set up a kingdom that could not be destroyed.[86]
Therefore Satan's offer of Parthia to Jesus is strategic, for by it he hopes
to subvert Daniel's prophecy. By offering Jesus only Parthia as the sum
of the first three kingdoms, he tempts Jesus to act too soon, to anticipate
his heritage by assuming rule over the first three monarchies, rather than
waiting to destroy the still more powerful fourth. But Jesus has already
spoken of the advantage of waiting:

> All things are best fulfill'd in due time,
> And time there is for all things, Truth hath said:
> If of my reign Prophetic Writ hath told
> That it shall never end, so when begin
> The Father in his purpose hath decreed,
> He in whose hand all times and seasons roll.
> (3.182–87)

In alluding to a reign without end, the Son refers to the prophecies of
Daniel (2:44, 7:14). But while Satan assumes that Daniel's prophecies

refer to the Son's first coming, the Son has discerned that they must apply to another time, that he must be tried in low estate before he can reign. The millenarians often made the point that the Messiah in his first coming must deny that very kingship that he will assume at his Second Coming. As Milton's Son refers to his future kingdom, he also alludes cryptically to the binding of Satan predicted in Revelation 20: "Know'st thou not that my rising is thy fall / And my promotion will be thy destruction" (3.201–02).

Moreover, when he rejects Parthia's military machinery Jesus renounces force as the means to establish his kingdom. Neither at his first nor at his Second Coming would Christ make use of military might *per se*. He comes to destroy the monarchies of earth, not to contest with them. Thus Milton's Son points out that before God's power "fleshly arm" or "fragile arms" (3.387–88) are frail and argue of human weakness rather than strength. Milton here aligns himself with John Owen and those who distrusted the claims of the Fifth Monarchists that military action would bring in the kingdom of Christ.

Inseparable from predictions of the millennium was the question of the Jews' return to their native seat. Seventeenth-century millenarians believed that the Ten Lost Tribes of Israel had to be restored before the Messiah's reign could be inaugurated. Brightman thought that the resurrection referred to in Revelation 20:11–12 was "no other thing but the full restoring of the Jewish nation."[87] The millenarians of the 1640s and 1650s warned that the prophecies of Daniel and Isaiah concerning Christ's kingship were often mistakenly connected with his first coming. In *Israels Redemption* Robert Maton (1607–53?) propounded the following paradox: that the Jews lacked faith in Christ's first coming, in which the Christians believed, but they were faithful to Christ's Second Coming, believing what the Christians doubted – that the Messiah would be king in Jerusalem.[88]

In offering Parthia as the means to install Jesus "in *David's* royal seat, his true Successor" (3.373), to deliver his brethren, and to reign "in full glory, / From *Egypt* to *Euphrates* and beyond" (3.383–84), Satan tempts Jesus to effect the restoration of the Jews. Jesus queries whether his rescue of the Jews is the necessary antecedent to his kingship:

> My brethren, as thou call'st them, those Ten Tribes
> I must deliver, if I mean to reign
> *David's* true heir, and his full Sceptre sway
> To just extent over all *Israel's* sons.   (3.403–07)

As the millenarians interpreted Daniel 10:26, Jesus was not destined to restore the Ten Tribes. At his first coming the Messiah must be killed and Jerusalem destroyed by the Romans so that the Messiah could return later to reign. The Jews, moreover, must be restored *before*, not after Christ's coming. When Christ comes, he is to rule in Jerusalem over the converted Jews together with the Gentiles.[89] This prophecy so excited Englishmen in the 1640s and 1650s that many pressed for the readmission of the Jews into England, hoping to effect their conversion as the first measure toward forwarding Christ's kingdom.[90]

Another key text was Isaiah 11:16. Although taken by most Christians to refer to the Jews' return from Babylon, millenarians such as Mary Cary interpreted it as a reference to the Jews' return to Jerusalem before the Second Coming.[91] Assuredly, Milton's Jesus alludes to the Babylonian captivity, asserting that the captive tribes returned thence neither humbled nor penitent, but he also hints that further contrition and conversion are necessary: "let them serve / Thir enemies, who serve Idols with God" (3.431–32). His words have often appeared harsh to critics. But Jesus is not rejecting his brethren; he is merely deferring both the Jews' return and his assumption of kingship over them to the time of their future calling. Paraphrasing Isaiah 11, Milton's Jesus predicts their eventual conversion:

> Yet he [God] at length, time to himself best known,
> Rememb'ring *Abraham*, by some wond'rous call
> May bring them back repentant and sincere,
> And at their passing cleave th' *Assyrian* flood
> While to their native land with joy they haste,
> As the Red Sea and *Jordan* once he cleft,
> When to the promis'd land thir Fathers pass'd;
> To his due time and providence I leave them.
>
> (4.433–40)

Alluding to Christ's kingship over the converted Jews, Milton pointedly names Jesus "*Israel's* true King" (3.441).

Rome is the fourth kingdom of Nebuchadnezzar's dream. Satan appears to offer Jesus the very kingdom he is destined to destroy. But as the millenarians insisted, it was not ancient Rome but papal Rome – the Babylon of Revelation, the little horn of Daniel – which Christ would topple. Clearly the magnificent but degenerate city that Satan lays before Milton's Jesus has an inevitable likeness to the Protestant version of papal Rome. Tiberius, the old lascivious emperor ruling without an heir, the "brutish monster," resembles the beast or Antichrist of Revelation who is to occupy the papal throne. When Jesus rejects Rome he echoes the outcry against Babylon in Revelation 17. His denunciation of the fleshly luxury which accompanies empire may have a yet subtler resonance, however. Contemporary critics of millenarianism denounced the Chiliasts' portrayal of Christ's future reign as luxurious and pleasure seeking. As though to answer these critics, Milton's Jesus specifically denies that his kingdom would possess such earthly shows: "Nor doth this grandeur and majestic show / Of luxury, though call'd magnificence, / More than of arms before, allure mine eye / Much less my mind" (4.110–13).

The Son also declines to liberate the Roman or any other people made effeminate by luxury: "What wise and valiant man would seek to free / These thus degenerate, by themselves enslav'd, / Or could of inward slaves make outward free?" (4.143–45). Critics often compare Jesus' indictment of the luxury-loving Romans with Milton's indictment in *The Readie and Easie Way* of his countrymen who welcomed the return of monarchy:

That a nation should be so valorous and courageous to winn thir liberty in the field, and when they have wonn it, should be so heartless and unwise in thir counsels, as not to know how to use it, value it . . . but . . . basely and besottedly to run thir necks again into the yoke . . . worthie indeed themselves, whatsoever they be, to be for ever slaves. (*CP* VII: 428).

The resemblance is important, not merely because denunciation of monarchical luxury was as timely in 1671 as in 1659. If Christ is to free his people from anti-Christian oppression, he must come to a people prepared to receive him – "saints" who have been spiritually renewed and recommitted to liberty. England must be ready for the millennium.

At this point Milton's Jesus alludes to two visions from Daniel which directly concern his future kingdom. Both occur in dreams of Nebuchadnezzar: the first is the vision of "a tree in the midst of the earth . . . that grew and was strong, and the height thereof reached unto heaven" (Daniel 4:10–11). The second vision is of the stone "cut out without hands, which smote the image upon his feet that were of iron and clay, and brake them to pieces," whereupon "the stone that smote the image became a great mountain, and filled all the earth" (Daniel 2:34–35). Daniel interprets the tree as Nebuchadnezzar, grown strong, the stone as a great kingdom that will destroy the four previous kingdoms, just as the stone broke the image to pieces. The stone itself will become a great kingdom which shall never be destroyed (Daniel 2:44). Milton combines the two prophecies:

> Know therefor when my season comes to sit
> On *David's* Throne, it shall be like a tree
> Spreading and over-shadowing all the Earth,
> Or as a stone that shall to pieces dash
> All Monarchies besides throughout the world,
> And of my Kingdom there shall be no end.
>
> (4.146–51)

Exegetes such as Tertullian interpreted the tree in Daniel as Christ's church, which would spread unto the ends of the earth.[92] Brightman connects it with Revelation's tree of life, which is Christ himself, its leaves the dissemination of the gospel throughout the earth: "Then shall the tree grow in the middest of the street of the holy City, whose leaves shall yeeld medicine and health to the nations, Reuel. 22.2."[93] Henry More comments that the tree in Revelation relates to trees which flourish in Psalms 1 and 72:7 and so signifies "these happy times of the *Messias* in the expected *Millennium*."[94]

According to millenarians the prophecy of the stone predicted Christ's destruction of the fourth monarchy. The stone is Christ, comments Archer, because he was not cut by hand but by God.[95] Mede refines the prophecy further, noting that Christ's final kingdom is not that of the stone (which denotes his present church) but the kingdom of the mountain, which is the future millenarian kingdom:

Lastly, that I may conclude; this is the most ample kingdom, which by *Daniels* interpretation, was foreshewed to *Nebuchadnezzar* in that Propheticall Statue of the foure kingdoms: not that of the *Stone* cut out of a Hill whiles yet the *Series* of Monarchies remained (for this is the present state of the kingdome of Christ) but of the *Stone* when they were utterly broken and defaced, to become a *Mountaine* and to fill the whole world.[96]

Henry More also divides the kingdom of the stone from that of the mountain, the latter given by Christ to the saints after the destruction of the little horn.[97]

Milton's Satan lacks the exegetical acumen to unravel Jesus' allusions to Daniel's promise of a kingdom. Refusing to enlighten him further, Jesus confidently asserts: "Means there shall be to this, but what the means, / Is not for thee to know, nor me to tell" (4.152–53). This reply echoes the response Jesus gave the apostles on being asked whether he would restore the kingdom to Israel. Robert Maton paraphrases the response as follows: it "ought not to be inquired of by you, nor to be revealed by me."[98]

The offer of Athens at this point is a tactical shift on Satan's part, for Athens does not fit the pattern of the other kingdoms, representing something other than a "worldly Crown." A realm of intellectual or spiritual eminence, Athens is not even a kingdom in the same sense as Parthia and Rome are. In effect such a "kingdom" was exactly what many commentators said the kingdom predicted in Revelation 20 denoted – a spiritual realm, the rule over the minds and hearts of men. In the soliloquy in Book 1 the Son not only rejects force but also aspires to spiritual authority: "Yet held it more humane, more heavenly first / By winning words to conquer willing hearts" (1.221–22). Jesus the future teacher chooses to gain his following among men by persuasion; Jesus before Pilate will deny that he seeks an earthly kingdom. Moreover, in *Paradise Lost* Michael told Adam that Christ was to destroy Satan not by military conquest but by destroying Satan's works in man, by "Obedience to the Law of God, impos'd / On penalty of death" (12.397–98).

Hence we are confronted with a paradox in the offer of Athens. In rejecting Athens, Milton's Jesus should affirm that his is a spiritual kingdom, on the Hebraic rather than the Hellenic model. But he does not do this. While he proclaims the supremacy of Hebrew prophets and poets over their Hellenic counterparts, he does not deny the earthly commonwealth and choose instead a spiritual kingdom. Indeed, he insists that spiritual vision must lead to active realization. Hebrew prophets were not unworldly dreamers, but "men divinely taught, and better teaching / The solid rules of Civil Government." He insists: "In them is plainest taught, and easiest learnt, / What makes a Nation happy, and keeps it so, / What ruins Kingdoms, and lays Cities flat; / These only with our Law best form a King" (4.357–58, 361–64). While praising the kingdom of the mind, Jesus has not opted for the role of philosopher over king, or denied his future kingship.

In response to Jesus' praise of ideal earthly kingship, Satan expresses skepticism, questioning whether Christ's kingdom is real or allegoric:

> A Kingdom they portend thee, but what Kingdom,
> Real or Allegoric I discern not,
> Nor when, eternal sure, as without end,
> Without beginning; for no date prefixt
> Directs me in the Starry Rubric set.   (4.389–93)

Milton has cast Satan in the role of the skeptics of his own time – Hall and Love, Edwards and Baillie, all of whom expressed doubt about or ridiculed the notion of a literal kingdom. Satan is unable to reconcile the Christ who suffers "reproaches, injuries, / Violence and stripes, and lastly cruel death" (4.387–88) with the king to reign on earth. Like the antimillenarians, he flatly declares the time and means of the prophecy's fulfillment unknowable: "Thou shalt be what thou art ordain'd, no doubt; / For Angels have proclaim'd it, but concealing / The time and means" (4.473–75). To Satan's skepticism Jesus simply responds: "I shall reign past thy preventing" (4.492).

In Book 5 of *Paradise Lost* the Son's anointing as Messiah had provoked Satan's envy and roused him to arms. In *Paradise Regained* others refer to Jesus as the Messiah, but Satan uses the term only once, questioning Jesus' right to be so called: "Of the *Messiah* I have heard foretold / By all the Prophets" (4.502–03). The millenarians of Milton's time believed the term Messiah had been used specifically in Daniel to denote Christ's role as future ruler of Jerusalem.[99] Daniel proves the key to Jesus' understanding of his Messiahship, for he determines thereby that the kingship promised will not be his until he institutes his millennial reign. Although he does not understand its time scheme, Satan determines to thwart Daniel's prophecy, taking Jesus to the city over which it has been prophesied he will rule. It is no accident that Jesus' final testing occurs in Jerusalem, where he is to be crucified as king of the Jews, and to which he will return to confirm his kingship.

Symbolically, on the temple's pinnacle Milton looks forward to Satan's fall and Christ's establishment of his kingdom. Replying to Satan, the Son affirms his future authority over him: "Also it is written, / Tempt not the Lord thy God: he said and stood. / But Satan smitten with amazement fell" (4.560–62). The victory of the incarnate Son on earth looks back to the eternal Son's victory over Satan in heaven: "with Godlike force indu'd / Against th' Attempter of thy Father's Throne" (4.602–03). But it also looks forward to Satan's future binding. Jesus warns Satan: "Lest he [God] command them [thee and thy Legions] down into the deep / Bound, and to torment sent before thir time" (4.631–32). The victory at the Temple recalls as well the prediction in Zechariah 6:13 of the Temple's rebuilding. According to some interpreters the prophecy foretells Christ's resurrection from the dead, but the millenarians believed it foretold Christ's inauguration of his kingdom.[100] Milton has it both ways in *Paradise Regained*, making Jesus' standing on the pinnacle preview both his victory over Satan at his resurrection and the establishment of his future kingship.

In 1659, in the first edition of *The Readie and Easie Way*, Milton issued his last strong blast of republicanism and millenarianism. But although he remained officially silent in the 1660s and 1670s, the unmistakable undercurrent of millenarianism in both epics speaks eloquently of the hopes Milton yet cherished. Millenarianism revived as a political force in the 1680s, fueled by the crisis of James II's accession after Charles II's death and spurred on by the approach of another prophesied era – the 1690s. Revelation was once again fervently invoked. Babylon would yet fall – many said it did when James II and his Catholic party fled. The saints are ruling, said the heirs of the Parliamentarians who took over the reins of government. Few expected that Christ himself would appear personally to inaugurate his reign on earth, but when William of Orange arrived from Holland on his white horse, many said he was the rider of Revelation 19 and a suitable stand-in for Christ.[101]

We cannot know how Milton might have reacted to the Williamite Revolution at the end of the century. In spite of defeat at mid-century, however, he remained steadfast and did not retreat into pessimism or passivism. Although neither *Paradise Lost* nor *Paradise Regained* sets forth a program of political action, both affirm the Son's future reign. Milton's persistent engagement with millenarianism in both of his epics functions to make his readers look expectantly to the future. After all, the millennium is a beginning, not an end.

NOTES

1. Henry Archer (also referred to as John Archer), *The Personall Reigne of Christ upon Earth* (London, 1642).
2. The Chiliasts believed the millennium, like the so-called Golden Age the pagans promised, would be an era of unparalleled peace and prosperity. Early Christians such as Eusebius deemed the emphasis on earthly pleasure too hedonistic, attacking Cerinthus as predicting an earthly kingdom where fleshly pleasure would be permissible. Augustine declared heretical the notion that Christ would return to rule an earthly kingdom. See Ernest Tuveson, *Millennium and Utopia. A Study in the Background of the Idea of Progress* (Berkeley, 1949), pp. 14–16.
3. Ibid., pp. 7–21.
4. [James I], *A Fruitefull Meditation, Containing. A plaine and easie Exposition, or laying open of the 7. 8. 9. and 10 verses of the 20. chap. of the Reuelation, in forme and maner of a Sermon* (London, 1603), B3ᵛ.
5. Ibid., sig. A6ʳ, A7ᵛ.
6. John Napier (or Napeir), *A Plaine Discouery of the whole Reuelation of Saint Iohn* (Edinburgh, 1593), pp. 240–41, 9–12. It was reissued several times, notably in the 1640s.

7. See Tuveson, *Millennium*, pp. 30–70, and Richard H. Popkin (ed.), *Millenarianism and Messianism in English Literature and Thought: 1650–1800* (Leiden, 1988).

8. David Pareus, *A Commentary upon the Divine Revelation of the Apostle and Evangelist John*, trans. Elias Arnold (Amsterdam, 1644), p. 504, and Arthur Dent, *The Ruine of Rome: or An Exposition upon the whole Reuelation* (London 1603), p. 271. Pareus also dates the millennium from the fall of Jerusalem to the papacy of Gregory VII (*A Commentary*, p. 525).

9. Thomas Brightman, *The Revelation of St. Iohn Illustrated*, in *The Workes of Thomas Brightman* (London, 1644), pp. 813–14, 824.

10. Pareus, *A Commentary*, pp. 504–05. Pareus comments: "BRIGHTMAN, *These thousand yeers*, saith he, *in which the Saints shall reign with Christ, do begin where the former ended*. Thus Satan should be bound a thousand years, and afterwards Christ should reign a thousand years. But I judge that one, and the same terme of a *thousand years* is denoted." He disagrees further with Brightman in identifying the angel who binds Satan with Constantine and the dragon as his pagan opponents. See *A Commentary*, pp. 506, 502. Dent also thought Satan's binding conditional during Christ's thousand-year reign: "the principles & grounds of true religion continued in the church, vntill the ful loosing of *Sathan*, though with many blotts, corruptions and abuses." See *The Ruine of Rome*, p. 272.

11. *Reverend Mr. Brightmans Iudgement or Prophesies what shall befall Germany, Scotland, Holland and the Churches adhering to them* (London, 1643). The author declares that Brightman was "persecuted and banished by the Bishops, and this Commentary condemned by them to the fire" (title page). This tract summarizes Brightman's commentary on chapter 3 of Revelation, adding also a summary of the commentary on chapters 18 and 19, as well as points in chapters 11–16.

12. *A Revelation of Mr Brigtmans' [sic] Revelation, Wherein is shewed, how all that which Mr. Brightman on the Revelation, hath fore-told concerning Germany, Scotland, and England, hath beene fulfilled, and is yet fulfilling, comparing his writings, and our Times together. In a Dialogue betweene a Minister of the Gospell, and a Citizen of London, wherein it is manifest, that Mr. Brightman was a true Prophet* ([London], 1641). The tract outlines the major points of Brightman's prophecies in dialogue form, pointing out their relevance to Protestants in the 1640s and particularly emphasizing the abuses of the bishops during this period.

13. Brightman's *Exposition on Daniel* was published in English in 1635 and reprinted with the commentary on Revelation in *Workes* in 1644 both in England and Amsterdam. See *Workes*, pp. 967, 824–25, 831.

14. David Owen, *Anti-Pareus, or, a Treatise in the Defence of the Royall Right of Kings: Against Pareus and the rest of the Anti-Monarchians, whether Presbyterians or Jesuits* (London, 1642).

15. In *The Reason of Church-Government*, Milton cites Pareus's view that Revelation is organized on the model of a tragedy: "this my opinion the grave autority of *Pareus* commenting that booke is sufficient to confirm" (*CP* 1:815).

16. Pareus, *A Commentary*, p. 525.

17. Ibid., pp. 515–16, 518.

18. In the 1640s and 1650s when they were most actively promoting millenarianism, Hartlib and Dury were close associates of Milton (see Popkin [ed.], *Millenarianism*, pp. 6, 75). They added prefatory material to an anonymous treatise entitled *Clavis Apocalyptica: or A Prophetical Key: By Which the Great Mysteries in The Revelation of St. John, and in the Prophet Daniel are opened; It being made apparent That the Prophetical Numbers com to an end with the year of our Lord, 1655* (London, 1651).

19. In 1638 Mede wrote to a friend that he was concerned that his papers on the issue of bowing to the altar had been published without his authorization. See Epistle XCVII in *The Works of the Pious and Profoundly Learned Joseph Mede* (London, 1664), p. 1081.

20. *The Key of the Revelation* (London, 1643) was reissued in 1650 with Mede's "A Coniecture Concerning Gog and Magog" appended. See Sarah Hutton's article on Mede in this book. See also Hutton, "The Appropriation of Joseph Mede. Millenarianism in the 1640s," in James E. Force and Richard H. Popkin (eds.), *The Millenarian Turn: Millenarian Contexts of Science, Politics, and Everyday Anglo-American Life in the Seventeenth and Eighteenth Centuries* (Dordrecht, 2001).

21. Johann Heinrich Alsted was born in Saumur in 1588, and he was appointed Doctor of Philosophy there in 1619. He founded an academy at Stuhl-Weiszenburg after the Thirty Years' War had devastated his native city. A prolific writer, he is especially important for his writings on education. Comenius was his student. See Percival R. Cole, *A Neglected Educator: Johann Heinrich Alsted* (Sydney, 1910).

22. Johann Heinrich Alsted, *The Beloved City, or The Saints Reign on Earth a Thousand Yeares* (London, 1643), pp. 7, 13, 57, 9.

23. Homes hoped to prove that belief in the millennium was orthodox, citing the salient features of millenarianism in the early church fathers Irenaeus and Lactantius, but dismissing Cerinthus, whom he calls a voluptuary. He summarizes the views of the leading millenarians, and refutes the objections of Baillie, Pareus, Prideaux, Hayne, and others. Homes thought the millennium imminent, as the subtitle indicates: *The Dawning of the Day-Star, About to rise, and radiate a visible incomparable Glory, far beyond any, since the Creation, upon the Universal Church on Earth, For a Thousand yeers. Yet to come, before the ultimate Day, of the General Judgement: To the raising of the Jewes, and ruine of all Antichristian, and Secular Powers, that do not love the Members of Christ, submit to his Laws, and advance his interest in this Design.*

24. Antimillenarians such as Robert Baillie said that the kingdom predicted in Daniel 2:44 was the spiritual dominion granted to Christ at his incarnation. See *A Dissvasive from the Errours of the Time* (London, 1645), p. 248.

25. See Mede, *Key* (1643), pp. 23–24.

26. In Daniel 12:6 the prophet asks the man clothed in linen how long it will be to the end of these wonders. The man (usually identified as Christ) replies:

"*it shall be for a time, times, and a half*" (Daniel 12:7). The commentators usually compute "*time, times, and a half*" as 1,290 days (i.e., years), calculated from the end of the daily sacrifice of the Jews to the beginning of the "abomination that maketh desolation" (Dan. 12:11). While some interpreters date the end of daily sacrifice to the destruction of the Temple under Titus, most date it as *c.* AD 360 in the reign of Julian the Apostate. Using the latter dating, Brightman assigns the calling of the Jews to 1650 in *A Most Comfortable Exposition of the last and most difficult part of the prophecie of Daniel* ([Amsterdam], 1635), pp. 84–85, and *Workes*, pp. 950–54. Goodwin agrees with Brightman's dating in *A Glimpse of Sions Glory* (London, 1641), p. 32. Alsted dates the millennium at 1694 (*The Beloved City*, p. 57). See also Archer, *Personall Reigne*, pp. 46–52, and Mede, *Daniels Weekes* (London, 1643). Other texts used by commentators include Daniel 8:13, 14 (which alludes to 2,300 days) and Daniel 9:24 (which alludes to 70 weeks determined for the holy city to make an end to sin). Homes summarizes the computations of the leading millenarians (*The Resurrection Revealed*, pp. 543–63).

27. Archer, *Personall Reigne*, pp. 49–52.

28. Commentators disagreed over whether the martyred saints alluded to in Revelation 20 ought to include the Protestant martyrs killed by modern Rome or only those of the early church martyred under the Roman empire.

29. William Bridge, *Babylons Downfall* (London, 1641), p. 28. Goodwin makes similar claims in *A Glimpse*, pp. 2–3.

30. *A Dissvasive* was reissued in 1646, 1647, 1648, and 1655. Baillie also attacked Anabaptists, Familists, Brownists, and other sects. See *Anabaptism, The True Fountaine of Independency, Antinomy, Brownisme, Familisme, and the most of the other Errours* (London, 1647). Among those who supported Baillie's critique of the Independents were John Trapp, *A Commentary or Exposition upon All the Epistles and the Revelation of John the Divine* (London, 1647), pp. 583–84; [Thomas Hayne], *Christs Kingdome on Earth, Opened according to the Scriptures. Herein is examined, What Mr. Th. Brightman, Dr. J. Alsted, Mr. I. Mede, Mr. H. Archer, the Glympse of Sions Glory, and such as concurre in opinion with them, hold concerning the thousand years of the Saints Reign with Christ, and of Satans binding. Herein also their Arguments are answered.* (London, 1645). Homes refuted Baillie's objections in *The Resurrection Revealed*, pp. 472–91.

31. Robert Baillie, *Errours and Induration, are the Great Sins and Great Judgments of the Time* (London, 1645), p. 11.

32. Baillie, *A Dissvasive*, pp. 224–52.

33. Ibid., p. 116.

34. Thomas Edwards, *Gangraena: or A Catalogue and Discovery of many of the Errours, Heresies, Blasphemies and pernicious Practices of the Sectaries of this time, vented and acted in England in these four last years* (London, 1646), pp. 125, 135–36.

35. Edwards, "Preface," part 3 of *Gangraena*, sig. [ ]$^{r-v}$. Edwards lists Chiliasts or millenaries as third in his list of errors (p. 15). In *The Word in Season to the Kingdom of England* (London, 1647), Mary Cary urges Edwards to moderate his attacks on the Independents (p. 11).

36. Edwards, *Gangraena*, p. 11.
37. The Fifth Monarchists were so called because of their belief that Christ was about to abolish the fourth monarchy (the rule of Rome) and set up his own monarchy – the fifth. Most millenarians interpreted the second chapter of Daniel as promising the destruction of papal Rome (the fourth monarchy) and the establishment on earth of Christ's kingdom (the fifth monarchy).
38. Christopher Love, *A Penitent Pardoned. Together with a Discourse of Christs Ascension into Heaven, and his coming again from Heaven. Wherein The opinion of the Chiliasts is considered, and solidly confuted* (London, 1649), pp. 149–50, 172. The sermon was posthumously reissued as "The Saints Advantage, By Christs Ascension," in *Grace, The Summe of XV Sermons* (London, 1652). See especially pp. 71–184.
39. Like Baillie, who had declared allegiance to Prince Charles after Charles I's execution, Love opposed the Independents and was inclining to the royalists. Convicted for having royalist correspondence in his house, Love pleaded innocence but was denied a pardon by Cromwell. Cromwell ordered Milton to answer Love's pamphlet writings. It was not Milton, however, but John Hall, newly employed by Cromwell, who undertook the response, in *A Gagg to Love's Advocate* (London, 1651).
40. [Joseph Hall], *The Revelation Unrevealed. Concerning the Thousand-Yeares Reigne of the Saints with Christ upon Earth* (London, 1650).
41. Ibid., p. 65.
42. Ibid., pp. 16–17.
43. Ibid., pp. 121–25, 35. Hall challenges Alsted's computation of the end of the fourth monarchy and its identification with modern Rome. He asserts that pagan Rome collapsed long ago, and that no fifth monarchy is to come (ibid., pp. 19–43). The only coming of Christ will be to judge, and that is a far-off event known only to God (ibid., pp. 218–19).
44. Ibid., pp. 102, 18, 209, 8.
45. Oliver Cromwell, *His Highnesse The Lord Protector's Speeches to the Parliament in the Painted Chamber, the one on Monday the 4th of September 1654* (London, 1654), pp. 12–14.
46. John Owen, *The Advantage of the Kingdome of Christ in the Shaking of the Kingdoms of the World* (Oxford, 1651), p. 5.
47. John Owen, *A Sermon Preached to the Parliament, Octob. 13, 1652. A Day of Solemne Humiliation* (Oxford, 1652), p. 18. See Michael Fixler, *Milton and the Kingdoms of God* (London, 1964), p. 177. In *A New and More Exact Mappe or, Description of New Ierusalems Glory* (London, 1651), Mary Cary supported the Fifth Monarchists, arguing that the saints may lawfully make use of the material sword to advance Christ's kingdom.
48. Owen, *A Sermon*, pp. 14, 19.
49. Ibid., pp. 41–44.
50. Cromwell, *His Highnesse*, pp. 14–15.
51. John Rogers, "An Epistolary Perambulation," in John Canne, *The Time of the End: Shewing, First, until the three years and an half are come (which are the last*

of the 1260 dayes) the prophecies of the Scripture will not be understood, concerning the Duration and Period of the FOURTH MONARCHY and Kingdom of the Beast (London, 1657), sig. a6ᵛ.

52. Laura Knoppers discusses Venner's fate in *Historicizing Milton: Spectacle, Power, and Poetry in Restoration England* (Athens, Ga, 1994), pp. 124–32. See also B. S. Capp, *The Fifth Monarchy Men: A Study in Seventeenth-Century English Millenarianism* (London, 1972), and P. G. Rogers, *The Fifth Monarchy Men* (London, 1966).

53. "The Epistle to the Reader," in Goodwin, *A Glimpse,* n.p. In the sermon Goodwin announces Babylon is fallen: "*God* is beginning the powring forth of the fifth Viall, namely, upon the Throne of the *Beast,* upon *Babylon*; this is the worke that is in hand: as soone as ever this is done, that *Antichrist* is downe, *Babylon* fallen, then comes in *Jesus Christ* reigning gloriously" (p. 2).

54. Stanley Stewart argues that Milton jettisoned the harsh remarks of the first edition because he shared allegiances with such zealots as the Fifth Monarchists. See "Milton revises *The Readie and Easie Way*," *Milton Studies* 20 (1984), pp. 205–24. See also Arthur Barker, *Milton and the Puritan Dilemma* (Toronto, 1942), p. 279.

55. William Hicks, "To the Christian Reader," *Quinto-Monarchiae, Cum Quarto OMOLOGIA: or, A Friendly Complyance between Christ's Monarchy, and the Magistrates* (London, 1659). Hicks remarks on the mistake of the Fifth Monarchists: "That they think it their duty to remove all Impediments and Obstacles that lie in their way (whether it be just Authority, or otherwise) to the obtaining of this their much longed for *Diana*: and so as much in them lie, endeavour the removing and pulling down of all the Horns, Powers, and Principalities, which they pretend to be the Supporters of the Kingdom of the Beast, and the great Whore." He reminds them, however, that it is the work of the horns, not the saints, to make the whore desolate. Therefore, while he asserts and maintains "the right and regular judgement of the *Quinto-Monarchians*; yet withal, that just obedience and tribute that is due unto Magistracy, as an Ordinance of God, and which will alwaies be due unto it, until the appearance of that great day of Christ, wherein his Fifth Kingdom shall radiate forth with a more incomparable glory then any of the former past Monarchies whatsoever" (n.p.). In his "Epistle Dedicatory" Hicks asserts that millenarians such as Archer, Homes, Maton, Mede, Alsted, and Hackwell did not espouse antimagistratical opinions.

56. More writes: "As for any *Fifth Monarchy,* in which *Jesus Christ* shall visibly and personally Reign as the *Monarch* thereof, or any one else as an *Universal Monarch* over all those many and large Kingdoms that shall then be *Christian*; (that the *Fifth-Monarchy-men* may not substitute this instead of the other) our *Exposition* is not at all favourable to any such conceit, as neither to that of the reign of the revived Martyrs upon *Earth* in the blessed *Millennium*. And I am so far from countenancing the Opinion, that these *Times* are to be brought in by the *Sword,* unless it be the *Sword* of the *Spirit,* which is the *Word of God*."

See "Preface to the Reader," in *Apocalypsis Apocalypseos; or The Revelation of St. John the Divine unveiled* (London, 1680), p. xxvi.

57. See Janel Mueller, "Embodying Glory: the Apocalyptic Strain in Milton's *Of Reformation,*" in David Loewenstein and James Grantham Turner (eds.), *Politics, Poetics, and Hermeneutics in Milton's Prose* (Cambridge, 1990), pp. 9–40.

58. Mede, *Key* (1643), p. 125.

59. William Twisse thought Mede's interpretation of Revelation 20 its most controversial aspect. See "Preface", *Key* (1643), a1ᵛ. The translator Richard More commented: "concerning the *1000* yeeres Raigne of Christ, grounded upon the *20th chapter* of the *Revelation*, with the authorities and reasons for the same, howsoever it be not received by many as Orthodox, yet is delivered with that moderation and subjection to the censure of the Church, that it can displease no man" ("The Translator to the Reader," *Key*, a4ᵛ). Twisse explains that he was puzzled that Mede should profess the opinion of the Millenaries that Augustine had rejected hundreds of years ago. Mede replied that he agreed with the opinion of Piscator that some [i.e., the martyred saints] should rise a thousand years before others and agreed with Alsted that Christ should reign on earth, only differing with him on whether the reign should occur after or during the Last Judgment: "*Medes* opinion was, that it should be *in & Durante die judicii*, in and during the day of judgement; which day of judgement should continue a thousand yeares, beginning with the ruine of *Antichrist*, and ending with the destruction of *Gog* and *Magog.*" See Twisse, "Preface" in Mede, *The Apostasy of the Latter Times* (London, 1644, the second edition corrected), sig. A2ᵛ–A3ʳ.

60. Mede, *Key* (1643), pp. 122–24. Variants are found in other millenarian writers. Archer thought the millennium began on the evening of the previous day and that the next day's dawning marked Christ's coming in judgment. See Archer, *Personall Reigne*, pp. 13–15, 39.

61. The millenarians particularly noted the congruence of Daniel 7:13–14 and Revelation 1:7, both of which refer to the Son of Man establishing a kingdom with the saints. *De Doctrina* cites Daniel 7:13–14 and 22, 27.

62. The dating of *De Doctrina Christiana* is discussed by William Hunter in this book in chapter 5 and John Shawcross in chapter 6. See also William B. Hunter, *Visitation Unimplor'd: Milton and the Authorship of "De Doctrina Christiana"* (Pittsburgh, 1998); Barbara K. Lewalski, "Milton and *De Doctrina Christiana*: Evidences of Authorship," *Milton Studies* 36 (1998), pp. 203–28; William B. Hunter, "The Provenance of the *Christian Doctrine*," *SEL* 32 (1992), pp. 129–42; and Gordon Campbell, "The Authorship of *De Doctrina Christiana*," *MQ* 26 (1992), pp. 129–30.

63. Citations of Milton's poetry are from *John Milton, Complete Poetry and Major Prose*, ed. Merritt Y. Hughes (New York, 1957).

64. The editor praises Mede's learning and piety, but warns that Mede "afforded too much countenance to the opinion of the *Chiliasts.*" He asserts that Mede tried to place the millennium elsewhere in deference to Augustine's view. He also maintains that Mede's view of the millennium was pure and peaceable

and that he did not try to win disciples for his view. See "Author's Life," in Mede, *Works*, pp. xvi–xxiv.

65. James Durham (1622–58), briefly chaplain to the future Charles II, was professor of divinity at Glasgow. See *A Commentarie upon the Book of the Revelation* (London, 1658), p. 714 (rptd. 1680).

66. More said that Christ was spiritually present in the millennium; he took Satan's binding as a parable "of his Children here on Earth" kept in "adamantine chains of rigid, severe, and inviolable Laws." See *Apocalypsis Apocalypseos*, pp. 206–07. See also the summary of More's views in *An Illustration of those Two Abstruse Books in Holy Scripture, The Book of Daniel, and the Revelation of S. John* (London, 1685): "The true Apostolick Church purged from Superstitious, Idolatrous and Tyrannical Principles and Practices will overspread the whole world in a manner. The Kingdoms of this world (as it is predicted in the Apocalypse) becoming the Kingdom of the Lord and his Christ" (pp. 18–19).

67. "Preface," in *An Answer to Several Remarks upon Dr. Henry More His Expositions of the Apocalypse and Daniel, as also upon his Apology. Written by S. E. Mennonite and Published in English by The Answerer* (London, 1685), sig. b2ᵛ. See also *Remarks on Dr. Henry More's Expositions of the Apocalypse and Daniel, and Upon his Apology: Defended Against his Answer to Them* (London, 1690). The anonymous author objects to More's political conservatism and his moderate interpretation of Revelation and Daniel, supporting instead a literal interpretation of Christ's future reign.

68. *A Scheme of the whole Book of the Revelation of Jesus Christ, of very great use, with the following Summarie of Daniels Visions, & cc. for the right understanding of the Parallel of that Book and the Revelation after set down* (1671), p. 3. The pamphlet agrees with Mede's view that Christ will come to reign personally on the morning of Judgment Day with the saints' bodily resurrection; it proposes the year of the Second Coming as 1700 ("Appendix," pp. 5, 9–10).

69. Brightman, *Workes*, p. 862. See also Archer, *Personall Reigne*, pp. 36–37.

70. In 1691 Richard Baxter published a reply to Thomas Beverley, who had argued that Christ's temporal reign would begin in 1697. Baxter not only denied that Christ would have a temporal reign, but also that "God's being All in All" implied a cessation of that reign. See Baxter, "Postscript," in *A Reply to Mr. Tho. Beverley's Answer to my Reasons Against his Doctrine of the Thousand Years Middle Kingdom, and of the Conversion of the Jews* (London, 1691), p. 15.

71. Joseph Mede, "A Coniecture Concerning Gog and Magog in the Revelation," in *The Key of the Revelation* (London, 1650), sig. Tʳ–T2ʳ.

72. Milton probably believed (as Pareus and others did) that different chapters of Revelation refer to the same event but from different viewpoints.

73. See Stella P. Revard, *The War in Heaven: Paradise Lost and the Tradition of Satan's Rebellion* (Ithaca, 1980), pp. 123–27, 132–34, 258–61; Paul Rovang, "Milton's War in Heaven as Apocalyptic Drama: 'Thy Foes Justly Hast in Derision,'" *Milton Quarterly* 28 (1994), pp. 28–35; and John T. Shawcross, "Stasis, and John Milton and the Myths of Time," *Cithara* 18 (1978), pp. 3–17.

74. Archer, *Personall Reigne*, p. 31.

75. See George Hughes, *VAE-EUGE-TUBA. Or the Wo-Ioy-Trumpet, Sounding the third and greatest woe to the Antichristian world, but the first and last joy to the Church of the Saints upon Christ exaltation over the Kingdomes of the World* (London, 1647), pp. 9, 11, 35–37, and M. [Mary] Cary, "Epistle Dedicatory," in *The Resurrection of the Witnesses; and Englands Fall from (the mystical babylon) Rome* (London, 1648), sig. A3–A4, (reissued 1653). In her "Postscript" Cary connects the victories of the parliamentary army with the saints' victories over the dragon in the war in heaven of Revelation 12. The Fifth Monarchist Christopher Feake commended her work. Mary Cary also published several tracts in 1651. In *The Little Horns Doom and Downfall* (London, 1651) she identifies Charles I's war with Parliament as that of the little horn with the saints.

   After the Restoration Psalm 2 continued to be cited as a millenarian text. See William Sherwin, *Logos peri logou; or the Word Written* (London, 1670), p. 9.

76. Pareus explains: "That more general Type of the *fourth Vision* noted, that the devill with his Angels, was so overcome by the death and resurrection of Christ, as neither he, nor they could suppresse the Church in its birth and growth. But this more speciall *Type* of the *last Vision denoteth*, that the Prince of devils was so bound in the first thousand yeers, that neither he himself, nor his emissary Angels could any longer uphold Paganisme, or hinder the course of the Gospell among the Gentiles." See Pareus, *A Commentary*, p. 504.

77. Mary Ann Radzinowicz identifies Psalm 2 as the source of the prophecy that the man-child is to rule the nations. See *Milton's Epics and the Book of Psalms* (Princeton, 1989), p. 146.

78. Alsted, *The Beloved City*, p. 55. Baillie argued that Revelation 19 did not apply to the millennium's beginning. See *A Dissuasive*, p. 249.

79. Hughes, *VAE-EUGE-TUBA*, pp. 11–12. Alsted comments that these verses describe the vanquishing of Antichrist's army. See *The Beloved City*, p. 56.

80. John Carter, *The Wheel turned by a voice from the throne of Glory* (London, 1647), p. 59.

81. Peter Sterry, *The Comming Forth of Christ In the Power of his Death* (London, 1650), pp. 8, 11–12, 26. See Revard, *The War in Heaven*, pp. 257–60.

82. Peter Sterry, *The Clouds in which Christ Comes* (London, 1648), p. 24.

83. See Stella P. Revard, "The Warring Saints and the Dragon: A Commentary upon Revelation 12: 7–9 and Milton's War in Heaven," *PQ* 53 (Spring 1974), pp. 181–94 (reworked in *The War in Heaven*).

84. James H. Sims, "Jesus and Satan as Readers of Scripture in *Paradise Regained*," *Milton Studies* 32 (1995), p. 187.

85. See Archer, *Personall Reigne*, p. 43; Goodwin, *A Glimpse*, p. 31; and *A Scheme of the whole Book of the Revelation of Jesus Christ*, p. 8.

86. See Archer, *Personall Reigne*, pp. 6–7; Barbara K. Lewalski, *Milton's Brief Epic* (Providence, 1966), p. 268; and Knoppers, *Historicizing Milton*, pp. 132–41.

87. See Brightman, *Workes*, pp. 832–33. See also *A Most Comfortable Exposition . . . of Daniel*, in Brightman, *Workes*, pp. 939–42.

88. Robert Maton, *Israels Redemption, or The propheticall History of Our Saviours Kingdome on Earth* (London, 1642), pp. 1–2. Alexander Petrie attacked Maton in *Chiliasto-Mastix* (Rotterdam, 1644), and Maton replied to Petrie's objections, point by point, in *Israels Redemption Redeemed, or Christs Personall Reigne on Earth, One Thousand Yeares with his Saints* (London, 1652).

89. See Maton, *Israels Redemption*, pp. 14–20, 58–60. See also John Owen, *Concerning the Kingdome of Christ* (Oxford, 1652): "I dare say there is not any promise anywhere of raising up *a Kingdome unto the Lord Christ* in this world, but it is either expressed or clearly intimated, that the beginning of it must be with the Iews" (p. 17).

90. Christopher Hill, "'Till the Conversion of the Jews,'" in Popkin (ed.), *Millenarianism and Messianism*, pp. 12–36.

91. See M. Cary, *New Jerusalems Glory* (London, 1651), pp. 20, 58–60. Together with Isaiah 11, Cary cites Zechariah 10:10–11 as describing the regathering of the Jews. See also Sims, "Jesus and Satan," pp. 202–03.

92. *Paradise Regained*, ed. Thomas Newton (London, 1752), note on 4.146: "The throne of David shall then *be like a tree* & c.; alluding to the parable of the mustard seed grown into a tree. Matt. xiii. 32 (and to what the parable also respects) Nebuchadnezzar's dream of the great *tree whose height reached into heaven, and the sight thereof to the end of all the earth*, Dan. IV. ii." See Sims, "Jesus and Satan," p. 204.

93. Brightman, "The confuting of that counterfait Antichrist, whom Bellarmine describeth," in Brightman, *Workes*, p. 649. Citing Ezekiel 17:24, Owen interprets the low and dry tree which God exalts as the "spiritual Kingdome of the Messiah." See Owen, *The Advantage*, p. 7.

94. More, *Apocalypsis Apocalypseos*, p. 236.

95. Archer, *Personall Reigne*, pp. 7–9.

96. Mede, *Key* (1643), p. 125. See also Humfry Ellis, *Two Sermons* (London, 1647), p. 9, and Goodwin, *A Glimpse*, p. 21.

97. Henry More, *A Plain and Continued Exposition of the Several Prophecies or Divine Visions of the Prophet Daniel* (London, 1681), pp. 48–49.

98. Maton, *Israels Redemption*, p. 4.

99. See Mede, *Daniels Weekes*, pp. 9–12.

100. Maton, *Israels Redemption*, sig. B^{r-v}. Mary Cary also cites prophecies from Zechariah (8:3–4 and 20) which predict Christ's return to Jerusalem. See *New Jerusalems Glory*, pp. 258, 289.

101. Benjamin Keach, *Antichrist Stormed: Or, Mystery Babylon the great Whore, and great City, proved to be the present Church of Rome* (London, 1689). Keach (1640–1704) cites Goodwin, Brightman, Mede, More, Du Moulin, Durham, Canne, and Jurieu. Pareus's prediction of a prince from the north who draws together a great army (earlier applied to Gustavus Adolphus) is now applied to William of Orange (pp. 190–91). Keach further states: "I am persuaded His present Majesty is raised to do great things for

Christ" (p. 188). Using the numbers of Daniel, he cites 1685 as the date when popery was enthroned in England and 1688 as the time of "Gods lifting up his hand by this present Providence" (p. 231). Matthew Mead also sees William as God's instrument in *The Vision of the Wheels, Seen by the Prophet Ezekiel; Opened and Applied . . . on Jan. 31, 1688/89 being the Day of solemn Thanksgiving to God for the great Deliverance of this Kingdom from Popery and Slavery, By His then Highness the Most Illustrious Prince of Orange. Whom God raised up to be the glorious Instrument there of* (London, 1689). Mead applies Ezekiel's vision apocalyptically, as it had been in the 1640s and 1650s.

4

Astronomical signs in Paradise Lost: Milton, Ophiucus, and the millennial debate

Malabika Sarkar

In one of his verse letters to the Countess of Bedford ("To have written then"), composed around 1609, John Donne declared "We have added to the world Virginia, and sent / Two new stars lately to the firmament" (ll. 67–68).[1] Editors have suggested that the reference to the "Two new stars" may be to two friends who had died recently, Cecilia Bulstrode and Lady Markham. It is also very likely a reference to the two supernovas which were the subject of intense speculation in the late sixteenth and early seventeenth centuries. One of these appeared in 1572 in the constellation Cassiopeia, the other in 1604 in the constellation Ophiucus. Taken in conjunction with the reference to Virginia, Donne's lines could be understood to refer to the two spheres of life in which the most spectacular discoveries of the Renaissance took place – navigation and astronomy. The appearance of the two new stars was not only an astronomical wonder but was also hailed as a miracle. In the excitement generated by the triumph of Protestantism and expectations of a new millennium in the seventeenth century, these two new stars were regarded as visible emblems of Christ's promised return. In another verse letter, this time to the Countess of Huntingdon ("Man to God's image"), Donne made an explicit reference to this possibility:

> Who vagrant transitory comets sees,
> Wonders, because they are rare; but a new star
> Whose motion with the firmament agrees,
> Is miracle; for, there no new things are, . . .
> As such a star, the Magi led to view
> The manger-cradled infant, God below.
>
> (ll. 5–8; 13–14)

These two new stars of 1572 and 1604 have a crucial role to play in *Paradise Lost* in communicating to us Milton's position in the millennial debate of the seventeenth century.

In her chapter in this book, Stella Revard has examined the political and theological dimensions of the millenarian fervor of the 1640s and 1650s. Milton's belief in the certainty, if not the imminence, of the millennium is apparent not only in the very open expectation of Christ's Second Coming in *Of Reformation* – "at that day when thou the Eternall and shortly-expected King shalt open the Clouds to judge the severall Kingdomes of the World" (*CP* 1: 616) – but also in his early poetry. His consciousness of ends of time generates the anxieties of sonnets such as "How soon hath time" and "When I consider how my light is spent." At the same time these anxieties are offset by the redemptive spirit enshrined in other poems of the time such as "On the Morning of Christ's Nativity" and "The Passion." As a result his poems of the 1620s and 1630s are essentially, in a broad sense, aligned to millennial ideas because the millennium is both an end and a new beginning. Nowhere is this so explicit as in *Lycidas*, where the destruction of the corrupt by the two-handed engine leads to resurrection, immortalization, and a new world order. While Milton's early faith in the coming of the new millennium is quite explicit, the failure of millennial hopes signaled by the Restoration must have had considerable impact on him. Even if he retained faith in the millennium through the 1660s and early 1670s as Revard argues, there would inevitably have been a sequence of questionings, analyses, and formulations of the reasons for its failure in the immediate present. Such questionings are an intrinsic part of *Paradise Lost*. In this process of inquiry which underlies and energizes the epic, Milton uses his knowledge of the controversy surrounding the appearance of the new stars, and the millennial debate revolving around their appearance, as means of diagnosis and discovery.

In 1572 a star of unusual brilliance appeared in the constellation Cassiopeia and was hailed by astronomers, astrologers, theologians, and others from many walks of life as a miracle. In the Aristotelian science of the sixteenth century, the regions above the moon were thought to be unchanging with neither generation nor decay.[2] Comets and other changeable phenomena in the sky belonged to the sublunary world. At such a time the appearance of a new star that indubitably belonged to the celestial sphere was fraught with extraordinary significance. Today, when sophisticated instruments like NASA's Hubble Space Telescope bring us pictures of embryonic stars, it is difficult to appreciate the enormity of the event.

The new star of 1572 was observed with great excitement by the Danish astronomer Tycho Brahe and, in Britain, by John Dee and his pupil

Thomas Digges. Among his unpublished manuscripts Dee listed one with the title "De stella admiranda in Cassiopeiae Asterismo," while in 1573 Thomas Digges published a work entitled *Alae seu Scalae Mathematicae* which contained a discussion of the new star in Cassiopeia.[3] The most extensive observations of the new star, however, were made by Tycho Brahe. His mathematical calculations led him to conclude that this celestial object was not a sublunary phenomenon but a new star in Cassiopeia belonging to the eighth sphere of the fixed stars. Recording his observations in *De Nova Stella* in 1574, he announced: "it is a star shining in the firmament itself – one that has never previously been seen before our time, in any age since the beginning of the world."[4] Inevitably prompted to think of the star that guided the magi, Tycho was filled with excitement as he declared that this new star was "a miracle indeed, either the greatest of all that have occurred in the whole range of nature since the beginning of the world, or one certainly that is to be classed with those attested by the Holy Oracles."[5]

Having observed that the new star shone brightly for a whole year, he wondered about its possible significance. He had no doubt that it was likely to produce "strange, great, and wonderful effects."[6] Yet he momentarily hesitated to speculate on the exact nature of these effects, declaring, like Raphael in Book 8 of *Paradise Lost*, that such speculations were beyond the range of human inquiry. The temptation to indulge in prognostications was, however, too great and almost immediately he ventured into a whole series of speculations. He suggested that "the joviall, cleere, and bright lustre" of the star "doth seeme to fore-shew a prosperous and peaceable estate of humane affaires." At the same time he detected a "Martiall fiery glittering thereof" which seemed to signify violence and trouble. With millenarian fervor Tycho declared:

By this joviall figure it seemeth to portend, a great alteration, if not an utter subversion of religion; so that those devices which by outward shewes and Pharisaicall Hypocrisie, have long time bewitched ignorant people, shall now come to their full point and end.

Curiously, he interpreted the fact that the star shone temporarily and then faded away as a paradigm of the fate of the "false Planets" – whose modus operandi seems similar to that of false prophets – and whose outward plausible appearance seduced men away from the light of truth until their eventual exposure and downfall.[7]

Tycho concluded by fixing both a time and a place where the cataclysmic changes heralded by the 1572 nova would occur. As to the place, his prediction was:

And as this Starre appeared in the highest heavens, to the full view of the whole world, so it is credible, that there shall happen a great Catastrophe and universall change throughout all the chiefe Nations of the Earth, especially those which are situated Northward from the Aequinoctiall.

After an astrological computation of time, he arrived at the very specific prognostication that "it is likely that the force and influence of this Starre, will chiefly show itself in the yeare of our Lord 1632."[8]

The partial translation of *De Nova Stella* that appeared in London in 1632 contained the prediction relating to the significance of that year as indicated by the 1572 nova. The translator's own verses pointed out:

> Astrologie is but the speech of Starres,
> Which doe fore-tell vs both of Peace and Warres,
> And by this Starre great Tycho did intend
> To shew the World was coming to an end.[9]

In the same year similar prognostications by Sibyl Tiburtina, Theodore Beza, and Paracelsus were republished.[10] These predictions, focusing on 1632, marked the climax that year of the career of King Gustavus Adolphus of Sweden, great reformer and champion of Protestantism against the Catholic Counter-Reformation. It was also the year of Gustavus's death, an event that many in England found difficult to accept.

Another treatise on the 1572 nova appeared in 1632, entitled *The New Starr of the North, Shining Upon the Victorious King of Sweden.*[11] The author was Alexander Gill the Younger of St. Paul's School in London, a man with whom Milton was on terms of close friendship and to whom he sent some of his Latin poems. Gill gave a detailed account of the publication history of *De Nova Stella* and an analysis of the contents. He suggested that "if Eclipses of the two great lights, and conjunction of Planets under some portions of fixed stars have at any time, or may portend events upon earth, much more may new Starrs moulded by the hand of God in the highest heavens challenge the like propheticall language." Gill also gave an account of the career of King Gustavus Adolphus of Sweden who, because of his virtue and valor, had become the "spectacle of the Christian world" and the man whose achievements appeared to have been heralded by Tycho's nova.[12] But he was convinced that the implications of the 1572 nova were in fact likely to be much greater. He reminded his readers that "by some it was deemed to be the very same Starre, which appeared unto the Sages of the East at the birth of our Saviour, and thereupon conjectured to be the neerefore-runner of the second coming of Christ, as that was the attendant of his first coming."[13]

Meanwhile, in 1604 another new star had appeared, this time in the constellation Ophiucus. This star was observed by Johannes Kepler, who noted that "the significance of this wonderful work of God's hand far exceeds that of the star of 1572," particularly as it was accompanied by the Great Conjunction of Saturn, Jupiter, and Mars.[14] But beyond suggesting that this new star signified "something of such exalted importance that it is beyond the grasp and understanding of any man," Kepler refused to be drawn into any speculation, concluding: "Time will teach us the true and actual meaning of this star."[15]

The 1630s initiated discussions on the millennial implications of the 1604 nova, and such discussions repeatedly brought together the 1572 and the 1604 novas. John Swan's popular treatise on astronomy, the *Speculum Mundi*, was printed in Cambridge in 1635 and then reprinted in 1643, 1665, and 1670. Like Alexander Gill, Swan declared that the 1572 nova was a celestial phenomenon the like of which had never been seen except "at our Saviour's birth." Its appearance, he suggested, could be said to "animate distressed Christians" two months after a sad event, "the cunningly plotted Massacre of the Protestants in France."[16] Predictably, his discussions included Tycho's prognostications about 1632 and the expected reference to King Gustavus Adolphus of Sweden. Swan hastened to bring into the orbit of debate also the other new star of extraordinary brilliance, the 1604 nova, pointing out that its appearance coincided with the discovery of the Gunpowder Plot. The implication is clear: that the new star in Ophiucus gave warning of "that damnable powder plot of the Papists."[17] Swan's conservative reading of the new stars as celestial warnings is very close to the traditional view of unusual sightings in the sky such as comets as signs of impending disaster. Although at times he does go a step further, regarding the new stars as bringers of comfort and hope for the distressed, he lacks Tycho's enthusiasm for interpreting the new star as a covenant or an assurance of the promised millennium.

In the same chapter, chapter 5, Swan referred to another celestial marvel, the comet of 1618, as belonging to the same celestial regions as the new stars. This comet had been examined and analyzed earlier in great detail by John Bainbridge in *An Astronomicall Description of the late Comet*.[18] Bainbridge was a fellow of Emmanuel College, Cambridge, and later the Savilian Professor of Astronomy at Oxford, where he was a contemporary of Robert Burton. His *Astronomicall Description* was primarily concerned with the position, trajectory, and other scientific matters relating to the 1618 comet. In a detailed analysis of the location of the comet, he noted that it was always in opposition to the sun and in the region of Scorpio and Libra. In the second part of *Astronomicall Description*, entitled *Morall Prognosticks or Applications of the late Comet or Blazing-Starre*, Bainbridge examined the 1618 comet as "not so much a cause of elementary alterations, as a celestiall signe of greater consequents."[19] He had already asserted that the comet was not a sublunary phenomenon but a celestial event like the appearance of the 1572 and 1604 novas. In a sustained passage of millennial faith and aspirations he declared:

That blessed Starre, which conducted the Magi to Christs poore, but sacred nurcery (of whose incarnation, and happinesse to mankinde thereby that Starre was an heauenly Harbenger) doth enforce me often to thinke that those many new stars and Comets, which haue beene more this last Century of the world, then in many ages before, did amongst other things signifie that glorious light of the Gospell, which hath lately illumined the whole world.

About the preaching of Luther were at least five Comets in tenne yeares, after which followed the happy departure of Germany, England, and many other Northerne parts from the spirituall Babylon. This new Comet doth give us hope, that the rest of Christendome before long will follow ...

Yea did not that admirable new Starre in Cassiopeia 1572 and that remarkable Comet 1577 plainly from heauen remonstrate, that howsoeuer the Euangelicall Churches in *France*, and the *Low-countries* might be for a time greiuously afflicted, yet maugre Sathan, and all his hellish Furies they should at length flourish, and triumph ouer their cruell aduersaries. ... I am verily perswaded that the new Star which appeared so long from 1604 to Ianuary 1606 in the foot of *Serpentarius*, hauing coincidance with the great conjunction of the three superior Planets ... giues us hope, that his other great promise shall shortly be accomplished ... the second coming of our blessed Sauiour.[20]

This network of associations assigned to comets a position of importance in the celestial regions and linked the comet of 1618 with the new stars and millennial hopes. There was an extant tradition according to which the star that guided the Magi was actually a comet. Analyzing Marsilio Ficino's *De Stella Magorum*, which examined both the significance of the star which guided the Magi and the role of the Magi themselves as "oriental astronomers," Stephen M. Buhler points out that the ancient tradition of regarding the star the Magi followed as a comet would explain the star's curious behaviour, as an ordinary star could not be expected to travel across the sky guiding them, or to appear, disappear, and reappear as that star seems to do in Matthew.[21] Such movements appear to be more in keeping with the parabolic trajectory of comets. He also highlights that, as a consequence of deliberating along these lines, Ficino asserted, citing many authorities, that comets were not necessarily evil omens. If this was indeed an established tradition, it is not surprising that, in the atmosphere of millennial expectations in the seventeenth century, the 1618 comet should have been regarded as a good omen.

What emerges from scientific and popular thought of the Renaissance is clearly this: that in the seventeenth-century debate about the advent of the millennium, the two new stars of 1572 and 1604 were seen as emblems sent to herald the great event. The millennium was after all a promised age of peace and prosperity, not a calendar event. The two new stars of 1572 and 1604, and the comet of 1618, were interpreted as celestial signs indicating the imminence of the millennium. The enthusiastic response to new stars and comets in the 1630s and the millennial speculations they inspired may be taken as providing the context for Milton's fabrication of the eternalizing myth in the closing section of his pastoral elegy of 1637, *Lycidas*. The resurrected Lycidas is likened to the "day-star" (1.168) or sun shining in the morning sky. He takes his place among the saints in heaven "that sing and singing in their glory move." The idea looks forward to Book 3 of *Paradise Lost*, where the angels circle around God "thick as stars" (3.61), singing hymns of praise. Lycidas's transformation into a "genius of the shore" guiding sailors lost at sea may be seen in this cultural context as his reincarnation into a star directing sailors to a safe haven.

In any event, millennial hopes in the seventeenth century centered on gifted individuals thought to be able to usher in the rule of saints. The repeated references to King Gustavus Adolphus of Sweden in discussions about the new stars and the 1618 comet point to this conviction. While the Swedish king was the centre of hope in the wider European context, in the context in fact of the entire Christian world, in Britain such hopes centred first on King James I, the "terrestiall Phoebus" to whom John Bainbridge dedicated his work on the 1618 comet. James had written commendatory verses for Tycho's *De Nova Stella*, part of which was reprinted by Alexander Gill. Later, millennial hopes focused on Oliver Cromwell. Marvell's "The First Anniversary," written in 1655, is an unequivocal celebration of Cromwell's prophetic destiny.

The failure of the Puritan cause signaled also the failure of millennial aspirations, and Milton's *Paradise Lost* presents a passionate questioning of the reasons for this failure. While its declared intention is "to justify the ways of God to men" (1.26), Milton's epic in fact explores the depths of loss, disorientation, and malaise.[22] *Paradise Lost* is essentially the story of uncreation. The moment of sin, "man's first disobedience" (1.1) marks the initiation of a degenerative process affecting the entire cosmos. In

Book 9, Eve's excited narration to Adam of her transgression brings the first sign of decay as the roses in the garland in Adam's hand fade and drop. As Adam joins Eve in the transgression, a whole series of changes take place. The harmonious relationship between them breaks down into discord as they point accusing fingers at each other. Animals turn predatory and seek to destroy each other. The balanced position of sun and earth is altered, with nights and days becoming unequal and eternal spring giving way to the alternation of the seasons.

These cataclysmic changes are brought about by the machinations of a character who projects himself time and again in the epic as millennial hero. Satan is the courageous leader of his troops as he energizes them with a show of faith and compassion. He is the wise counselor of Eve to whom he apparently reveals the actions and motivations of the highest powers. He is the bold adventurer discovering new lands like a Renaissance navigator or new cosmic worlds as Galileo did looking through his telescope (*PL* 1.283–95) and is thus able to capture the imagination of readers. With his apparent leadership abilities, compassion, insight, and pioneering qualities, Satan is the archetypal millennial hero. This self-fashioning as millennial hero needs to be understood in the light of the widespread millennial aspirations that marked seventeenth-century Puritanism. Satan becomes a travesty of the kind of heroism displayed by Cromwell and King Gustavus Adolphus of Sweden.

Throughout *Paradise Lost* we are always conscious of Satan's dissembling, of the disjuncture between his real and projected selves. The many disguises he adopts are only the physical manifestations of a more pervasive condition of personality, a compulsive role playing, which becomes intensified during his visit to the new cosmos. While Satan deceives even his followers in hell with a show of loyalty and compassion, his self-fashioning moves into a higher mode as he turns his attention to man and the new cosmos. There, in the two temptations of Eve, he presents himself as one who brings enlightenment and deliverance. His adoption of the prophetic role marks him out as the archetypal false prophet. This self-fashioning also completes the series of patterned oppositions in the poem between the divine and the diabolical – the divine and devilish trinities, Christ's bright cosmic chariot and Satan's dark "car of night" (9.65), the promised return of the Messiah and Satan's projected image of himself as millennial hero.[23]

Milton depicts Satan's self-presentation as millennial hero in the new world within two framing images, the comet in Ophiucus in Books 2 and 4 and the new star in Ophiucus in Book 10. These are defining images of enormous significance in *Paradise Lost*. Their significance emerges when they are examined in the context of millennial speculations of the time regarding the new stars and the comet of 1618. The comparisons with these phenomena accomplish a narrative fashioning much more complex than Satan's self-presentation alone, since they both facilitate Satan's projection of himself through these images of celestial phenomena (image as disguise) and provide an ironic commentary (through the act of comparison) on the entire millennial issue. More than once in the epic Milton compares Satan and his followers to comets and falling stars. There is, for instance, the memorable description in Book 1 of how Mulciber fell from heaven and in the evening "Dropped from the zenith like a falling star" (1.745) and in the same book Satan's flag unfurled shines "like a meteor streaming to the wind" (1.537). Comets and falling stars, however, were generally regarded as sublunary phenomena in Milton's day and while these could also have millennial implications signifying the fall of Antichrist,[24] the comparison of Satan to the new stars which clearly belonged to the celestial sphere is a deeply troubling one as it seems to connect Satan with the promised Second Coming. It is in the same celestial region that Bainbridge locates the 1618 comet in Ophiucus in his treatise of 1619. The millennial implications of the two framing images of Satan as the new star and the comet in Ophiucus are therefore both powerful and provocative.

   As Satan confronts Death on his way out of hell in Book 2, Milton describes his awesome presence thus:

> Incensed with indignation Satan stood
> Unterrified, and like a comet burned,
> That fires the length of Ophiucus huge
> In the Arctic sky, and from his horrid hair
> Shakes pestilence and war.   (2.707–11)

Bainbridge explains the position of the comet in detail with the help of a planisphere which shows the comet stretching from the equinoctial line to the north, the cometary line running parallel to Ophiucus. It seems likely that this is the comet in Milton's mind in Book 2, since he gives it a specific location that matches the location of the 1618 comet: "That fires the length of Ophiucus huge / In the Arctic sky." That Milton had a keen interest in astronomy is by now fairly well established. In the circumstances he is more than likely to have been familiar not only with Bainbridge's treatise but also with references to this comet in popular encyclopedias such as Swan's *Speculum Mundi*. He would have been conscious also of the tradition that regarded the star of Bethlehem as possibly a comet, and comets – particularly the comet of 1618 – as not just good omens but, even more, signs of the coming millennium. In a poem that is unusually alert to both traditional cosmology and the new astronomy, Milton's orthodox view of comets as bringing "pestilence and war," combined with a deliberate reference to Ophiucus, is not without a special significance. The allusions provide a direct and open refutation of the millennial hopes raised both by the 1618 comet and the 1604 nova.

The image of Satan shining like an unusually brilliant comet looks forward to his appearance at the end of Book 4. Discovered by the touch of Ithuriel's spear, Satan starts up like a keg of gunpowder unexpectedly set on fire and "with sudden blaze diffused, inflames the air" (4.818). As he confronts Gabriel we see his immense stature:

> On the other side Satan alarmed
> Collecting all his might dilated stood,
> Like Teneriff or Atlas unremoved:
> His stature reached the sky. (4.985–88)

This flaming figure at the end of Book 4 stands directly below the constellation Libra at midnight in the same part of the hemisphere again as the constellation Ophiucus, which would be directly below Libra at that hour. While the image of gunpowder which precedes the exchange between Satan, Zephon, and Gabriel emphasizes Satan's destructive potential throughout, it also strategically reinforces Milton's earlier refutation in Book 2 of millennial aspirations heralded by the comet of 1618. Bainbridge's treatise raises such expectations linking the Ophiucus comet to the promised millennium and Swan's encyclopedia interprets the significance of the same comet as a providential warning, but to Milton's disillusioned mind it is neither promise nor warning but the first visible sign or appearance of the agent of destruction. Seventeenth-century readers, familiar with contemporary astronomy and astrology from scientific treatises, almanacs, textbooks, and encyclopedias of the time would not have failed to make the connection between the two passages in Books 2 and 4 and contemporary speculations about the 1618 comet.

While Satan's appearance as a comet in Ophiucus in Books 2 and 4 is a potent reminder of the failure of millennial hopes raised by the 1618 comet, a more insidious and ironic reminder comes through the Ophiucus image in Book 10. There Satan is on his way back from paradise after having successfully corrupted Adam and Eve and thus achieved apparent success in his devious war against God. Sin and Death meet him:

> And now their way to earth they had descried,
> To Paradise first tending, when behold
> Satan in likeness of an angel bright
> Betwixt the Centaur and the Scorpion steering
> His zenith, while the sun in Aries rose:
> Disguised he came, but those his children dear
> Their parent soon discerned, though in disguise.
>
> (10. 325–31)

He steers his course between the Centaur and the Scorpion, that is, in the part of the heavens where the constellation Ophiucus is to be found and in which the new star had appeared in 1604. Satan appears "in likeness of an angel bright." The likeness is not to an angel resembling a human form with wings, as such a figure would have attracted immediate attention and exposure. Satan appears instead as a new angelic star in Ophiucus. In many passages in *Paradise Lost* the angels are identified with stars, and Milton's portrayal of Satan as a star here is reinforced by Satan's position between the Centaur and the Scorpion. This startling appearance justifies the emphasis on the word "behold" in the passage, its sharply explosive impact indicative of both the sense of surprise in the reaction of Sin and Death and the expression of irony as the dominant feeling of the narrator's consciousness.

Indeed, Satan retains his star disguise even after he reenters Pandemonium:

> At last as from a cloud his fulgent head
> And shape star bright appeared, or brighter, clad
> With what permissive glory since his fall
> Was left him, or false glitter: all amazed
> At that so sudden blaze the Stygian throng
> Bent their aspect, and whom they wished beheld,
> Their mighty chief returned.   (10.449–55)

Milton's use of "aspect" here is deliberate. It is a word whose astrological significance with reference to the planets and stars was widely known in the Renaissance and it invests the whole host of fallen angels with a "permissive glory" which enables them to shine like stars until their final transformation into a colony of hissing serpents.

Within the context of seventeenth-century millennialism, the appearance of Satan as the comet and the new star in Ophiucus enhances our perception of him as powerful and compelling, but also as deceitful and evil. Helen Gardner has written of a progressive degeneration of Satan indicated through his disguises of cherub, toad, and serpent.[25]

Yet these disguises are but instances of cunning and expediency. Satan's self-fashioning is proactive and he uses disguise for the purpose of negotiation and control. There is a clear distinction, however, between two modes of self-fashioning that he undertakes. There are moments when all his faculties are concentrated on seeking, devising, and insinuating, as in his conversation with Uriel and the two temptations of Eve, when motivation is more important than image and apparent degradation through disguise may be expedient. After all, as an inferior he was likely to gain greater indulgence. There are other situations when his energies are concentrated on a self-conscious projection of a public image of himself to impress those whom he encounters before and after the Fall. In the modes of self-fashioning through which he projects himself to an audience he wishes to impress, whether it be Sin and Death, or Gabriel and the angels, or the devils in Pandemonium, Satan undergoes not degradation but a reinvention of himself as celestial phenomena of millennial value. The process involves exploitation of both biblical myth and history as these strategies of simulation are at once expressions of loss, a hallucinatory attempt to recover earlier cosmic positions – as an angel Lucifer had once been like a star in heaven – and at the same time subtle negotiations of empowerment. They are mimetic acts that skillfully manipulate the texture of beliefs associated with celestial phenomena that energized the millennial aspirations of the century.

In depicting Satan's self-presentation as millennial star or comet, Milton is able to focus attention on the millennial debate of the seventeenth century, not to subvert millennialism itself but implicitly to criticize those who misread the signs. In his state of despair and disillusionment at the failure of the Puritan cause, Milton looks back at those earlier celestial signals and their interpretations and, in a process of diagnosis and discovery, sees those earlier interpretations as misreadings. His own version of those celestial signs as being linked with Satan rather than the Second Coming is almost a regressive step in astronomical terms, reverting to the earlier view of celestial changes as bad omens. He now sees these celestial phenomena as diabolical manipulations of cosmic signs. The cosmic signs that lit up the sky for almost a hundred years were signs not of hope but of deceitful illusions.

The identification of Satan with the new stars thus provides for the millennial hopes of the century Milton's personal ironic commentary. It is a fierce indictment of the false hopes raised of the immediate advent of the promised millennium and the misreadings of celestial signs that fueled such hopes. Moreover, seventeenth-century millennialism had become inextricably connected with achievements in intellectual inquiry, as the millennium was expected not only to restore the rule of the saints, leading to the Second Coming of Christ, but also to recover, for man, the encyclopedic knowledge and power over nature that Adam had enjoyed in paradise before the Fall. In the circumstances, Milton's passionately felt sense of betrayal of millennial hopes could not have been more eloquently expressed than by using a landmark event of the new astronomy as the text for the expression of his sense of failure.

NOTES

1. Citations of Donne's poems are from A. J. Smith (ed.), *John Donne: The Complete English Poems* (Harmondsworth, 1971).
2. For the extent to which Aristotelio-Ptolemaic cosmology continued to dominate astronomical thought in the sixteenth century and even in the seventeenth, see Francis R. Johnson, *Astronomical Thought In Renaissance England* (New York, 1968).
3. Ibid., p. 156.
4. Tycho Brahe, *De Nova Stella*, rptd. in H. Shapley and H. E. Howarth, *A Source Book in Astronomy* (New York and London, 1929), p. 19. Tycho gave a detailed analysis of all books written about the new star in Cassiopeia in his *Astronomiae Instauratae Progymnasmata* (Prague, 1602). A partial translation of *De Nova Stella* appeared in London in 1632 as *Learned Tico Brahae his Astronomicall Coniectur of the new and much Admired Starre*.
5. *De Nova Stella*, p. 13.
6. Tycho Brahe, *Astronomicall Coniectur*, p. 14.
7. Ibid., p. 15.
8. Ibid., pp. 16–17.
9. "The Translatovr To The Reader," in ibid.
10. See B. S. Capp, *Astrology and the Popular Press* (London, 1979), p. 168.
11. Alexander Gill, *The New Starr of the North, Shining Upon the Victorious King of Sweden* (London, 1632).
12. Ibid., pp. 21, 22.
13. Ibid., pp. 8–9.
14. Johannes Kepler, *A Thorough Description Of An Extraordinary New Star Which First Appeared In October Of This Year, 1604*, trans. Judith V. Field and Anton Pestl, in *Vistas in Astronomy* (Oxford, 1977), vol. XX, p. 333.
15. Ibid., pp. 336–39.
16. John Swan, *Speculum Mundi* (London, 1635), pp. 114, 107.
17. Ibid., p. 115.
18. John Bainbridge, *An Astronomicall Description of the Late Comet from the 18 of November 1618 to 16 of December following* (London, 1619).
19. Ibid., p. 28.
20. Ibid., pp. 30–32.

21. Stephen M. Buhler, "Marsilio Ficino's *De Stella Magorum* and Renaissance Views of the Magi," *Renaissance Quarterly* 43 (1990), pp. 348–71.
22. All citations from *Paradise Lost* are from *The Complete Poems of Milton*, ed. John Carey and Alastair Fowler (London, 1968).
23. The phrase "car of night" is discussed in my note on "Satan's Astronomical Journey, *Paradise Lost* IX 63–66," *Notes & Queries*, New Series, 26 (1979), pp. 417–22.
24. Ken Simpson's chapter in this book examines the millennial implications of comets and falling stars in *Paradise Regained*, in particular the powerful impact of the simile comparing Satan to an "Autumnal star" falling from heaven.
25. Helen Gardner, "Milton's Satan and the Theme of Damnation in Elizabethan Tragedy," in Gardner, *A Reading of Paradise Lost* (Oxford, 1965).

5

The millennial moment: Milton vs. "Milton"

William B. Hunter

The biblical promise of the millennium held for John Milton and many of his contemporaries a far more immediate expectation of fulfillment than the word does for most of us today; we define it merely as beginning on an even totality of a thousand years. In Milton's day Christians understood the millennium prophesied in Revelation 20 to be the appearance of the Word of God in heaven which would initiate a thousand years of universal peace and prosperity. It could begin at any moment, not like ours only in coincidence with every tenth century.

Although apocalyptic promises appear in various other New Testament passages and especially in the last six chapters of the Old Testament prophet Daniel, the millennium proper is defined only in the Book of Revelation. There the narrator, John, hears at the end of a series of visions a voice declaring (19:7) that "the marriage of the Lamb [understood as the Son of God] is come, and his wife [understood as the true Christian church] hath made herself ready" for it by the overthrow of the whore of Babylon (19:2) or, as many English Puritans interpreted her, the Roman Catholic faith, which they thought they were achieving as they worked towards a final cleansing of the English church from any remaining impurities of Rome.

These Puritans found in the promised marriage of the Lamb with his purified church a major text to validate their efforts against Charles I and the Laudian establishment. As the narration of Revelation continues, the Son as the Word of God will appear on a white horse in the heavens (19:11–16), leading to the overthrow of the beast of Revelation 13, which with all its followers is cast into a "Lake of fire" burning with brimstone (19:20). Thereupon an angel appears to bind Satan for a thousand years (20:1–2), the millennium. Interpreting their efforts as the effectuation of this prophecy, Puritans accordingly stressed the millenarian age of peace and prosperity which would follow as the consequence of their success and prove the righteousness of their cause. Milton has long been recognized as one of those who in the 1640s held such millenarian expectations.

There is no suggestion of them, however, in Milton's Cambridge days. He is so firmly fixed as a Puritan in critical opinion that one forgets there is no evidence to support a dissident position until *Lycidas*.[1] Proof of his support of the current political and religious regime is obvious in his celebration of the foiling of the Gunpowder Plot, his poems commemorating the bishops of Winchester and Ely, and his sworn acceptances of the standards of the Church of England for both his degrees.

Although the Nativity Ode may be read as millenarian, as Barbara Lewalski and Stella Revard have done in this book, it is questionable whether it is an exception in supporting the validation that Puritans found in the biblical text.[2] It centers, of course, on the birth, not the Last Judgment. But as the sixteenth stanza summarizes: "The Babe lies yet in smiling Infancy, / That on the bitter cross / Must redeem our loss," the sacrifice that will lead to our glorification at the end of time.[3] To arouse for it "those ychain'd in sleep," the dead, "The wakeful trump of doom must thunder through the deep." This image does not derive from Revelation but from two of St. Paul's letters: "we shall all be changed . . . at the last trump: for the trumpet shall sound, and the dead shall be raised incorruptible" (1 Cor. 15:51–52) and when "the trump of God" sounds the dead and those still alive will be "caught up together . . . to meet the Lord in the air" (1 Thess. 4:16–17) which, amalgamated with the "great white throne" of the Last Judgment in Revelation 20:11 provides Milton's line 164: "The dreadful Judge in middle Air shall spread his throne." Some limitation of "th'old Dragon" indeed began with the birth being celebrated, as Milton goes on to list at length examples of the disappearance of the pagan gods. This is not, however, the total imprisonment of Satan in hell, as the Bible describes his incarceration for a thousand years (Rev. 20:2); for the Milton of these earlier years "our bliss / Full and perfect is" only at the Last Judgment, foreseen now with the birth, not at the millennium, to which he seems indifferent.

Well after his university days, however, when he had to face the exigencies of the Laudian church, Milton reconsidered the event as being more immediate to his life, finding in it as other Puritans did authorization for resisting that church. Thus in *Of Reformation* he expected that "some one [obviously John Milton] may perhaps bee heard offering [works that] sing and celebrate thy *divine Mercies*, and *marvelous Judgements* in this Land" with the overthrow of those whom he judged to be unworthy prelates. At that time Christ, "the Eternall and shortly-expected King[,] shalt open the

Clouds to judge the severall Kingdomes of the World ... proclaiming thy universal and milde *Monarchy* through Heaven and Earth" (*CP* 1: 616) – a day associated with England's struggle for religious freedom that will inaugurate the thousand years of peace.

Again, in *Animadversions* he prayed that the Lord would proceed through the current Puritan efforts to achieve this perfection on earth, to celebrate which he himself would "perhaps take up a Harp, and sing thee an elaborate Song" (*CP* 1: 706). Then the "Prince of all the Kings of the earth" will appear and "take up that unlimited Scepter which thy Almighty Father hath bequeath'd thee; for now the voice of thy Bride [the church] calls thee" (*CP* 1: 707). As Arthur Barker pointed out, "it is the religious issue which forms the center of the argument" in Milton's political pamphlets.[4] Indeed, in such a position state and church cannot be separated.

Not many Christians, however, shared in such a specific application of the verses in Revelation. As the *Oxford Dictionary of the Christian Church* observes: "Millenarianism properly so called was but rarely met with," appearing only among such groups as the Anabaptists, the Bohemian Brethren (with whom Milton found much in common), and the English Independents.[5] One must recognize the fundamental differences between the inauguration of millennium and Judgment. The former would begin with a period of social and religious amelioration. It would conclude violently after a short period of satanic domination on his release from hell (Rev. 20:7–8), which would end with his defeat and the inauguration of a newly renovated heaven and earth (Rev. 20:10–21:4). Major Continental dogmatists ignored the millenarian aspects, collapsing it into its sequel, the Last Judgment, in part because it is found only in Revelation – not elsewhere in the Bible, where the emphasis is entirely on the Judgment. Furthermore, in contrast with English Independency, they had no state church in opposition to which it could be effectively applied. Among those following this line of thought, which ignored the millennium preceding the Last Judgment with which they were concerned, were William Ames and Johannes Wollebius. Ames, in the account of final events in his *Medulla* (chapter 41) found no occasion even to mention it; Wollebius's longer discussion in his *Compendium* (chapters 34–36) paid no attention to any of its details.[6]

De Doctrina Christiana, traditionally assigned to Milton, has long been recognized as deriving in large part from some chapters from Ames and Wollebius. In its treatment of the millennium especially, it falls squarely into this Continental tradition of indifference rather than the English

Independent activist one. In his characterization of angels, its author cites the millennial passage in Revelation but only to locate the evil ones in hell (*CP* VI: 349). Its chapter on "Incomplete Glorification" (chapter 25) – that to be achieved in this life – never suggests that the living might extend their efforts to purify the church to a great climax and conclusion with the appearance of the equestrian Word in heaven. Thus its author would not have dreamed in the early 1640s of celebrating in verse its actualization. Seven chapters later (chapter 33) he considers "Complete Glorification [and] Christ's Second Coming," which is to celebrate the conclusion of the thousand years following the Word's first appearance. Like contemporary dogmatists he does not distinguish the Judgment that begins the thousand years from the one that follows, and assumes (*CP* VI: 623–25) that during that time the Son will be occupied judging the evil angels and the resurrected martyrs, as Revelation forecasts it will begin (20:4–6). With Ames and Wollebius his interest focuses rather on the final Judgment, preceded by the "false prophets, false Christs, wars, earthquakes, persecutions, plague, famine," and so on of Satan's reign (*CP* VI: 616; Wollebius's text is essentially identical), catastrophic events not foreseen by English Puritans, who instead expected an increasing betterment of their political and religious circumstances which would herald the appearance of the Word to begin a thousand years of peace.

In the years which followed, however, actual political developments seem to have forced Milton, like many of his contemporaries, to abandon belief in the immediate (but not necessarily the ultimate) realization of these millenarian hopes. With Barker we can observe that "As the revolution progressed, Milton's confidence diminished; but . . . the idea of the kingdom remained fixed in his mind." He concluded that for Milton: "The reign of Christ might itself be impossible to establish, as Christianity then went; but its desirability is an underlying motive in the political pamphlets [continuing from the earlier antiprelatical ones], for it provided an ideal pattern of government by the wise and good."[7] Even in his near despair before the coming Restoration of Charles II, Milton could still adumbrate in *The Readie and Easie Way* that with the governmental reform he projected in it, "peace, justice, plentifull trade and all prosperitie" should ensue, and "shall so continue . . . even to the coming of our true and rightfull and only to be expected King . . ., the Messiah, the Christ" (*CP* VII: 445) heralding the millennium, quite different from the interval of satanic domination which would precede the Last Judgment according to Revelation.

Although this is the last extended reference to the millennium I have found in his works, others have interpreted as millenarian several passages in *Paradise Lost*. In Book 3 the Son prophesies that after his death and resurrection he "through the ample Air in Triumph high / Shall lead hell captive" and "then with the multitude of my redeemed / Shall enter Heav'n long absent" (3.254–61). Alastair Fowler's long note in his edition interprets this last "difficult line" as a conflation of the Son's "first with his second coming."[8] Such a reading seems probable, though in any case there appear to be no millenarian allusions in the passage.

Again, in Book 12 after his resurrection:

> to the Heav'n of Heav'ns [the Son] shall ascend
> With victory, triumphing through the air
> Over his foes and thine [the Father's]; there shall surprise
> The Serpent, Prince of air, and drag in chains
> Through all his Realm, and there confounded leave;
> Then enter into glory, and resume
> His Seat at God's right hand.   (12.451–57)

In his annotation of these lines in his edition, Roy Flannagan thought they referred to the binding of Satan by the angel in Revelation 20:1–2, while Stella Revard argues in this book that references to Satan's chaining in *Paradise Lost* generally allude to the millennium.[9] However, this passage echoes 2 Peter 2:4: "God spared not the angels that sinned, but cast them down to hell, and delivered them into chains," conflated with Colossians 2:12–15: believers "are risen with him [Christ]" thanks to God, who also "raised him from the dead"; he, in turn, "having spoiled principalities and powers [orders of fallen angels], made a show of them openly, triumphing over them in it." As Milton's reliance on these passages indicates, the lines in *Paradise Lost* do not refer to Christ's later millennial appearances.

Immediately following these lines is an account of the Second Coming and its accompanying Last Judgment: the Son from heaven

> shall come,
> When this worlds dissolution shall be ripe,
> With glory and power to judge both quick and dead,
> To judge the unfaithful dead, but to reward
> His faithful, and receive them into bliss.   (12.458–62)

William Empson thought that in this passage Milton doubted the millennium.[10] Instead, it describes the events of the succeeding Last Judgment; for, to repeat, at the Judgment that begins the millennium according to Revelation only the martyrs are restored to rule with the

Son (20:4). Everyone else must wait (20:5). Since the unfaithful and the faithful are judged together in this passage of the poem, it must refer to the final judging of everyone as recounted in Revelation 20:12–13.

The last account in the poem, of the final rather than the millennial Judgment, repeats the previous one: the Son appears "in the clouds from Heav'n" to "dissolve Satan with his perverted World," an event to be followed by the creation of "New Heav'ns, new Earth" (12.545–49), as foretold in Revelation in association with the final Judgment (21:1). None of these examples associated with the end of time alludes to its antecedent thousand years. One may conclude that, with most other interpreters, Milton at this later date had melded the Judgment of Revelation 20 with the final one a thousand years later, probably because this is the only one foretold elsewhere in the Bible.

A case can also be made for understanding as millennial the War in Heaven, which occupies the last half of Book 5 and all of Book 6, as Stella Revard has fully documented from contemporary texts; for its biblical origin is certainly Revelation 12, which, like the rest of the book, is devoted to "last things."[11] At the conclusion of the war as Milton recounts it, Satan and his followers are all "rowling" in hell's fiery lake (1.52) just as they are in the biblical account of the beginning of the millennium in Revelation 20:1–2. Such similarities, however, are not sufficient to justify interpreting the war as millennial. In the Bible no relationship is drawn between the war of Revelation 12 and the binding of Satan in chapter 20. Furthermore, Milton places his war just after the beginning of time, not near its end. In the poem the Son single-handedly wins the battle, whereas in Revelation 12 it is Michael and the good angels, and in chapter 20 there is no battle and a single angel (who only at a stretch might be the Son) binds Satan. At the end of the war of Revelation 12 Satan is merely "cast out into the earth" (9–10), not to hell. Nor does he remain there for a thousand years in the poem: the Father releases him after nine days (1.48) so that "with reiterated crimes he might / Heap on himself damnation" (1.214–15).

Even so, Milton's biblical authority for the war (as he freely interprets it) is certainly this chapter of Revelation and thus is originally associated with final matters. It occurs at the very center of Revelation, just as Milton located it centrally in his poem. The similarities I have pointed out he must have created quite deliberately, inviting his readers to interpret the war as meaningful at the beginning of time as his plot requires, and at its end where the Bible places it. Furthermore, Milton provides substantial evidence for a third interpretation at the middle of time, the three days of the war matching those from Good Friday through to Easter Day.[12] No such period is suggested in Revelation. Thus, in brief, on the evening before the battle begins, the Christian Maundy Thursday, all the angels good and bad participate in a "sweet repast" (5.630). In a slight revision of the passage added in 1674 to make clearer the allusion to Christ's passion, Milton added two lines: "They eat, they drink, and in communion sweet / Quaff immortalitie and joy" (5.637–38), with the word "communion" conveying the special eucharistic meaning for its Christian readers.

Then, significantly, the Son disappears completely from the narrative as he remains under the power of death from the crucifixion to the resurrection, the heavenly forces being led as in Revelation by Michael – indecisively in the poem, victoriously in the Bible. Only at dawn on the third day (6.699, 6.748) does the Son appear again when he "Ascended" (6.762) to overcome alone Satan and his force. It is not an accident that this word begins the second half of the poem in the lineation of the 1667 edition. In short Milton invites his readers to view the War in Heaven as God in eternity could: as simultaneously present at the beginning of time (the surface narrative), at its center (the subtext of the passion and resurrection), and at its end (the source narrative in Revelation). I see no evident way to include in this profoundly complex creation an additional allusion to the millennial chaining of Satan followed by a long period of peace and prosperity.

An interesting fact which does not appear to have been hitherto noticed is how totally unlike Milton the author of *De Doctrina Christiana* is in his indifference to the account of the War in Heaven in Revelation. His citations of verses from it (*CP* VI: 315, 347, 349, 350) are only as prooftexts which describe angelic natures; for him the war itself holds no interest at all.

The evident progressive loss after the early 1640s of Milton's belief in the realization of the biblical millennium has been seen in this total lack of interest in that event which one finds in *De Doctrina*, which he is thought to have been especially occupied with during the two years leading up to the Restoration, when political and religious realities must have forced upon him reconsideration of its imminence. Rather than the Word appearing on a horse in the sky, Charles II came on a boat from France. Hence Michael Fixler, in some perplexity, recognized the conflict between Milton's professed earlier belief in the gradual transformation of mankind to millennial glorification by political activities in the 1640s, and its absence from *De Doctrina*, which would be explained

by these historical facts. As Fixler summarizes, in his antiprelatical position and to a lesser degree throughout his political arguments Milton
"evidently believed that the coming of the Kingdom of Glory and
the manifold spiritual and material perfection proper to it was immanent." His "constant belief" then was that perfect glorification would
involve "the total renovation of Man and nature" and there would be a
"progression toward perfect glorification [which] would gradually transform not only men, but also the conditions under which they lived."[13]

Considering how different from this is the position of *De Doctrina*,
which he accepted with everyone else as Milton's work, Fixler could only
conclude that "Milton abandoned these [earlier] assumptions" because
of historical developments; for in the treatise "Collective spiritual
progress... is absent as the bridge or continuum between the imperfect
glorification" within which Puritans believed they were striving "and the
perfect one." Furthermore, the treatise strongly affirms that the Second
Coming is quite unforeseeable, "in sharp contrast to the assumptions
behind the prayers in *Of Reformation* and *Animadversions* and which appeared as well in scattered references as late as *Eikonoklastes*," portending
for Milton the expected appearance in heaven of the Word.[14]

Against such apparently obvious paralleling of Milton's loss of conviction about the millennium with the indifference to it of the treatise,
however, Maurice Kelley in his edition of *De Doctrina* (*CP* vi) showed its
very close, often verbatim parallels with Wollebius's *Compendium* on this
subject. Indeed, a glance at his extensive notes to chapter 33 provides immediate proof of such "influence." But, as Kelley had also clearly demonstrated (*CP* vi: 18–19), such close dependence proves that these pages date
from the early 1640s, when Milton was occupied with his public attacks
on the governance of the Church of England and with his private school,
years when he believed in an imminent millennium – not from the late
1650s when actual political developments were forcing some modifica-
tion or surrender of such expectations. In brief, Kelley concluded that
De Doctrina developed from what Milton's nephew-student-biographer
Edward Phillips called "A perfect system of divinity," associated with
dictation of it in Milton's classroom and heavily dependent upon such
digests of dogma as those of Ames and Wollebius. They are the origin
of the many direct quotations, especially from the latter, which are so
prominent in chapter 33. Accordingly it must date from the early 1640s
rather than the disillusioned period of the late 1650s.

When Kelley came to consider Fixler's parallels of the suppos-
edly late treatise indifferent to the millennium with Milton's probable

disenchantment, he had to recognize that on this subject the treatise for once cannot provide a gloss for the canonical works. Like Wollebius's book, the treatise is indifferent to millennial hopes, though in its similarity to Wollebius's ideas it must date from just those years in the earlier 1640s when Milton's hopes for an English millennium were at their highest. Kelley then necessarily had to discount Fixler's argument: "the similarity [of chapter 33] to Wollebius ... suggests that Milton's [indifferent] views on the second coming [in the treatise] may have been espoused as early as 'A perfect System,' which is to be dated early 1640s or before, and that the 'marked reorientation' that Fixler finds in the *Christian Doctrine* may not be reorientations at all" (*CP* vi: 615, n. 2). One must conclude that it echoes in the 1640s Wollebius's indifference to the subject, which is quite inconsistent with what we know were then Milton's own very different thoughts. Kelley simply left unargued such obvious contradictions on this subject between the chapter of the treatise that dated from the early 1640s and the tracts of the same period.

But one should recognize also that the "Perfect system" which Phillips reported from his schooling with Milton in the early 1640s was probably not the teacher's own "tractate" but one which each student was set to work out for himself, the foundations of its thirty-third chapter being provided by quotations dictated by the teacher from Wollebius's *Compendium*, which the students would then annotate and support by proof-texts. Anyone of Milton's education and experience then would have long graduated from such an elementary exercise as Phillips reported from his classroom. In *Doctrine and Discipline of Divorce*, which dates from just these years, Milton judges the capacity of his opponents not to go beyond "the easie creek... of a Medulla" (*CP* ii: 232–33) such as Ames's.[15] From this point of view one need not accept the blatant inconsistency in Milton's thought that Kelley had to postulate: two different authors easily account for the two different positions he had to recognize. Alternatively, Barker and Fixler could account for the seeming concurrence regarding the millennium only by assuming what Kelley has shown to be an inconsistently late dependence on Wollebius for the composition of this part of the treatise. Again, recognition of two different authors resolves the difficulty.

NOTES

1. See William B. Hunter, "Herbert and Milton," *South Central Review* 1 (1984), pp. 22–31, especially pp. 22–23.
2. See Barbara Lewalski's chapter and Stella Revard's chapter in this book.

3. Citations of Milton's poetry are from John T. Shawcross (ed.), *The Complete Poetry of John Milton* (Garden City, 1971).
4. Arthur Barker, *Milton and the Puritan Dilemma, 1641–1660* (Toronto, 1942), p. 124.
5. F. L. Cross (ed.), *Oxford Dictionary of the Christian Church* (London, 1966), pp. 900–1.
6. William Ames, *Medulla Theologica* (1629), trans. John D. Eusden as *The Marrow of Divinity* (Boston, 1968), and Johannes Wollebius, *Compendium Theologiae Christianae* (1626), trans. John W. Beardslee, in *Reformed Dogmatics* (New York, 1965).
7. Barker, *Milton and the Puritan Dilemma*, pp. 195, 197.
8. Alastair Fowler (ed.), "*Paradise Lost,*" in John Carey and Alastair Fowler (eds.), *The Complete Poems of John Milton* (London, 1968), p. 575n.
9. Roy Flannagan (ed.), *The Riverside Milton* (Boston, 1998), p. 703n. See also Stella Revard's chapter in this book.
10. William Empson, *Milton's God* (London, 1961), p. 127.
11. For Revard's case that the War in Heaven has millennial implications, see her chapter in this book.
12. See W. B. Hunter, C. A. Patrides, and J. H. Adamson, *Bright Essence* (Salt Lake City, 1971), pp. 115–30.
13. Michael Fixler, *Milton and the Kingdoms of God* (London and Evanston, 1964), p. 213.
14. Ibid., pp. 214, 215.
15. See my *Visitation Unimplor'd: Milton and the Authorship of "De Doctrina Christiana"* (Pittsburgh, 1998), p. 31.

6

Confusion: the apocalypse, the millennium

John T. Shawcross

The two words apocalypse and millennium are used with some kind of interchangeability in critical circles. They are not synonymous: the second is only part of the first in the Bible. While this chapter is primarily a response to William Hunter's essay preceding it, it is necessary, I think, to examine the issues involved, expanding into much discussion which relates to that essay but which, at the same time, offers a separate essay on the subject of this collection.

The first of the two words "Apocalypse, Revelation" comes from the Greek αποκαλυπσις, meaning "revelation" from the verb "to uncover." In religious terms it is identified as a prophetic disclosure, and the last book of the New Testament, allegedly by St. John the Divine of Patmos (where these visions were said to have been communicated), is called The Apocalypse or The Revelation. Its first verses speak of "The Revelation of Jesus Christ, which God gave unto him, to show unto his servants things which must shortly come to pass; and he sent and signified it by his angel unto his servant John: who bare record of the word of God, and of the testimony of Jesus Christ, and of all things that he saw. Blessed is he that readeth, and they that hear the words of this prophecy, and keep those things which are written therein: for the time is at hand" (Rev. 1:1–3). But a careful reader should immediately recognize a potential confusion: to reveal (or uncover) something that is to occur, "this prophecy" as the words delineate it, is not to manifest its existence or the existence and power of that God, which would seem to be its intent. Only through faith that the revelation will become manifested will the confusion disappear, and only when the "time" has "shortly come to pass" will such manifestation occur, if it does. The apocalyptic vision is only potential; any revelation involved here is also only potential and not some revealed reality.

The problem became a transitional point for the seventeenth century as belief in the revelation of God resolved into the manifestation of God – a manifestation most usually seen in natural things, nature and the world around humankind. The questions concerning the earth (triggered surely by the denial of a geocentric universe in the sixteenth century) which emerge in the opposed writings of Godfrey Goodman and George Hakewill and in such theories of the earth as Thomas Burnet's developed the deistic principle that dominates late seventeenth-century and eighteenth-century thinking, leading to transcendental and pantheistic concepts as the nineteenth century loomed.[1] The effects upon literature are well demonstrated as the ancients vied with the moderns in critical debate and mimesis vied with imitation, and (let it be especially noted) as vatic poetry (the line of vision) gave way for a while to the line of wit, so praised by critics such as F. R. Leavis.

A further aspect of the dual way of knowing God's existence lay in the expectation that the "millennium" was about to occur, usually suggested as around 1655–57 or so, whereby his revelation and manifestation would coincide.[2] The year of occurrence was predicted through dating of biblical events, primarily from the birth of Christ, considered then to be 0, and backward to the creation depicted in Genesis 1:1–3, and then forward through such prophecies as the Apocalypse. While apocalypticism persisted, the nonmanifestation of the expected millennium was compensated for by manifestations of God within nature, and belief in the biblical millennium declined. The lack of occurrence, of course, set up confusions in religious thinking and also in the political world, for the expected changes in the political world which the reign of Christ would have effected did not occur. Confusions resulted in scrambling for religio-political positions, and in the decline of the Fifth Monarchists (who were active through 1661) as a political force. Negated, too, and thus not significant as political public argument, were the imminent conversion of the Jews and the incarceration of the devil, who had long before been identified with Satan and also with Lucifer. The hope in and expectation of millennium, and its subsequent failure to arrive, intensified deistic thinking and gave, for many, a death knell to revelation as proof of God and his works. In its place observation of his manifestation in natural things as a sign of his presence increased.

The Book of Revelation concerns prophecy, through visions and similitudes (or allegory), and it finds its sources in such Old Testament books as Daniel, as many people have pointed out, and in apocalyptic writings that appear between the two testaments (and after the Apocrypha, which also intervenes).[3] The writers of these apocalyptic books (the Pseudepigrapha) assumed the name of a dead hero who rewrote purported history in terms of prophecy. Among them are the Books of Enoch, which speak of the coming of the Messiah and the Day of Judgment; the Assumption of Moses, with prophecies of the birth of Christ; and the Sibylline Oracles, which present the downfall of oppressors and the dawn of the messianic age. Anyone familiar with Revelation can see the influence upon it of these books, and the composite (and not always coherent) nature of this last book of the New Testament has been acknowledged by biblical scholars for a long time.[4] According to *The Interpreter's Bible*:

Apocalypticism . . . is basically a belief in two totally distinct and different ages: this present age is temporal and irretrievably evil because it is under the control of the author of evil; whereas the new age will be eternal and perfectly righteous because it will be under the direct governance of God. It was but natural . . . that as the Messiah became more important in apocalyptic thinking a temporal kingdom should be assigned to him.[5]

Important here is the fusion of the Judaic belief in a Messiah in some linear future and the Christian belief in the Christ who was the incarnated Son of God and who taught the way to achieve salvation. His reign in the millennium is thus understood as a fusion of Judaic and Christian thought, not as part of any prior plan of God for humankind.

The only reference to the millennium in the Bible occurs in Revelation 20:1–10, specifically six times in verses 2–7. The word means "a thousand years," but the variation in spelling that one finds – one n or two – attests to some of the uncertainties besetting the term. It relates to the Latin *millenarius*, meaning "of a thousand," and derives from the New Latin formation of *mille* plus *anni*, "thousand" plus "years." The word does not appear in classical Latin. It is a Latin translation of the Greek χιλιοι, "thousand," and ετος, "year," of the New Testament (written in Greek). Belief in this future time of the appearance of Christ on earth is thus called millenarianism (with one n) or chiliasm, defined as the "belief that Christ will reign personally on the earth with his saints for one thousand years or an indefinitely long period before the end of the world."[6] As *The Interpreter's Bible* remarks:

The doctrine [of millenarianism] itself is an outgrowth of the prophetic view of the day of the Lord, when the enemies of the Jews would be defeated and the righteous theocracy of Israel as God's people would be re-established here on earth in this present age of human history, a belief that developed into the expectation of the kingdom of God. (519)

To be specifically noted here is that the teaching of Christ in the New Testament is *not* millenarian. His coming (as recorded in Mark 1:15) is identical with the Last Judgment, and the renewal of the world is connected with the Last Judgment (Matt. 19:28); there is no period of a thousand years intervening before the Last Judgment. "Of Paul, it may at least be said," according to Schaff's and Herzog's discussion of "Millennium, Millenarianism," "that by his doctrine of a limited reign of Christ (1 Cor. XV.25 sq) he gave a foothold in the Church for chiliastic expectations. But their main support was in the apocalyptic teaching of John (Rev. XX.4 sqqq), completely misunderstood as the passage has been by many commentators from Augustine down." It should be especially remembered that early church Fathers such as Eusebius held the Book of Revelation to be spurious.[7]

As I remarked above, the idea of a millennium in which "the dragon, that old serpent, which is the Devil, and Satan" would be "bound... a thousand years, and cast into the bottomless pit, and shut...up, and set a seal upon him, that he should deceive the nations no more, till the thousand years should be fulfilled" derives from various writings of the Pseudepigrapha.[8] In 1 Enoch 10:4–6, for example, we read:

And again the Lord said to Raphael: "Bind Azâzêl hand and foot, and cast him into the darkness: and make an opening in the sert, which is in Dûdâêl, and cast him therein. And place upon him rough and jagged rocks, and cover him with darkness, and let him abide there for ever, and cover his face that he may not see light. And on the day of the great judgment he shall be cast into the fire."

Here it should be recognized that "for ever" (εις του αιωνα) may denote various periods of time, not only "eternity."[9] Azazel was the chief offender and leader of the first rebellion, punished by imprisonment and later by fire. "The whole earth has been corrupted through the works that were taught by Azâzêl: to him ascribe all sin" (1 Enoch 10:9). The name derives from the combination of words meaning "goat" and "to go," that is, "scapegoat." All of this is recorded in the perspective statement in Jude 6: "And the angels which kept not their first estate, but left their own habitation, he hath reserved in everlasting chains under darkness unto the judgment of the great day." There is, however, no thousand-year reign of Christ announced.

Although biblists sometimes deny the point, "This brief but significant episode, like the expulsion of Satan from heaven, has a mythological base" (*The Interpreter's Bible*, 12, 517–18). In all, the "combination of Messianism and apocalypticism in Judaism is provided by II Esdras 7: 26–30," and "according to II Baruch 39–40, the Messiah will establish his kingdom, after the Antichrist is destroyed, and his kingdom will endure as long as this world of corruption endures" (519). A thousand years is a nice round figure. The idea of the loosing of Satan after a period of time, we should understand, comes with the Greek concept of cyclic time clashing with Hebrew linear time, and ultimately defeats the point of the myth that "time will be no more," that a stasis will be reached with the good ascending to heaven and the evil being doomed to hell.[10] It is clear from what has just been recalled that the episode of the millennium in Revelation 20:1–10 is a kind of insertion into the picture of the last days in Revelation 19 and its continuance in Revelation 20:11–15 and onward.

The question of apocalypse and the question of the millennium beset religious thinkers from the early church Fathers on, and intensely so in Milton's time. A significant point for the ensuing discussion, I believe, is recognition that millennium is only one element – and that a somewhat brief one – within the vision: it is an inserted "vision," when compared with other accounts of the punishment of the "bad" angels. The sources of the Book of Revelation in the last mystical books of the Old Testament, in the Apocrypha, and especially in the often repudiated Pseudepigrapha, caused many to ponder the religious truth of that book, some treating it as spiritual allegory only, not as historic truth. That is, not all literally believed that a millennium would come to pass in the 1650s, although many apparently did. Uncertainty over the meaning of "a thousand years" and the extent of the span's actual duration is an obvious upshoot; uncertainty over the concept of the defeat of Satan (Rev. 20:2) and yet a loosing of him and his evil forces sometime "a thousand years" later (Rev. 20:3, 7) tends to negate belief in the efficacy of his ensuing captivity after some unnamed period of time (Rev. 20:10). The Last Judgment is to follow the millennium, but curiously sometime after Satan had again gone out after a thousand years and deceived the nations, not upon the ending of the thousand years. On account of such illogic in the world of biblical good and evil, the "last" Judgment, it seems, may not achieve the stasis in heaven for the good which Revelation goes on to recount (Rev. 21–22:1–5)!

This long preamble to my remarks has seemed necessary, for certain concepts arise to confute William B. Hunter's chapter in this book, "The millennial moment: Milton vs. 'Milton'." In the immediate past Professor Hunter has presented a number of arguments to question and indeed to reject the authorship of *De Doctrina Christiana* (hereafter *DDC*) for John Milton.[11] His thesis is that the author of that treatise and Milton in his accepted writings differ in attitudes toward millennium. In the treatise

Hunter finds general indifference, but he finds belief in its promise, particularly in its effect on religio-political matters, in Milton's other works. My remarks do not engage with other arguments against authorship, each of which should be taken up separately to ascertain its validity and significance for the issue. I am here dealing only with millennial thought presented in this essay.

Professor Hunter's basic argument is that Milton shows a belief in the millennium in its political manifestations (for example, in the antiprelatical tracts), while *DDC* not only does not, but almost ignores the millennium. He finds backing for this argument in discussions by Arthur Barker and Michael Fixler, and in relation to theological treatises by Johannes Wollebius and William Ames, which do not examine the political/social import of millennium and which seem "indifferent" to it. This latter point seems to suggest corroboration that *DDC* derives from European provenance, not English, and thus from a another author, not from Milton. My preamble has pointed out the uncertainty about Revelation 20:1–10 in theological thought, the expectation and failure of the millennium's coming to pass in the 1650s (its nonmanifestation), and its intrusive position within the Apocalypse, with which it is not coterminous. Barker and Fixler ignore these matters and then, writing about the apocalypse in Milton's work, are dismayed that Milton has not, in *DDC*, presented a politically significant millennium. They have confused the Apocalypse with the millennium by expecting the part to be the whole. As I read Hunter's discussion, he has done the same.

But two other problems are more troublesome: Hunter does not pay attention to the failure of millennium to come in the 1650s, which nullified such ideas as Charles I as Antichrist and the Interregnum period serving as preludes to the Second Coming and he (with Barker and Fixler) ignores what a theological treatise such as Wollebius's, Ames's, or *DDC* is.[12] It is not a polemical work like *Of Reformation*; it is a presentation of a "theological system," and it engages theological polemics by offering a refutation of alleged errors of *doctrine*. However, it does not (or should not) fall under the classification of "debate" or "oration" that characterizes Milton's divorce tracts and antimonarchical volumes. It does disagree with other presentations of "theological systems" (including Wollebius's and Ames's on certain points), but it is offered as "further purification" and "exposition of almost all the chief points of Christian doctrine," to be "accepted or rejected" according to one's "absolute conviction by the clear evidence of the Bible." (I use the words of the "Epistle" to *DDC*,

slightly altered for expression.) It is not "polemical" as *Areopagitica* or
Tetrachordon are, but "educative" of theological matters. Such also are the
"theological systems" of Wollebius and Ames.[13]

The author of *DDC* is, like Johannes Wollebius and William Ames
before him, attempting to make sense of the scriptures: he has been dis-
satisfied with "sometimes brief, sometimes more lengthy and methodical
expositions of almost all the chief points of Christian doctrine" but believes that "God has revealed the way of eternal salvation only to the individual faith of each man, and demands of us that any man who wishes
to be saved should work out his beliefs for himself" (*DDC*, "Epistle";
CP VI: 117–18). He notes early in chapter 1 that he aims "only to assist
the reader's memory by collecting together, as it were, into a single book
texts which are scattered here and there throughout the Bible, and by
systematizing them under definite headings, in order to make reference
easy" (*CP* VI: 127). His methodology offers various prooftexts for statements of doctrine; for example, "Christian doctrine is the doctrine which,
in all ages, Christ…taught by divine communication, for the glory of
God and the salvation of mankind…" (I.1; *CP* VI: 126) is then "proved"
by scriptural texts elaborating "Christ" and "by divine communication,"
and by an exegesis of the words themselves, such as: "Understand the
name Christ as meaning also Moses, and the prophets who foretold his
coming, and the apostles whom he sent." The aim of the treatise is the
presentation of valid Christian doctrine for the reader, an educative intent and a hope in eradicating from people's thought what the author
finds to be not valid.

Both the author of *DDC* and Milton are concerned with the meanings
of the texts of the Bible (we remember *Tetrachordon* as one overt instance)
and both recognize the inherent problems those texts can cause. The var-
ied and often improbable identity of the angel who recorded the visions
of Revelation through St. John, and the inconsistencies and disjunctions
posed by the millennium, problematize the treatise's discussion.[14] But
the angel and the scriptural statements are fully accepted. (In *Paradise
Lost* 4.1–2 Milton cites that "warning voice, which he who saw /
Th'*Apocalypse*, heard cry in Heaven aloud."[15]) In Book I, chapter 5
(*CP* VI: 255ff.) the author looks at the difficulties of the very first verses
of Revelation (noting incidentally that the angel "is described in almost
the same words as the angel in Dan. x. 5, etc."). He cites Theodore
Beza's conclusion that some verses of Revelation "had been disordered
and transposed by some Arian," and disputes that throughout the Bible
angels "assume[ ] the person and the very words of God, even without

taking the name of Jehovah or God, but with the name of an angel only, or even of a man" (*CP* VI: 256).

In chapter 33 of Book I, *DDC* investigates "Complete Glorification, also...Christ's Second Coming, the Resurrection of the Dead, and the Conflagration of This World," defining the Last Judgment as the time at which "CHRIST WITH THE SAINTS, ARRAYED IN THE GLORY AND THE POWER OF THE FATHER, WILL JUDGE THE FALLEN ANGELS AND THE WHOLE HUMAN RACE" (*CP* VI: 621). The author comments:

At the time of this last judgment it seems that the often-promised and glorious reign of Christ and his saints on this earth will begin. I say *at the time of*, rather than *on the day of*, because the word *day* is often used to mean some indefinite period of time, and because it does not seem likely that so many millions of angels and men could be assembled and judged within the space of a single day. (*CP* VI: 623)

The treatise continues: "Christ's reign, then, will extend from the beginning to the end of this time of judgment, and will continue for some time after the judgment has finished, until all his enemies are subdued" (*CP* VI: 623–24). The author is aware of the impossibility of equating biblical time durations with contemporary notions of time, and he answers questioners of the biblical text by asserting that "there will be no end to his kingdom *for all ages*, that is, while the age of the world endure, until *time will be no more*, Rev. x.6, . . . Thus his kingdom will not *pass away*, like something ineffectual, nor will it be *destroyed*" (*CP* VI: 627). As these quotations indicate, the author of *DDC* accepts the commonplace reading of Revelation 20 and rejects those (even such theologians as Beza) who interpret it to cast doubt on Christ's reign on earth. He does not, however, employ the words "millennium" or "χιλιαετος": his words are "mille annos" and, in his quotation, "anni mille."

Like the Book of Revelation, the author has a lot to say about the Second Coming, which is interrupted by the statement of the millennium, and the last chapter of Book I (*CP* VI: 615–33) is devoted to this apocalyptic vision. Christ's coming is evidenced by "signs": 1) "The common signs are those which are common to the destruction of Jerusalem, the *type* of Christ's second coming, and his second coming itself" (*CP* VI: 616; my emphasis); 2) "Secondly, the revelation of antichrist and his destruction through the spirit of Christ's mouth" (*CP* VI: 617); 3) "Some authorities think that a further portent will herald this event, namely, the calling of the entire nation not only of the Jews but also of the Israelites" (*CP* vi: 617): "Christ will be slow to come... [but see 2 Peter 3:3, 4, etc.] where the reason is given why the Lord will put off the day of his coming" (*CP* vi: 618); and 4) "His coming will be full of light" (*CP* vi: 618). The resurrection and Last Judgment, following upon the Second Coming, are discussed in *CP* vi: 619–27. Throughout he accepts God's revelations according to scripture, and thus Satan's loosing after the thousand years is noted on p. 625, but little is made of it, just as it plays a small role in the whole of the scriptural account. The author of *DDC* has, like other commentators, recognized the problems of Revelation 20:1–10 in making sense, following as it does upon 19:19–21 and of its own illogic of supposed narrative, and simply iterates it as part of scripture.

In chapter 33 (*CP* vi: 619–27), the author restates scripture and answers various skeptics. He does not spend a great deal of time on Satan's loosing upon the earth, for his subject is Christ's Second Coming, the resurrection of the dead, and the conflagration. The author thus implies a most justified uncertainty about this illogical, "*inserted*" vision. It appears in Revelation 20:1–10 and is therefore recounted and not questioned in *DDC*; the "punishment of the wicked" is fully laid out according to biblical texts. He proceeds with the glorification of the righteous and with a vision of heaven, as does Revelation. The uncertainties of the Bible on the "abolition of the world's substance, or only a change in its qualities," is noted but dismissed, quite rightly, as not his concern in this treatise on Christian *doctrine*.

And here is the nub of the disagreement I have with Hunter's reading: the treatise is not remotely concerned with anything like a premillennial appearance by the Son foreseen by English Puritans. I do not state that the author was not concerned with this; we cannot know. But such discussion would be out of place in this treatise, just as it would be in the statements of Christian doctrine by Wollebius or Ames. *DDC* is not a duplication of Continental Calvinists in this matter: the intentions of the work are far different from Milton's intentions in the antiprelatical tracts or in *The Tenure of Kings and Magistrates*.

Dating may also have significance here (see note 2). We do not know when *DDC* was written: it may have been first explored, if Milton's, in the 1640s, but further developed (and some have said begun) in 1658–60, and I would caution that the manuscript's corrective parts (with hands other than just that of Milton's amanuensis Jeremy Picard's) suggest continuing attention. If the millennium was expected around 1655–57, its failure to appear, and the subsequent lack of religious and political reforms hoped for previously, would have dismissed such earlier views from consideration in the late 1650s onward – like all the apocalypses that have been foreseen but have not come to pass. The expected millennium did not occur, but this does not negate apocalypticism itself. While there still might be hope that sometime in the distant future a reign of Christ on earth will occur, it was not foreseen in terms of specific manifestation after the late 1650s; instead, as I indicated earlier, deistic principles spread and intensified. The employment of Jude 6 in the treatise (as well as Revelation 20:10) recalls only the punishment of the bad angels (*CP* VI: 348) because of their not having kept their first estate; it does not imply an affinity with the "millennium" of Revelation 20:2–7. Nor do the citations of 20:2, 3 (*CP* VI: 349) deal with millennium, only with punishment.

Divorcing Milton's belief in and attitude toward millennium from the apocalypse and its treatment in Revelation 20 are the numerous references to the text in Milton's acknowledged works.[16] We should also note commentators' references to these texts in the two epics.[17] Hunter bases his argument not only on the confusion between apocalypse and millennium, not only on the misassignment of what texts laying forth Christian doctrine educatively cover and do, and not only with inattention to dating, but also upon criticism offered by Michael Fixler and Arthur Barker, who are treating apocalypticism and who, understandably, make reference to the reign of Christ as the Bible does in St. John's vision.[18] Hunter sees the interest of Calvinists as centering in the events following the millennium, which was not central to their interpretation of the reign of Christ. Following Fixler, he worries that the treatise has "some marked reorientations of emphasis [indicating] that Milton abandoned these assumptions" [of political changes].[19] Fixler, however, has paid no attention to the intentions of *DDC*, no attention to dating and the failure of millennium, and slights the extensive reference to apocalypticism in the treatise.[20]

While overt politicism is not included in the words of *DDC* – nor should it be – certain comments on the signs preluding millennium – for those who wish to interpret them as politically contemporary – do exist: "the destruction of Jerusalem" (for which read the English monarchy?), the "false prophets, false Christs, wars, … persecutions, … dwindling of faith and charity right down to the last day itself." Furthermore, the "special signs are extreme carelessness and impiety, and almost universal rebellion" (*CP* VI: 616), with a prooftext from I Timothy 4:1: "*the day of Christ will not come, unless rebellion comes first …*" And in the 1640s, of course, there was rebellion followed by the theocracy under Cromwell.

Steps toward millennium could be interpreted by the hopeful – until mid-1653, at least, when the Protectorate was proclaimed. From 1659 onward it was clear that the millennium was not occurring and that the events of the past were not signs, common or special. Universal rebellion was not on the immediate horizon, and by 1660 a new "Antichrist" had appeared.

Milton believed in the apocalypse; so did the author of *DDC*. None of the references in *DDC* imports a contemporary millennium, although there are indications of the reign of Christ for a thousand years as part of the apocalypse which will come in both Milton's works and in the treatise. Hunter's quotations of *The Readie and Easie Way* in terms of the Good Old Cause and a continued hope in its accession do not have anything to do with millennium, only with apocalyptic thinking.[21] Some of the Fifth Monarchists may still have looked forward to an imminent millennium, but most did not, and Milton shows no evidence of Fifth Monarchist thinking on this point in the late 1650s onward. The opening lines of Book 4 of *Paradise Lost*, lines 1–5, specifically allude to St. John's vision in Revelation and in chapter 20; *DDC* also cites Revelation 20:1–10. Milton and the author of the treatise both accept the passage, strong believers as they are in the scriptures. A passage in Book 12, lines 537–51, implies the same text, and continues, as does Revelation 21, with the new heavens and new earth which will arise.[22] These are futural, but not imminently futural, events. Similarly Hunter's quotation of 12.451–57 and 12.458–62 is good evidence of Milton's belief in the apocalypse and the ascent of the Son to the right hand of God after his work on earth has created a "Paradise, far happier place / Then this of *Eden*, and far happier daies" (12.464–65). But there is nothing here to imply any immediacy – nothing about *the* millennium.

The chiliastic underpinnings of various works of Milton up to around 1657 look forward to a millennium envisioned by, among others, the Fifth Monarchists. By around 1671 there have been "republican" advances on government, and thought of *imminent* millennium, bringing radical change, has disappeared.[23] Importantly, in an incisive statement Michael Wilding draws attention to "the contradictions that arose when [Milton] renounced the attempt to establish by military means a radical Kingdom of Heaven on earth, and turned instead to the private preparations of the soul for the paradise within."[24]

In this chapter I have challenged the thinking that Miltonists have shown in connection with the concept of the apocalypse and of the millennium, encased therein, to argue that *DDC* exhibits a strong belief in and use of Revelation 20–21 while reinterpreting those scriptural passages when others have denied their truth; to set forth that Milton's apocalyptic concepts do not change except for a lack of belief in an imminent millennium past 1657; and therefore to confute the argument that Milton and the author of *DDC* of necessity are different because of these supposed differences in millenarian thinking. The nature of a theological system likewise excludes the political polemic the millennium conjured up for people, including Milton, in the 1640s. The question of the authorship of the treatise must be taken up separately and in great detail, but Hunter's argument concerning the significance of the millennium in that question is simply specious.

NOTES

1. See Godfrey Goodman, *The Fall of Man, or the Corruption of Nature, Proved by the Light of Our Naturall Reason* (London, 1616); George Hakewell, *An Apologie or Declaration of the Power and Providence of God in the Government of the World* (Oxford, 1627); and Thomas Burnet, *Telluria Theoria Sacra* (London, 1681), trans. as *The Theory of the Earth* (London, 1684) and *The Sacred Theory of the Earth* (London, 1691).

2. Apparently it is necessary to remind the reader of this expectation. As David Masson writes in *The Life of Milton* (London, 1873), vol. III, p. 153, in discussing the millenaries or Chiliasts: "The purport of their doctrine was that in the year 1650, or, at the furthest, 1695, Christ was to reappear in human form at Jerusalem, destroy the existing fabric of things in a conflagration, collect the scattered Jews, raise martyrs and saints from their graves, and begin his glorious reign of a thousand years." See also vol. V (1877), pp. 16–17, under "Fifth-Monarchy Men." Henry Archer in *The Personall Reigne of Christ Upon Earth* (1642) argued that the conversion of the Jews (a required event to prelude the millennium) would occur in 1650 or 1656 (dependent upon the date of Julian the Apostate's reign, 360 or 366), and that the papacy would disappear in 1666 (recalling the number of the beast). William Aspinwall's 1653 text presented *A Brief Description of the Fifth Monarchy, or Kingdome, That shortly is to come into the World*, and in it he alleges that the "uttermost durance of Antichrist's dominion will be in the year 1673," although he cannot determine the precise year. In 1657 was published John Canne's *The Time of the End; and the planned revolt set forth in A Standard Set Up Whereunto the true Seed and Saints of the Most High may be gathered together into one, out of their several Forms* (London, 1657) as the expected turning point. See P. G. Rogers, *The Fifth Monarchy Men* (London, 1966), and B. S. Capp, *The Fifth Monarchy Men: A Study in Seventeenth-Century English Millenarianism* (London, 1972). See also the chapter by Barbara Lewalski in this book which cites additional contemporary prognostications.

Aware of the proffered date of 1655–57, one understands Milton's Piedmont sonnet (Sonnet 18, May 1655) as seeing the massacre in Italy as indication of a potential catalyst for the millennium; we note his use of the parable of the sower (Matt. 13:3–23) and Tertullian's "Blood of martyrs is the seed of the Church" (*Apologeticus* 50). The events of October 1655, when twelve major-generals were officially announced to organize and patrol the several counties of England against infractions of various "blue laws" became a sign that the millennium was at hand, though all Milton could do was "serve" by standing and waiting (Sonnet 19, "When I consider how my light is spent"). The Fifth Monarchists were antagonistic to Cromwell's assumption of all controls, basically through military rule, as well as his reaffirmation as Protector in June 1657.

3. See also my "Stasis, and John Milton and the Myths of Time," *Cithara* 18 (1978), pp. 3–17, and remarks in Barbara Lewalski's and Stella Revard's chapters in this book.

4. See such studies as Norman Cohn's *Cosmos, Chaos and the World to Come: The Ancient Roots of Apocalyptic Faith* (New Haven and London, 1993), and Bernard McGinn's "Early Apocalypticism: The Ongoing Debate," in C. A. Patrides and Joseph Wittreich (eds.), *The Apocalypse in English Renaissance Thought and Literature: Patterns, Antecedents and Repercussions* (Manchester, 1984), pp. 2–39.

5. *The Interpreter's Bible* (Nashville, 1957), vol. XII, p. 519.

6. *The New Schaff-Herzog Encyclopedia of Religious Knowledge*, ed. Samuel Macauley Jackson, et al. (New York and London, 1910), vol. VII, p. 374.

7. See *Historia Ecclesiastica*, III, 25.2–4. Augustine in *The City of God*, 20.1–9, construes the verses in Revelation 20 as spiritually meant, not historical.

8. Sources for the millennium from the Pseudepigrapha and rabbinical writings are cited from David Noel Freedman (ed.), *The Anchor Bible Dictionary* (New York, 1992), IV; "the thousand year span is the time from the birth of Christ until his parousia" (833). Noted also are Victorinus of Petau (d. *c.* 304), who took Revelation 20:4–6 literally, and Jerome (342–420 CE), who altered the reading and took it allegorically. See also such studies as Norman Cohn's *The Pursuit of the Millennium* (London and New York, 1957).

9. Similarly 2 Esdras 7: 36–31 talks of the world as asleep for seven days and then it shall be raised up and the corrupt shall die; while 2 Baruch 39–40 recounts the vision and the coming of the Messiah, and declares that the principate of the Messiah "will stand for ever, until the world of corruption is at an end."

10. See my discussion in note 3.

11. See Hunter's *Visitation Unimplor'd: Milton and the Authorship of "De Doctrina Christiana"* (Pittsburgh, 1998) and various other essays since then.

12. One might also add the rejection of opening up the country to the Jews (a concern of the mid-1650s) and thus taking a first step toward their conversion. Hunter does acknowledge that circumstances finally forced Milton reluctantly to relinquish his belief in the immanence of the millennium, but fails to examine the significance further. (Milton does not abandon

millenarian thought and expectation.) Instead he continues with Milton's "apocalyptic view" (with which I certainly agree) but as if it were equivalent to that failed concept of millennium in the 1650s.

13. A problem is that a theological system advanced should not involve such political/social argumentation, yet *DDC*, for example in Book I, chapter 10, does go beyond its purported intent of presenting "Of the Special Government of Man Before the Fall." It adds "Dealing also with the Sabbath and Marriage," and after relatively brief and direct statements on those two subjects, backed up by prooftexts, the text moves into a disputation about marriage and divorce.

14. See Michael Bauman's listing of citations of Jude 6 and Revelation 20:1–10 in *A Scripture Index to John Milton's* De Doctrina Christiana (Binghamton, 1989).

15. Citations from Milton's poetry are from John T. Shawcross (ed.), *The Complete Poetry of John Milton* (Garden City, 1970).

16. The concordances to Milton's poetry and English prose record that Milton *never* used millennial, millenarian, or millennium, or even a thousand years/days to mean the reign of Christ. We do find "Apocalypse," "Revelation(s)" (but none refers to the millennium), and "reveal."

17. See James H. Sims, *The Bible in Milton's Epics* (Gainesville, 1962).

18. See Michael Fixler, *Milton and the Kingdoms of God* (London and Evanston, 1964), and Arthur Barker, *Milton and the Puritan Dilemma, 1641–1660* (Toronto, 1942). Hunter misrepresents the first quotation from Barker by not quoting it fully: "his theological treatise, like Calvin's, considers political theory as an integral part of Christian doctrine" (p. 124), but Barker is wrong, in that the treatise is not concerned with the political, as Hunter later confirms. Hunter's use of the quotation points up, correctly, that political theory and Christianity were intertwined.

19. I quote Fixler, *Milton*, p. 214; this quotation does not appear in Hunter's article.

20. Hunter cites Maurice Kelley's remark in *CP* VI that points out Fixler's wrong conclusions because of such inattention.

21. Compare Barbara Lewalski's reading of this passage in her chapter in this book.

22. Bauman lists citations of Revelation 21 as 6.483, 567, 628, 629 (2), 631, 633 (2), and 739. The quotation from *PL* Book 12, of course, looks forward to the Last Judgment, not millennium.

23. Compare my *John Milton: The Self and the World* (Lexington, 1993), pp. 164, 238.

24. Michael Wilding, *Dragons Teeth: Literature in the English Revolution* (Oxford, 1987), p. 258.

Apocalypse

7

John Martin's apocalyptic illustrations to Paradise Lost

Beverley Sherry

The achievement of John Martin (1789–1854) as apocalyptic painter is manifest in his numerous oil paintings, from the early *Belshazzar's Feast* (1820, private collection) to the late work *The Great Day of His Wrath* (1852, Tate Gallery). This is Martin the artist of cataclysm, which is the characteristic mode of his oil paintings. However, when he came to illustrate *Paradise Lost* in 1824–27, Milton's poem tamed the artist of cataclysm as Martin responded to Milton's paradise and also to the broad eschatological dimensions of the poem, dimensions which encompass Apocalypse as both holocaust and beatitude, both hell and heaven. His illustrations were executed not in colour but in the black-and-white medium of mezzotint, and this essay explores how, in his manipulation of the light and darkness of mezzotint, Martin achieved his apocalyptic illustrations to *Paradise Lost*.

In 1823, already well known as an apocalyptic painter, he was commissioned by the London publisher Septimus Prowett to engrave twenty-four illustrations for an edition of *Paradise Lost*. Each image was about 8 × 11 inches. Within a year Prowett commissioned a second set, each of about 6 × 8 inches; there are minor differences in design between the two sets. Martin worked with the soft steel plate newly developed by Thomas Lupton in 1822. What is unusual is that his mezzotints are originals; that is, they are not engravings of paintings but were designed directly on to the plates; each is lettered "Designed & Engraved by J. Martin Esqr." From March 1825 Prowett began selling the work in parts as Martin proceeded with his commission. The project was completed by January 1827 and the book published in two volumes as *The Paradise Lost of Milton with Illustrations, Designed and Engraved by John Martin*. It was sold in four separate formats: an imperial folio and imperial quarto each with the larger plates, an imperial quarto with the smaller plates, and an imperial octavo with the smaller plates. Prowett also sold loose proofs and prints of the mezzotints. This ambitious project was an unqualified commercial success.[1]

Martin's *Paradise Lost* illustrations have proved to be also an enduring artistic success. Since 1688 numerous illustrations of the poem had appeared, both in editions and as independent paintings.[2] The first illustrators, in an effort to render as many incidents of the narrative as possible, adopted a synoptic method: within a single frame a particular incident is depicted in the foreground and a series of others in the background. By the early nineteenth century, illustrators had abandoned this method, although they still created a series of pictures which followed the general narrative line. Joseph Wittreich argues that they were by then more concerned "with elucidating Milton's vision and with defining the essential qualities of his art."[3] Martin's twenty-four illustrations are unevenly distributed across the twelve books of *Paradise Lost* but they form an entire oeuvre which is a "portrayal" of the poem. Wittreich, whose approach is that illustrations are a "form of nonverbal criticism," concludes that, in "elucidating" Milton's vision, "Henry Fuseli captured Milton's sublimity, John Martin his vast spatial dimensions," while Blake achieved "the fullest exploration and the deepest comprehension of the Miltonic vision."[4] The superior genius of Blake must be acknowledged, but his comprehension of Milton's vision is peculiarly his own, and some of his illustrations are clearly personal attempts to "correct" *Paradise Lost*.[5] Martin's illustrations have been considered the truest or most "Miltonic" of all and, while "not as independently intriguing as Blake's, . . . still probably the best that Milton ever got."[6]

Part of their truth is that Martin does not focus overly on Milton's characters, who defy visual representation, but on Miltonic space, which can be more easily visualized. Both Blake and Fuseli meet head-on the challenge of Milton's characters by portraying them as splendid Michelangelesque figures. By contrast, Martin, who had limited ability in figure drawing but exceptional ability with perspective and cosmic drama, did not concentrate on Milton's characters but rather on their place in various settings. In her book *Milton and English Art*, Marcia Pointon rightly claims that "Martin is the only artist to portray Adam and Eve fully in the context within which Milton presents them."[7] She also observes that, while Martin does not show the psychological conflicts of Milton's characters by means of figure drawing and facial expression, he has other means, in his mastery of mezzotint, of conveying those tensions.[8] This relates to my argument that Martin's manipulation of the light and darkness of mezzotint conveys central concerns of *Paradise Lost*.

Images of light and darkness, and of height and depth, are pervasive in Martin's illustrations. Light and darkness are the most defining characteristics of Martin's encounter with Milton. This essay does not study illustrations as "a form of nonverbal criticism," a translation, a copy of a literary text, or, on the other hand, as "independent imaginative structures."[9] My approach is that illustrations are at once a portrayal of a literary work and a meeting or crosscultural encounter between an artist and a writer. Martin's nineteenth-century illustrations of Milton's seventeenth-century poem constitute a striking example of such an encounter.

The Miltonic culture of Martin's time and of his life; the cult of the sublime; the industrial, scientific, and archaeological climate of the day were some of the avenues by which Martin came to *Paradise Lost*.[10] For the purpose of this study, the millenarian and apocalyptic enthusiasms of Martin's context are particularly significant. He came from a family environment of heady Protestantism, with tendencies, particularly in his younger brother Jonathan, to prophetic dreams and visions.[11] The late eighteenth and early nineteenth centuries marked a period of popular millenarianism in England, and Martin both responded to it and helped fuel it. A number of his paintings on apocalyptic themes – *The Fall of Babylon* (1819), *Belshazzar's Feast* (1820), *The Destruction of Pompeii and Herculaneum* (*c.* 1822), *The Seventh Plague of Egypt* (1823), *The Deluge* (1826), *The Fall of Nineveh* (1829) – date from the same decade as his *Paradise Lost* engravings, while his last paintings, the trilogy of *The Great Day of His Wrath* (1852), *The Last Judgment* (1853), and *The Plains of Heaven* (1853), form a spectacular conclusion to his apocalyptic canon. People queued to see these canvases and thousands purchased reproductions. In his book *The Second Coming: Popular Millenarianism 1780–1850*, J. F. C. Harrison makes the interesting distinction that, whereas millenarian pamphlets "sold in their hundreds, John Martin's apocalyptic scenes were viewed by thousands when exhibited in London and by many more when reproduced as engravings in the annuals, *Forget Me Not*, *Friendship's Offering*, *The Keepsake*, and in illustrated editions of the Bible."[12]

So, apocalyptic painter meets Milton's *Paradise Lost*, a poem which appeared (in 1667) "at an historical high point of millennial speculation."[13] Even though Milton's hopes for the millennium had dimmed by this time, he still believed in it, and this is testified by "covert" passages in *Paradise Lost*, as Stella Revard has argued.[14] More importantly, there is a general eschatological perspective in the poem, a stance of "*[w]aiting for apocalypse*."[15] The heavenly "Paradise of eternal rest" (12.314), transcending both the paradise of Eden and the "paradise within" (12.587), is a veiled presence in the poem, and recurring passages look forward to the end of time, to the apocalypse as cataclysm but, even more, to the apocalypse as a renewed heaven and earth, the "golden days" when "God shall be All in All" (3.337–41).[16] Catherine Morris Westcott, in her study "The Sublime and the Millennialist in John Martin's Mezzotints for *Paradise Lost*," gives evidence for Martin's millenarianism, including his connection with the early nineteenth-century millenarian group known as the British Israelites. She also notes that, if Martin's engineering plans – for pure air and water for London, efficient sewerage, inland drainage, ventilation of coalmines – had been implemented they "would have contributed towards the development of the secularized utopia – the New Jerusalem – looked for by the Millennialists."[17] Her study does not explore, however, how Martin's illustrations portray the apocalyptic dimensions of *Paradise Lost*.

That portrayal has much to do with his handling of light and darkness. For Martin, as for Milton, light had an intense significance throughout his life. As a youth growing up in Northumberland, he roamed the hills at dawn, delighting in the effects of light and shade, and in his very last days on the Isle of Man, according to his son Leopold, he sat "with a fixed gaze on the sea and the sky, watching the effects of light and shade."[18] His older brother William was an anti-Newtonian who held that light is the mystic dwelling place of God.[19] John's apocalyptic paintings show that he shared his brother's belief: they typically represent a source of divine power as dramatic emanations of light from on high. This is striking in *Belshazzar's Feast* with its rays of light streaming from the mysterious writing on the wall – an "indescribable effulgence" in Martin's own words.[20] The light is even more striking in the mezzotint version completed in 1826. Leopold recorded that the "glorious blaze of light" in the *Belshazzar's Feast* mezzotint, "the splendid burst of sunlight" in the 1827 mezzotint of *Joshua Commanding the Sun to Stand Still*, and "the awful light" in the 1828 mezzotint of *The Deluge* were chiefly the result of his father's close supervision of the use of particular inks in the printing process.[21]

Martin's fascination with light relates to his early experience in glass painting. Samuel Taylor Coleridge disparagingly commented: "It seems as if [Martin] looked at Nature through bits of stained glass."[22] His employment as a glass painter in 1806–11 made a lasting impression on him. In evidence he gave in 1836 before a Select Committee on Arts and their Connection with Manufacture, he placed stained glass as "far superior to oil-painting or water-colours, *for by the transparency we have the means of bringing in real light*" (my italics).[23] In the Middle Ages stained glass was regarded as creating "windows of miraculous light"; even a modern artist has explained that the image with the light going *through* it takes on a "timeless quality," and stained-glass artists refer to themselves as "painting with light."[24] The indwelling presence of "real light" in the medium is what fascinated Martin, and for similar reasons he was drawn to mezzotint.

As distinct from line engraving and etching, mezzotint creates an image through shades of light and darkness and includes a tonal range from the richest velvety black to incandescent highlights. Martin was the first artist to illustrate *Paradise Lost* in this medium and, as Michael Campbell observes, he exploited "the dramatic tonal range which only mezzotint could create and which is so noticeably absent in the linear work of earlier illustrators."[25] Commenting on Martin's illustration for Book 7 of *Paradise Lost*, Campbell writes: "[t]he title of this work, *Creation of Light*, is almost the definition of the mezzotint process."[26] It is the only engraving method in which the artist in effect begins in darkness, and creates a picture by working from black to white. Like stained-glass work, it is a kind of painting with light in that it involves a progressive wiping away of the ink, burnishing the metal plate to uncover or create areas of light. At the time of Martin's *Paradise Lost* illustrations, 1824–27, the impact of his glass-painting experience was still strongly felt.[27] Perhaps he found in mezzotint, with its process of uncovering light, something analogous to stained glass. Certainly, in the focal areas of light in both his paintings and his mezzotints, he seems to strive for an effect of translucency analogous to that in stained glass.

The train of connections I want to suggest is this: Martin's lifelong fascination with light, his treatment of light as a source of supernatural power in his apocalyptic paintings, the lasting impression upon him of "real light" in stained glass, and his creating light out of darkness in working the mezzotint plate. These factors then met *Paradise Lost*, which had come out of its own cultural context, a context shaped fundamentally by the darkness of Milton's daily life with memories of light. This is projected in the poem as a longing for light, a worship of God as light, and a pervasive use of images of light and darkness in the action of the poem. Composing in a manner analogous to that of the mezzotint artist, who begins with the pure black of the metal plate, Milton creates areas of light out of darkness and composes a poetic vision out of his blindness. As David Masson observed more than a hundred years ago: "the very physical scheme and conception of the poem as a whole seems a kind of revenge against blindness." Or, as William Kerrigan more recently argued, blindness was Milton's strength and *Paradise Lost* "was inaugurated by, not despite," it.[28]

Light and darkness are not only metaphors in the poem but become active presences in the drama. Isabel MacCaffrey's comments are still perhaps the best we have:

> Shot through the contrasting regions of the epic . . . is a balance between an upper world of air and purity, and a hidden, monster-haunted world of dark perplexity. The conflict between darkness and Milton's powerful living light pervades most of these contrasts and is . . . his most potent instrument for making concrete the drama of *Paradise Lost*: the struggle of opposites that brings about the Fall.[29]

Dominant in Martin's understanding of Milton's vision is an imaginative response to these vertically operating elemental forces of light and darkness. He expresses this response through the chiaroscuro medium of mezzotint. The finished product might be regarded as a series of visual correlatives of the poem which importantly include something of himself – a creative portrayal, personal and unique.

As his publisher and reading public might have expected, his illustrations function first as a series defining the narrative line of *Paradise Lost*. What happens in the poem is represented in spatial perspectives and images created out of the tonal range of mezzotint.

Martin's first mezzotint, *The Fall of the Rebel Angels* (1.44; figure 1), is startling and dynamic, depicting heavenly light expelling Satan and his followers down to infernal darkness. For Books 1 and 2, five illustrations follow which build up around Satan associations of yawning gulfs, tunnels, and ever deepening darkness. Then, in *The Heavenly City and Light of God* (3.365; figure 2) and *Satan and the Stairs of Heaven* (3.501; figure 3), Martin achieves a visual analogue to a major modulation in the poem: he moves, partly with Satan, always with Milton as narrating bard, from the dark depths of hell up to the expansive "realms of Light." Following upon this, the transition to Book 4 is announced in the mezzotint of *Eve at the Pool* (4.453): here paradise and especially Eve are bathed in light from above and the landscape of paradise merges with heaven. When Satan arrives Martin shows darkness beginning to encroach upon paradise in *Satan Prying at Adam and Eve* (4.502). Surprised at the ear of Eve, Satan springs up in a sudden blaze which Milton associates with gunpowder (4.813–19) and Martin depicts, in *Satan Surprised by Ithuriel and Zephon* (4.813), as a dim glow compared with the radiance of the unfallen angels. As Zephon reminds Satan: "Think not, revolted Spirit, thy shape

Figure 1. John Martin, *The Fall of the Rebel Angels* (*PL* 1. 44). Proleptic of the Last Judgment, with light as the wrath of God, this illustration conveys the "utter darkness" and "bottomless perdition" into which Satan is hurled. Reproduced by permission of the Victoria & Albert Museum, London.

the same / Or undiminisht brightness" (4.835–36). With the dawning light and Satan's temporary departure, Adam and Eve are again bathed in rays of light from above in *Adam and Eve at Morning Prayer* (5.136). Satan's chief opponent in the battle for Adam and Eve is the archangel Raphael. Unlike Satan, he is a true light-bearer, coming to Adam and Eve like "another Morn / Ris'n on mid-noon" (5.310–11); his visit is

Figure 2. John Martin, *The Heavenly City and Light of God* (*PL* 3; 365). As in Martin's apocalyptic paintings, the center of power is a seemingly endless source of light from on high. Reproduced by permission of the Victoria & Albert Museum, London.

Figure 3. John Martin, *Satan and the Stairs of Heaven* (*PL* 3. 501). Responding to *Paradise Lost* as a poem of exile, Martin here depicts Satan's alienation and his acute sense of the loss of light. Reproduced by permission of the Victoria & Albert Museum, London.

Figure 4. John Martin, *The Bridge Over Chaos* (*PL* 10, 312–47). The engineering technology of Martin's day, the age of Telford and Brunel, meets *Paradise Lost* in this visual analogue of the measureless depths of chaos. Reproduced by permission of the Victoria & Albert Museum, London.

signaled by Martin as a beneficent glow of light, welcomed by Adam and Eve, in *The Approach of the Archangel Raphael* (5.308) and *Raphael Discoursing with Adam and Eve* (5.519).

Before the turning point of the Fall comes Martin's *Creation of the Sun and Moon* (7.339). It is a cosmic perspective which shows the bringing up of light out of darkness, and at this juncture redefines the elemental forces at work in the poem. With the next mezzotint, *The Temptation of Eve*, darkness engulfs paradise. This is the illustration to line 780 of Book 9 ("So saying, her rash hand in evil hour..."). It is the climactic moment of the Fall, for Martin as for Milton, and the engraving is noticeably darker than the following one which depicts Eve giving the fruit to Adam. The judgment follows, *Adam and Eve Hiding from the Voice of God*, the illustration to 10.108 ("Come forth"). This shows the once expansive garden reduced to a tunnel-like glade, paradise taking on the carceral contours of hell, with Adam and Eve hiding from a livid glare of light. Next is the darkest mezzotint of the entire series, *The Bridge Over Chaos* (10.312–47; figure 4). It extends through an enormous tunnel, at the end of which is visible a small light of our world. That world is depicted as overcome with darkness in the next mezzotint, *Adam Rejects Eve* (10.863).

There are three remaining mezzotints in the series and one might expect them all to be dark, but the very next one, *The Regions of Heaven*, is a glorious vision filled with light. Martin's line reference is to 11.78 ("*Amarantin* Shade, Fountain or Spring"), but in its context this line follows an allusion to the apocalypse and a proleptic image of the Last Trump:

> the bright Minister that watchd...blew
> His Trumpet, heard in *Oreb* since perhaps
> When God descended, and perhaps once more
> To sound at general Doom. Th'Angelic blast
> Filld all the Regions: from thir blissful Bowrs
> Of *Amarantin* Shade, Fountain or Spring,
> By the waters of Life, where ere they sate
> In fellowships of joy: the Sons of Light
> Hasted,...   (11.73–81)

Martin's illustration depicts heaven here as pre-eminently a natural landscape, similar to his scenes of paradise before the Fall and quite different from the architectural perspectives of his earlier *Heavenly City* (3.365; figure 2). Following upon *Adam Rejects Eve* – the final illustration for Book 10 which shows paradise so hopelessly changed and darkened – *The Regions of Heaven* could well be titled, "this other Paradise," a reminder that after the Fall the heavenly paradise still exists and that the apocalypse will

Figure 5. John Martin, *The Expulsion (PL* 12. 641). This mezzotint is most like Martin's apocalyptic paintings, yet the peaceful winding river in the distance conveys the hope suggested in Milton's words, "the world was all before them, where to choose / Thir place of rest." Reproduced by permission of the Victoria & Albert Museum, London.

come, when "the Earth / Shall all be Paradise" (12.463–64) and "wrauth shall be no more" (3.264).

Martin's next illustrations, the last two of his series, return to the immediate story of Adam and Eve and God's wrath. Celestial light, a powerful actor in the drama, becomes foreboding and alienating. *The Approach of the Archangel Michael* (11.226) seems to signal cataclysm: dramatic rays, with a suggestion of lightning, emanate from the approaching archangel, while Adam and Eve, standing on the brink of what appears to be a dark abyss, turn away in fear from the light. In the Book 12 mezzotint, *The Expulsion* (figure 5), lightning streaks across the sky and explosive rays shoot from the walls of paradise. Light as the wrath of God banishes Adam and Eve, as it had banished Satan in Martin's first mezzotint. The world they descend into, while not the sheer depths of darkness depicted in the first mezzotint, is lower and much darker than paradise. Martin conveys a sense of cataclysm here and, of all the twenty-four mezzotints, this is most like his apocalyptic paintings. His specific line reference is 12.641, the elegiac "They looking back, . . ." At the same time, in response to the closing lines of the poem, there is a suggestion of hope in the peaceful winding river and lake in the distance and the tiny illuminated figures on the heights, perhaps trees, perhaps guardian angels.

As an unfolding sequence Martin's illustrations thus respond to light and darkness as shaping powers in the action of *Paradise Lost* and interconnect the Fall of Adam and Eve with Satan's story. They portray *Paradise Lost* as a poem of exile, of banishment, and in this respect differ markedly from Blake's Christocentric illustrating of the poem.[30]

They are, however, more than just a series. Most of these engravings carry multiple associations, evoking other areas of the poem and frequently comprehending Milton's wider vision. They depict events happening in time, as part of the unfolding narrative, but, through Martin's mastery of mezzotint and perspective, they also place these events in relation to areas of ever receding light and ever deepening darkness where endless space becomes endless time. In this way they intimate the double perspective of *Paradise Lost*, temporal and eternal.[31] James Tread-well has commented specifically on those areas in Martin's mezzotints "where physical delineation gives way to areas of tonal blankness" of either light or darkness; he argues, however, that this leads the viewer away from the poem, creating "the conditions for the free play of individual imagination."[32] Perhaps this is so, but I would argue rather that these areas of infinite light and infinite darkness are a response to the eschatological perspective of *Paradise Lost* and that it is here notably that Martin the artist of apocalypse meets Milton's apocalyptic poem.

These images recur throughout Martin's series. In *Satan Calling up his Legions* (1.314), the dark vortex of hell seems to spiral downwards interminably. In the stunning mezzotint of *Satan on the Throne of Pandemonium* (2.1), the darkness behind and below Satan recedes indefinitely. In *Satan Prying at Adam and Eve* (4.502), the human pair are bathed in rays of light falling from an area of ever receding light above the landscape. This connection of the unfallen pair with a seemingly translucent light at the top of the picture is emphasized in *Eve at the Pool* (4.453) and *Adam and Eve at Morning Prayer* (5.136), while a vortex of light through the clouds is the focus of power in *The Creation of the Sun and Moon* (7.339). There are four mezzotints, however, where Martin excels in creating an artistic illusion of infinite light and infinite darkness.

In the first of the series, *The Fall of the Rebel Angels* (figure 1), the apocalyptic darkness is dramatically evoked. The bodies of angels hurled through space convey a sense of something happening at a point in time, as with Martin's *The Expulsion* (figure 5). But the lower darkness of this plate shows something else as well. Ever smaller figures are depicted hurled into an immense black void, and because of the three-dimensional effect of the perspective and the velvety blackness of pure mezzotint, this area is immeasurable in space. Martin makes us see the "bottomless perdition" (1.47), the "utter darkness" (1.72, 5.614). In *Paradise Lost* these depths *are* Satan's torment and Milton insists that they go on for ever. At the apocalypse Satan will not be annihilated. He will be "quell[ed]" (12.311), trodden "at last under our feet" (10.190), the mouth of hell will be obstructed and sealed up "[f]or ever" (10.637), but the fire of hell is "[u]nquenchable" (6.877). Satan and "his perverted World" – our world – will be "dissolve[d]" (12.546–47) but Satan himself will not be destroyed, only "his works / In [Adam and in his] Seed" (12.394–95).[33] At his moment of truth, his anguished soliloquy on Mount Niphates, Satan is acutely aware of this: "And in the lowest deep a lower deep / Still threatning to devour me opens wide" (4.76–77). The devouring deep, yawning into infinity, is powerfully suggested in Martin's first illustration. Indeed the mezzotint can be taken as a Last Judgment, in the tradition of Rubens's *The Fall of the Damned into Hell* (1619, Alte Pinakothek, Munich). An art historian, writing on Martin's illustrations, refers (with justifiable inexactness) to the Last Judgment as occurring in Book 1 of

Paradise Lost.[34] It does occur there, proleptically, as also at the end of Book 6.

Martin did not design a mezzotint for Book 6 but *The Fall of the Rebel Angels* doubles for the terrifying expulsion in that book. The glaring "lightning" (6.849) issuing from the Son's chariot is the banishing light, and the "pernicious fire" (6.849) is proleptic of the final conflagration. Martin's line reference for his first mezzotint (1.44) points specifically to images in Book 1 – "Him the Almighty Power / Hurld headlong... / With hideous ruin...down / To bottomless perdition" (1.44–47) – but these relate to images in Book 6 of angels falling "headlong...to the bottomless pit," "Hell [seeing] / Heav'n ruining from Heav'n...Hell at last / Yawning" to receive them (6.864ff.). The fall through chaos in the first mezzotint opens out to yet another part of *Paradise Lost*, the image of another almighty "sling" of the Son's "victorious arm" in Book 10: "at one sling / Of thy victorious Arm, ... / Both *Sin* and *Death*, and yawning *Grave* at last / Through *Chaos* hurld," (10.635–36). Chaos is there "at [the] last," at the apocalypse. Like the "bottomless pit" of hell, it is at the end of time and beyond, deep, dark, "[i]llimitable...where length, breadth, & highth, / And time and place are lost" (2.892–94).

The other mezzotint notable for measureless depths of darkness is *The Bridge Over Chaos* (10.312–47; figure 4), of all Martin's prints the most prized by collectors today. In his discussion of Martin's illustrations as "aesthetic constructs," James Treadwell comments closely on this work and its "abyss of pictorial space,"[35] but he does not relate it to the dynamics of Milton's poem. Milton early on gives an eerie indication of the depths of chaos when he tells the reader that, but for "the strong rebuff of som tumultuous cloud," Satan would be falling through chaos "to this hour" (2.934–36). Martin responds to this imagination. His mezzotints are "aesthetic constructs" and more: they are visionary portrayals, and *The Bridge Over Chaos* is a visual correlative of the timeless depths of darkness which Satan himself describes as the "unreal, vast, unbounded deep" (10.471), to which he is drawing mankind and into which he himself, despite having the freedom of our world until the end of time, is condemned forever to fall.

Martin's two exemplary illustrations of infinite light are for Book 3. The first is *The Heavenly City and Light of God* (figure 2). Martin's line reference is 3.365 ("Then Crown'd again thir gold'n Harps they took"), the moment after the dialogue in heaven. In the foreground angels take up their harps and begin "[t]hir sacred Song" (3.369), but the centre of power, as in Martin's apocalyptic paintings, is a dramatic emanation of light at the top of the picture. Above the heavenly city rays of light pour from a focal point which recedes indefinitely, while on the right a dark cloud shades the light. This seems to be an attempt to illustrate the angels' description of God in their hymn:

> Fountain of Light, thy self invisible
> Amidst the glorious brightness where thou sit'st
> Thron'd inaccessible, but when thou shad'st
> The full blaze of thy beams, and through a cloud
> Drawn round about thee like a radiant Shrine,
> Dark with excessive bright thy Skirts appeer.
>
> (3.375–80)

The mezzotint also evokes the blind bard's hymn to light, particularly the image of "Bright effluence of bright essence" (3.6). Having "venture[d] down / The dark descent" to hell, the bard reascends and "feel[s]" with relief God's "sovran vital Lamp" (3.19–22) – feels it, that is, with his senses and approaches divine light, even though God "never but in unapproached light / Dwelt from Eternitie" (3.4–5). The source of light receding infinitely in the mezzotint parallels the "bright essence" drawing the blind bard. Because of the combination of perspective and Martin's polishing of the metal plate to produce an area of incandescent light, there is an illusion of translucency which approximates the timeless effect of light passing through stained glass.

   The second illustration for Book 3, *Satan and the Stairs of Heaven* (figure 3), opens out still further into the poem. Its specific line reference is 3.501 ("farr distant he descries"); it depicts Satan looking from a distance at the steps leading up to heaven, and has rightly been considered a superlative design.[36] James Treadwell analyzes it, with the Book 10 illustration of *The Bridge Over Chaos*, to support his argument that Martin's illustrations take us beyond the poem rather than back to it.[37] I would argue rather that this is one of the arch-images of Martin's series which portray central themes of Milton's poem. Responding to *Paradise Lost* as a poem of exile, Martin here conveys Satan's acute sense of the loss of light, so poignantly expressed in Books 1, 2, 4, and 9, as well as his feeling of alienation and exile, his utter loneliness. This is thrown into relief by the companionship of the unfallen angels moving in groups up the stairs toward the heavenly light. The radiance streaming from above also evokes an image at the end of Book 2 where Milton as narrating bard moves with Satan up toward the regions of light and breathes a sigh of relief in the lines: "But now at last the sacred influence / Of light appears, and from the walls of Heav'n / Shoots farr into the bosom of dim Night / A glimmering dawn"

(2.1034–37). Unlike Satan, he is not exiled but is able to approach and benefit from the "sacred influence."

This mezzotint also conveys dramatically the dual perspective of *Paradise Lost*. The light falling through the cosmos, the angels walking up the stairs, Satan watching from a distance – all this is happening in time; but in the lower left the darkness beneath Satan is unending and, dominating the picture, the deepening "effulgence" at the top, as in *Belshazzar's Feast*, suggests a source of power transcending the particularities of space and time. As in the other Book 3 illustration, Martin has combined his powers of perspective with his skill in working the entire tonal range of mezzotint. The metal plate has been polished to uncover more and more light. It is a product and process of *disclosure*, and in Martin's hands this mezzotint becomes a revelation of light.

Light and darkness are, mysteriously, at once temporal and eternal in Milton's epic. Born in time, darkness or night is "eldest of things" (2.962) yet "*Eternal*" (3.18). Light is "first-born" (3.1), "first of things" (7.244), yet one with the eternal "bright essence increate" (3.6). While Martin's unfolding series shows light and darkness operating in time, shadowing forth the temporal action of the poem, his images of ever receding light and ever deepening darkness represent dimensions of timelessness which correspond to the apocalyptic perspectives of *Paradise Lost* and the "mystery at the end of the universe."[38]

All this is not a translation of the poem, far less a copy. Insofar as it represents an interpretation of the poem, it might be regarded as analogous to literary criticism. Criticism, however, is a logical, rhetorical, discursive discipline. Illustration is not. It responds to a literary text in its own medium, in its own way. Milton insists that poetry is, compared with logic or rhetoric, "more simple, sensuous, and passionate,"[39] and Martin the artist is in tune with the sensuous power of *Paradise Lost*, preeminently its shaping images of light and darkness. Molded by his particular cultural context – the apocalypticism of his times and of his own paintings, the cult of Milton and the sublime, the industrial climate, his fascination with light in nature, his experimenting with light in various art forms – he encountered *Paradise Lost*. Then, working in mezzotint, with its process of uncovering light from darkness, he achieved a unique visual analogue which is revelatory rather than explanatory. It evokes the grandeur and sublimity of *Paradise Lost*, the themes of exile, the vertical dynamics of light and darkness, the gathering darkness over mankind in the temporal world, and the everlasting darkness and everlasting light in the eternal world.

APPENDIX

Martin gave only book-and-line references with each engraving; the titles below are used throughout this essay.

1. *The Fall of the Rebel Angels* (Book 1, line 44)
2. *Satan on the Lake of Fire* (Book 1, line 192)
3. *Satan Calling up his Legions* (Book 1, line 314)
4. *The Building of Pandemonium* (Book 1, line 710)
5. *Satan on the Throne of Pandemonium* (Book 2, line 1)
6. *Satan, Sin and Death* (Book 2, line 727)
7. *The Heavenly City and Light of God* (Book 3, line 365)
8. *Satan and the Stairs of Heaven* (Book 3, line 501)
9. *Eve at the Pool* (Book 4, line 453)
10. *Satan Prying at Adam and Eve* (Book 4, line 502)
11. *Satan Surprised by Ithuriel and Zephon* (Book 4, line 813)
12. *Gabriel Discerns the Approach of the Angel Guards* (Book 4, line 866)
13. *Adam and Eve at Morning Prayer* (Book 5, line 136)
14. *The Approach of the Archangel Raphael* (Book 5, line 308)
15. *Raphael Discoursing with Adam and Eve* (Book 5, line 519)
16. *The Creation of the Sun and Moon* (Book 7, line 339)
17. *The Temptation of Eve* (Book 9, line 780)
18. *The Temptation of Adam* (Book 9, line 995)
19. *Adam and Eve Hiding from the Voice of God* (Book 10, line 108)
20. *The Bridge Over Chaos* (Book 10, lines 312–47)
21. *Adam Rejects Eve* (Book 10, line 863)
22. *The Regions of Heaven* (Book 11, line 78)
23. *The Approach of the Archangel Michael* (Book 11, line 226)
24. *The Expulsion* (Book 12, line 641).

NOTES

1. For a detailed account, see Thomas Balston, *John Martin 1789–1854: His Life and Works* (London, 1947), pp. 95–99; J. Dustin Wees, *"Darkness Visible": The Prints of John Martin* (Williamstown, Mass., 1986), pp. 18–19. For the twenty-four subjects of Martin's illustrations, see the Appendix to this chapter. Reproductions of the complete series, of both the larger and smaller plates, may be found in Michael J. Campbell, *John Martin: Visionary Printmaker* (York, 1992). Illustrations in this book are from Martin's first series of mezzotints, the larger plates, and are reproduced from proofs held in the Victoria & Albert Museum, London. For reproductions of the series on the Internet, see http://www.stedwards.edu/hum/klawitter/milton/martin/martinindex.htm.

2. See Joseph Wittreich's comprehensive catalogue of Milton illustrators in William B. Hunter et al. (eds.), *A Milton Encyclopedia*, 9 vols. (Lewisburg and London, 1978), vol. IV, pp. 55–78.

3. Ibid., vol. IV, p. 57.

4. Ibid., vol. IV, pp. 56, 57.

5. For colour reproductions, see Martin Butlin, *The Paintings and Drawings of William Blake*, 2 vols. (New Haven, 1981), vol. II (Plates), nos. 632–59.

6. Martin Meisel, *Realisations: Narrative, Pictorial, and Theatrical Arts in Nineteenth-Century England* (Princeton, 1983), p. 174. See also *Literary Gazette*, 2 April 1825, p. 220 (review of the first part published by Septimus Prowett in March 1825); C. H. Collins Baker, "Some Illustrators of Milton's *Paradise Lost* (1688–1850)," *The Library*, 5th Series, 3 (1948), pp. 1–21, especially p. 2, and pp. 101–19; Kester Svendsen, "John Martin and the Expulsion Scene of *Paradise Lost*," *SEL* 1 (1961), pp. 63–73, especially p. 72; Edward Hodnett, *Image and Text: Studies in the Illustration of English Literature* (London, 1982), p. 114; James B. Twitchell, *Romantic Horizons: Aspects of the Sublime in English Poetry and Painting, 1770–1850* (Columbia, Mo., 1983), p. 112; Wees, "*Darkness Visible*," p. 3; Campbell, *John Martin*, p. 41; and George Klawitter, "John Martin's Revolution and Grandeur: A New Direction for Milton's Early Illustrators," *Explorations in Renaissance Culture* 24 (1998), pp. 91–117, especially p. 92.

7. Marcia Pointon, *Milton and English Art* (Manchester, 1970), p. 179.

8. Ibid., pp. 179–83.

9. Wittreich's term, "a form of nonverbal criticism" (*Milton Encyclopedia*, vol. IV, p. 56), signifies an approach developed in his *Angel of Apocalypse: Blake's Idea of Milton* (Madison, 1975). It is particularly useful with Blake's illustrations because of their wealth of symbolic interpretive detail, and is exemplified in Irene Tayler's analysis of Blake's *Comus* illustrations, "Say First! What Mov'd Blake? Blake's *Comus* Designs and *Milton*," in Stuart Curran and Joseph Wittreich (eds.), *Blake's Sublime Allegory: Essays on* The Four Zoas, Milton, Jerusalem (Madison, 1973), pp. 234–48. Stephen Behrendt applies the approach strenuously in *The Moment of Explosion: Blake and the Illustration of Milton* (Lincoln and London, 1983). See also Ernest W. Sullivan, "Illustration as Interpretation: *Paradise Lost* from 1688 to 1807," in Albert C. Labriola and Edward Sichi, Jr. (eds.), *Milton's Legacy in the Arts* (University Park and London, 1988), pp. 59–92. Edward Hodnett follows the approach of illustration as translation and subjects Martin's series to a "plate-by-plate image-to-text scrutiny" (*Image and Text*, p. 107); consequently he condemns Martin on the one hand for omitting parts of the poem and on the other for introducing "merely incidental" material (ibid., p. 122). James Treadwell uses the terms "aesthetic constructs" and "independent imaginative structures" in "Blake, John Martin, and the Illustration of *Paradise Lost*," *Word & Image* 9 (1993), pp. 363–82, 379, 380; he sees Blake's and Martin's illustrations as a "medium for looking beyond the poem (rather than back to it)" (p. 371).

10. For the Miltonic culture of the late eighteenth and early nineteenth centuries, see Stephen C. Behrendt, "*Paradise Lost*, History Painting,

and Eighteenth-Century English Nationalism," *Milton Studies* 25 (1989), pp. 141–59, 148, 157; James G. Nelson, *The Sublime Puritan: Milton and the Victorians* (Madison, 1963), chapter 4; Pointon, *Milton and English Art*, pp. xxxii–xxxvi; and Lucy Newlyn, Paradise Lost *and the Romantic Reader* (Oxford, 1993), chapter 1. For the abiding presence of Milton in Martin's life, see Leopold Charles Martin's *Reminiscences of John Martin*, KL (1889), cited in Balston, *John Martin*, p. 161, and Pointon, p. 178. For Martin and the sublime, see Morton D. Paley, *The Apocalyptic Sublime* (New Haven and London, 1986), chapter 6. For Martin's engineering projects and his annexing of *Paradise Lost* to industrial concerns of his day, see Balston, *John Martin*, chapter 15; Svendsen, "John Martin," pp. 66–67, 71–73; Francis D. Klingender, *Art and the Industrial Revolution* (revd. edn., Frogmore, 1972), pp. 104–10 and figs. 52, 53; John Dixon Hunt, "Milton's Illustrators," in John Broadbent (ed.), *John Milton: Introductions* (Cambridge, 1973), p. 216; and William Feaver, *The Art of John Martin* (Oxford, 1975), pp. 77–81.

11. See Balston, *John Martin*, pp. 15–16, and Paley, *The Apocalyptic Sublime*, pp. 127–28.

12. J. F. C. Harrison, *The Second Coming: Popular Millenarianism 1780–1850* (London, 1979), p. 131.

13. Paul J. Korshin, "Queuing and Waiting: The Apocalypse in England, 1660–1750," in C. A. Patrides and Joseph Wittreich (eds.), *The Apocalypse in English Renaissance Thought and Literature: Patterns, Antecedents, and Repercussions* (Manchester, 1984), p. 253.

14. See above p. 58.

15. Joseph Wittreich, *Visionary Poetics: Milton's Tradition and his Legacy* (San Marino, 1979), p. 212. See also David Loewenstein, *Milton and the Drama of History: Historical Vision, Iconoclasm, and the Literary Imagination* (Cambridge, 1990), pp. 111–25.

16. Citations from Milton are from *The Riverside Milton*, ed. Roy Flannagan (Boston, 1998). See also 3.260–65, 3.321–41, 6.730–33, 11.42–44, 12.537–51, 12.555–56.

17. Catherine Morris Westcott, "The Sublime and the Millennialist in John Martin's Mezzotints for *Paradise Lost*," *Athanor* 13 (1995), pp. 54, 55.

18. Balston, *John Martin*, pp. 21, 238.

19. See Ruthven Todd, *Tracks in the Snow: Studies in English Science and Art* (London, 1946), p. 97.

20. From Martin's descriptive pamphlet which accompanied the painting, cited in Paley, *The Apocalyptic Sublime*, p. 132.

21. Campbell, *John Martin*, p. 2. See also Paley, *The Apocalyptic Sublime*, p. 138.

22. *Table Talk*, 30 May 1830, in Carl Woodring (ed.), *The Collected Works of Samuel Taylor Coleridge*, 16 vols. (Princeton, 1990), vol. XIV, p. 152.

23. Balston, *John Martin*, p. 30.

24. Beverley Sherry, *Australia's Historic Stained Glass* (Sydney, 1991), pp. 9, 10.

25. Campbell, *John Martin*, p. 40.

26. Ibid., p. 57. For the mezzotint process see also Wees, "*Darkness Visible*," pp. 14–15, and Paley, *The Apocalyptic Sublime*, pp. 137–38.

27. His *Belshazzar's Feast* was translated into stained glass *c.* 1821 (now at Syon House, London), and in 1824, upon the death of his former employer Charles Muss, Martin supervised the completion of Muss's glass-painting commissions. See Feaver, *The Art of John Martin*, p. 52 and fig. 32; Paley, *The Apocalyptic Sublime*, pp. 189–90; and Balston, *John Martin*, p. 79.
28. David Masson (ed.), *The Poetical Works of John Milton*, 3 vols (2nd edn., London, 1882), vol. II, p. 54, and William Kerrigan, *The Sacred Complex: On the Psychogenesis of* Paradise Lost (Cambridge, Mass., 1983), p. 133. Masson's lengthy discussion of Milton's blindness as a "positive qualification" for *Paradise Lost* (pp. 51–57, 51) bears interesting resemblances to an account of the mezzotint process: "in all this what else have we than the poet making districts in the infinitude of darkness in which he himself moved, and, while suffering some of the districts to remain in their native opaque, rescuing others into various contrasts of light?" (p. 54).
29. Isabel Gamble MacCaffrey, Paradise Lost *as "Myth"* (Cambridge, Mass., 1959), p. 169. For the metaphysics of light Milton inherited from classical and Christian hermeneutics, see D. C. Allen, "Milton and the Descent to Light," *JEGP* 60 (1961), pp. 614–30. See also Don Cameron Allen, *The Harmonious Vision: Studies in Milton's Poetry* (revd. edn., Baltimore and London, 1970), chapters 5 and 7, and Michael Lieb, *Poetics of the Holy: A Reading of* Paradise Lost (Chapel Hill, 1981), chapter 9.
30. See Wittreich, *Angel of Apocalypse*, pp. 93–94.
31. For "Milton's characteristic double vision" in *Paradise Lost*, see Marshall Grossman, *"Authors to Themselves": Milton and the Revelation of History* (Cambridge, 1987), p. 154. Wendy Furman has discussed "human *chronos* and divine *kairos*" in relation to three illustrations of the expulsion – Blake's, Carlotta Petrina's, and Mary Groom's – "'With Dreadful Faces Throng'd and Fiery Arms': Apocalyptic 'Synchronisme' in Three Illustrations of *Paradise Lost*," *Coranto* 25 (1990), pp. 20–33, 22.
32. Treadwell, "Blake, John Martin," pp. 376, 381. See also Klawitter, "John Martin's Revolution and Grandeur," p. 94, for his comment on the "infinity" of the background in Martin's mezzotint of *Satan on the Throne of Pandemonium*.
33. See Juliet Cummins's interpretation of "dissolve" in this book, pp. 175–179.
34. Westcott, "Sublime and Millennialist," p. 55, n. 43.
35. Treadwell, "Blake, John Martin," pp. 377, 379.
36. Campbell, *John Martin*, p. 49. It is used as the cover of Campbell's book, and as the frontispiece of Leslie E. Moore's *Beautiful Sublime: The Making of* Paradise Lost, *1701–1734* (Stanford, 1990).
37. Treadwell, "Blake, John Martin," pp. 377–79.
38. The phrase is Paul Davies's in *The Mind of God: Science and the Search for Ultimate Meaning* (London, 1992), pp. 223, 226.
39. *Of Education* (1644), in Flannagan (ed.), *The Riverside Milton*, p. 984.

8

The enclosed garden and the apocalypse: immanent versus transcendent time in Milton and Marvell

Catherine Gimelli Martin

> But it is here as in Gaming, where, tho the Cheat may lose for a while, to the Skill or good fortune of a fairer Player, and sometimes on purpose to draw him in deeper, yet the false dice must at the long run Carry it, unless discovered, and when it comes once to a great Stake, will Infallibly Sweep the Table.
>
> Andrew Marvell, *An Account of the Growth of Popery, and Arbitrary Government in England*

> And though all the windes of doctrin were let loose to play upon the earth, so Truth be in the field, we do injuriously by licencing and prohibiting to misdoubt her strength. Let her and Falshood grapple; who ever knew truth put the wors, in a free and open encounter.
>
> John Milton, *Areopagitica* (*CP* II: 561)

This essay proposes that the temperamental differences so obvious in the two quotations above are also temporal: that implicit in Milton's and Marvell's quite different attitudes toward fate and chance are fundamentally different conceptions of time. Further, it will suggest that the difference between Milton's temporal commitment to an immanent, active, and progressive revelation of truth and Marvell's transcendental and/or apocalyptic determinism largely accounts for their profoundly different pastoral landscapes. Finally, it will also show that these distinctions hold even after accounting for the fact that these quotations respond to two very different historical situations. Milton is cited from *Areopagitica*, a work written at the height of England's millenarian optimism, while Marvell is cited from *An Account of the Growth of Popery, and Arbitrary Government*, a work written in the depths of her post-Restoration cynicism. Yet their divergent attitudes toward human contest, fallibility, and capacity for recovery in time remain substantially the same both before and after the Restoration. Milton's early conviction that the champions of truth will always ultimately be rewarded is generally consistent with the trust his post-Restoration poems place in the inevitable victories of "Patience and

Heroic Martyrdom" (*PL* 9.32).[1] By the same token, Marvell's enduring skepticism about these rewards is evident in even his most optimistic pre-Restoration poems, "An Horatian Ode" and "The First Anniversary of the Government under His Highness the Lord Protector." Many of these disparities have been noted before, but rarely with any real awareness that they go so far beyond "mere" temperamental differences as to suggest an important ideological schism within their otherwise shared belief systems.[2]

The enclosed garden may at first seem an unlikely place in which to explore how two different views of time and temporal renewal – one immanent, the other transcendent – can produce the alternate poetic as well as ethical and political universes that ultimately emerge within its walls. Yet as Jane Brown reminds us, the enclosed garden has provided a privileged place for exploring the intersection of eternity, temporality, and ideology throughout most of Christian history. As she observes in *The Pursuit of Paradise*: "All the dreams of the secret garden are encapsulated in this precious image: the perfect garden, an encounter with an angel, the treasure within – both Mary herself and the child in her womb – the implied blessing on philosophic debate, intimations of death and the blind windows and barred gate which keep the world at bay." Unsurprisingly, Brown shows that the image of the garden as a space of temporal/spiritual fulfillment particularly dominates the "golden age" of English landscape gardening, the period between 1570 and 1770 when the Protestant millenarian revival began to reshape England's political and religious landscape.[3] This revival is already evident in Shakespeare's early political tragedies, which set the stage by prophetically depicting the overthrow of a tyrant/king like Richard II as a prelude to restoring this "other Eden, demi-paradise," this England.[4]

According to Katharine R. Firth the religious impetus to reestablish the second Eden or New Jerusalem in England begins with John Bale's 1544 chronicle of Lollard martyrs, to which he appended a previously peripheral prophecy attributed to Joachim of Abbas (*c.* 1342). Here Joachim predicts that the latter days of the church will be governed by the spread of liberty, learning, and spiritual reform, which Bale interprets to include not just the establishment of true religion but the overthrow of the Roman Catholic church. John Foxe's later memorialization of the English martyrs of Mary's reign in his *Book of Martyrs* and *Acts and Monuments* further confirmed Bale's identification of the millennium with the increase of pure worship and learning, and also prepared the way for later scholars – Thomas Brightman, Joseph Mede, and in a more secular sense, Francis Bacon – to look forward to the apocalypse as a time of renewal rather than as merely the final destruction of all earthly things. Afterward, the heirs of this radical Protestant tradition envisioned the apocalypse as an event within, not outside of, time, where it had been placed by earlier theologians who considered its temporal dimension already complete at the moment of Christ's resurrection.[5]

Not just the epigraph above but Milton's *Areopagitica* as a whole testifies to his debt to this phase of English millenarianism. Early works like *Of Reformation* and *Animadversions* draw directly on the views of Mede (the most prominent Fellow during his residence at Cambridge), Brightman, and Foxe, and his Cambridge prolusions further fuse them with Baconian millenarianism.[6] This commitment is not abandoned in late works such as *The Readie and Easie Way*, a treatise written while he was still closely associated with Marvell, the talented protégé who became his friend and lifelong supporter. Both as the son of a minister with strong Puritan leanings and as tutor to the Independent General Fairfax, Marvell's religious and political adherence to this camp (despite some earlier, rather loose Royalist sympathies and friendships, and despite Fairfax's refusal to consent to king-killing) was already well-established before he became Milton's assistant Latin secretary under Cromwell. His progressive/millenarian credentials were further confirmed by his poetic tributes and political adherence to the Lord Protector while the regime lasted, and afterward by his continuing support for the causes of individual and religious liberty equally paramount for Milton. Historically these commonalities are so abundantly well-documented that at least one Marvell scholar, Warren Chernaik, finds no philosophical divide between the two poet/politicians whatsoever. Despite Marvell's greater pessimism or – to put it another way – his greater realism about the "fairer Player[s']" chances of winning in this world, Chernaik follows Wordsworth's venerable lead in placing "the later Sidney, Marvell, Harrington... and others who called Milton friend" in a common "Puritan libertarian" camp.[7]

Chernaik stands on firm ground here: not just Wordsworth but the majority of Milton's and Marvell's contemporaries made similar claims. A publisher's preface to the 1697 volume of *Poems on Affairs of State* announces: "The following poems, writ by Mr. *Milton*, Mr. *Marvell*, & c... will shew us, that there is no where a greater Spirit of Liberty to be found, than in those who are Poets," because they have taken the lead in denouncing "those pernicious Principles which lead us directly to Slavery." Given that Marvell spent most of the Restoration picking up the Miltonic gauntlet of antiabsolutist and antiprelatical pamphleteering, often at great personal cost, this claim is only partially hyperbolic.[8] For the key tropes of "Puritan libertarianism" are as frequently encountered in Marvell's garden poetry as in Milton's pastorals. Both typically feature a good pastor or gardener as an archetypal Puritan individualist who symbolically withdraws from the common plain to shepherd his own vision of the good. Yet neither exclusively valorizes the *vita contempliva*, which both ultimately reject by heeding the higher call of the *vita activa* to complete real works in the real world. Just as Milton cannot praise a "fugitive and cloister'd vertue, unexercis'd & unbreath'd, that never sallies out and sees her adversary, but slinks out of the race, where that immortall garland is to be run for, not without dust and heat" (*CP* II: 515), Marvell cannot cloister himself for ever at Nun Appleton House, but goes on to serve the Commonwealth government defended by Milton with all the labors of his left hand and loss of his sight. Later, "they also serve" after the Restoration, albeit Milton mainly by standing and waiting as the muse lends new eyes to guide his right hand.

Both poets thus clearly recognize that "the garden is not enough," as Christopher Hill remarks of Marvell; that "the life of the community demands the death of the individual, rest is obtainable only through and by means of effort, eternal vigilance is the price of liberty, freedom is the knowledge of necessity."[9] Given these shared ethical and political commitments, the distinctly different designs assumed by Miltonic and Marvellian gardens must be traced to another source, the most likely of which is their distinctly different conceptions of millennial "rest." Marvell's most complete vision of this rest appears in "Bermudas," a prime example of how in his ideal *hortus conclusus*, both time and space are quite literally concluded. In this fully enclosed, "remote," and "unespy'd" (ll. 1–2) retreat, an active God supplies his passive people's every possible want. Free from the "rage" (l. 12) of both waters and prelates, its visionary elect safely "ride" the island's providential waves in perfect harmony with their floating haven, with heaven, and with a musical "time" that is fully theirs to "keep" (l. 40). This reciprocal, reversible, and ultimately static space/time is protected by both the island's "eternal Spring" (l. 13) and its living temple, which sustain this truly New Jerusalem with miraculous new fruits. Oranges "light" its temple's "golden Lamps," while apple "plants of such a price, / No Tree could ever bear them twice" (ll. 23–24) cancel out all possibility of future transgression. Growing at the feet, not above the reach, of this unfallen people, the pineapple symbolizes all that it literally "bears": perfect hospitality, harmony, and fertility. Nor is this vision such a unique example of Marvell's pastoral art

as some critics would suggest, for the apocalyptic, solitary, idyllic, and
serenely "idle" enclosures of "Bermudas" reappear in visionary moments
in "The Garden," "Upon Appleton House," and the vast majority of his
other secular and spiritual pastorals. Significantly, these moments only
turn tragic when their "comic" closure is ruptured, as it is for Marvell's
complaining Nymph and his mown Mower.[10]

These idyllic enclosures typically lack not just the mutability and temporality of Milton's Eden but also the strenuous activity of its gardeners.
Supplying not only their own wants but those of a largely absent, inscrutable, yet dialectically demanding God, Milton's Adam and Eve
cultivate a highly un-Bermudan paradise presided over by a distinctly
different kind of deity. Alone upon a heavenly throne whose radiance
only the Son can fully penetrate, this God relates to his earthly children chiefly by guiding them toward the same positively self-questioning
attitude to his providential design expected of all his children, including
the first-begotten. This questing forms the common bond uniting the
unenclosed spaces of both the earthly and the heavenly paradise, which
commonly participate in an open-ended, monistic cosmos. United by a
dynamic "one first matter," this cosmos achieves its final "flowering" in
the same godhead who provides its *prima materia* (*PL* 5.469–82). Because
this cosmic continuum is also ethical, neither paradise can exclude the
physical and spiritual temptations so markedly missing from Marvell's
ideal gardens. Because (as *Areopagitica* declares) Milton regards incom-
pletion and open-endedness as intrinsic ingredients of perfection, like
that "fair field of Enna" where Persephone was ravished, his Eden is
and must *remain* accessible not only to time but also to its ravages. Yet
even this temporal monism takes on a potentially positive valence for
Milton, who does not regard time as the traditional enemy but rather
as an ultimately benign ingredient of eternity, which it measures along
with "all things durable" (*PL* 5.580–81).

Milton's physical, ethical, and temporal monism culminate in his distinctly un-Marvellian conception of eternal rest. As he declares in *The
Reason of Church Government*, mutability must be the precondition of all
true "delight" even in the highest heavens. For it is not to be "conceived
that those eternall effluences of sanctity and love in the glorified Saints
should . . . be confin'd and cloy'd with *repetition of that which is prescrib'd*, but
that our happinesse may orbe it selfe into *a thousand vagancies* of glory and
delight, and with *a kind of eccentricall equation* be as it were an invariable
Planet of joy and felicity" (*CP* 1: 752; my emphasis). The "eccentrically"
mutable eternity enjoyed by these "glorified Saints" is later echoed in the

epic celebrations of his heavenly angels, which are similarly compared to the "dances" of the eternally harmonious yet temporally "irregular" planets, in their "mazes intricate / Eccentric, intervolv'd, yet regular / Then most, when most irregular they seem" (*PL* 5.621–24). This endlessly movable feast might well perplex a more conventional Christian reader – a perplexity Marvell in fact confesses in his poem "On Mr. Milton's *Paradise Lost*" (ll. 5–8). But Milton's temporal paradoxes follow consistently enough from the simultaneously immanent and transcendent nature of his God, who at once fills infinitude and retires "uncircumscrib'd" from time and space (*PL* 7.168–70). Even his divine foreknowledge seems ambiguously mutable and/or retractable, at once capable of predicting the future and of withdrawing from his active knowledge (*PL* 3.117–18), a schema which permits a maximally dialectical model of divine providence.[11]

Thus, like Milton's God, divine providence can intersect with time and space and at the same time transcend them. For rather than merely decreeing, this God tentatively outlines a providential plan which must be actively completed by the creatures he has independently enabled to apprehend and interpret his natural and divine laws. The principal model for this interaction is naturally provided by the Son, who in Book 3 dialectically "helps" God decide how to amend the human lapse. This highly cooperative covenant between the deity and his free agents/subjects is immanently, but not transcendently, "fated" to be good, because in Milton's definition true freedom is ultimately indistinguishable from true goodness (Sonnet 12, ll. 10–12). As a result his God can paradoxically but rightfully proclaim that "Necessity and Chance / Approach not mee": for while there is no "necessity" in the details of his providential plan, there is also no chance that its overarching design will ultimately deviate from the benign laws of freedom and fecundity he has decreed from eternity, which alone "is Fate" (*PL* 7.172–73).[12]

Despite its theological idiosyncrasies, this conception of divine providence is historically consistent with the apocalyptic innovations of Bale, Brightman, Foxe, and Mede. Like the early English revolutionaries in general and his fellow Independents in particular, Milton regarded contemporary events as a gradual, uncertain, but also historically inevitable "unfolding" of the New Jerusalem along the lines established in Mede's *The Key of the Revelation*.[13] According to this school of thought, the imminent arrival of this "unfolding" (as the word apocalypse literally means) is itself "unfolded" in the people's active sense of vocation. The rationale behind this conviction is implicit in William Twisse's preface to the *Key*, which declares: "when darknesse covered the earth, and grosse darknesse the people; the Lord hath risen upon us, and his glorie hath beene seene upon us."[14] Although the darkness preceding the apocalypse makes the exact nature of the events leading up to it highly uncertain, the active participation of God's people in the great cleansing work provides a clear sign of its approaching "glorie." The vagueness surrounding these manifestations not only permitted highly diverse interpretations of its signs and their meaning even among such closely allied Puritan libertarians as Milton and Marvell, but also led many to stress the fundamental open-endedness of the divine plan much as Milton did.

However, as his "The First Anniversary" indicates, Marvell placed his hopes in a specific Cromwellian "king" and/or law-giver who would single-handedly establish a classical republican or "mixed" government – an ideal blend of monarchic, aristocratic, and democratic elements. Although equally indebted to the classical republican tradition, Milton's much more conditional providentialism made him reluctant to identify the kingdom of God with any single party or "hero," a position which fortunately did not require major alterations after the Commonwealth failed.[15] His consistency in this respect is shown by the fact that his first work on the subject, *Of Reformation*, imagines the kingdom of God as a "universal and mild *Monarchy*" ruling both "Heaven and Earth" (*CP* 1: 616), in terms later echoed in both *The Readie and Easie Way* and *Paradise Lost*, which also imagine an ideally "mixed" government being established at both the beginning and the end of time.

In epic time this ideal is fulfilled as the Son takes on his "mild monarchial" rule as a kind of first among equals, "United as one individual Soul" (*PL* 5.610). As the Father's perfect "Similitude" (*PL* 3.384), the Son is at once the almighty King's perfect mediator and the perfect subject, who according to Abdiel now "One of our number thus reduc't becomes." Because "reduc't" refers both to his stepping down among his brethren and to his leveling of the old angelic hierarchies (both of which Satan resists), the Son is best understood as a kind of Supreme-Subject-in-Chief ruling through laws to which he is himself subject, "His Laws our Laws" (*PL* 5.843–44). Later, the archangel Michael indicates that the unfallen Adam might have performed a similar role for his earthly sons had he not usurped divine authority, thereby paving the way for the historical rise of "unbrotherly" monarchies of the satanic type (*PL* 11.342–48, 12.63–74). Nevertheless, the ideal pattern of mixed government is not canceled out but merely deferred to a later date, when the Jews at last set up their "Senate" in "the wide Wilderness" (*PL* 12.224–25). *Of Reformation* had similarly associated the revival of this natural/providential pattern with the "ancient Republick of the Jews," which through a "mild Aristocracy of elective Dukes, and heads of Tribes," naturally evolves (via a detour into monarchy) into a true "Jewish Senat at home" under the "Roman Senat from without" (*CP* 1: 574–75). Before, as after, the Restoration, then, Milton's providentialism is grounded in a cooperative view of evolutionary history in which human energies cyclically but inevitably restore the divine republican plan.

Although Marvell usually shows little inclination – philosophical, personal, or political – to view human history as operating in close conjunction with providential time, in "The First Anniversary" God's unseen hand does ideally and explicitly guide Cromwell's. Significantly, however, this event is described as a transcendent intervention rather than as an immanent evolution toward the ideal state. As such it represents an abrupt break with the usual state of affairs, in which the divine plan is not only inscrutable but often flatly incompatible with human aims, desires, and wishes.[16] Stoically, Marvell does not consider this situation unjust but simply necessary, an effect of the human fall that has severed human desires from divine designs for ever. The apocalypse will eventually come and Eden will be restored, but the date, course, and most certainly the details of that conclusion are fixed by a divine Fate that does not interact with human efforts through legible natural laws or individual "callings." Both in "The First Anniversary" where that Fate is identified with Cromwell and in "Bermudas" where it is not, the kingdom of God simply and abruptly "arrives."[17] Yet given the near absolute "darkness" in which the divine plan is shrouded, in the Protectorate poems Marvell was at least briefly able to consider that the Second Coming might surprise him by appearing in his own lifetime. The fact that such optimism goes largely against the ideological grain is indicated by the notorious tensions and ambiguities of these poems. As most commentators have noted, these tensions disappear only in Marvell's elegy for the Lord Protector, where his optimism is no longer strained to its previous pitch.

Christopher Hill explains this apparent incongruity by suggesting that Marvell's acceptance of blind necessity made him actually a "truer Cromwellian . . . than Milton, who could not accept the new tactics" associated with the waning years of the Protectorate, much less the later cynicism of Restoration politics, a climate in which Marvell survived and even thrived, honored by the new king as by the old Protector. Yet, like Chernaik, Hill betrays a somewhat sentimental wish to reunite the old allies at the expense of some important facts. For according to Hill, Marvell shared or even exceeded "Milton's sense . . . of good through evil, of the impossibility of good without evil, of the meaninglessness of rejecting good because of concomitant evil."[18] But unfortunately there is little evidence that Marvell ever believed that good emerges from evil, a view that his dualist sense of time would alone inhibit. In fact Marvell's beliefs lead him to precisely the opposite position: that "one good must destroy another" in this world. John Carey sensibly links this belief to Marvell's dichotomizing habits of mind, but fails to note how his characteristic spatial oppositions – garden/wilderness, nature/art, body/soul – also extend to time.[19] Because in thoroughly un-Miltonic fashion Marvell regards both mutability and history as irremediable evils not to be altered by either the sufferings or even the successes of the saints, his view of time remains closer to Calvin than to Mede. Like Milton's, Marvell's eschatology is consistent with his ethics, which, unlike his friend's, are essentially Calvinist in character.

More specifically, Marvell seems to have been influenced by the secular Calvinism of Thomas Hobbes, who by regarding the human/divine covenant as a temporally limited, one-sided agreement without any option for further renegotiation, severely restricted man's present-tense cooperation with God. Hobbes logically derived these restrictions from the very nature of Calvin's ultra-transcendent, ultra-inscrutable deity, which would logically exclude divine providence from human time and understanding until the unknowable Last Day. Outside of both time and space, this God decrees history from on high as a form of necessity in which man must act to fulfill his ethical obligations without being able to contemplate, much less to promote his grand but unknowable design.

Marvell's adherence to a highly similar theology is evident in *The Rehearsal Transpros'd*, where he insists: "There is first of all a necessity . . . that was pre-eternal to all things, and exercised dominion not only over all humane things, but over *Jupiter* himself and the rest of the Deities and drove the great Iron nail thorough the Axle-tree of Nature."[20] Here "Jupiter" serves as a conventional figure for fate, God's "deputy" in nature, which because it is ultimately ruled by him, is similarly all-ruling. In his "Definition of Love," this force regularly rules our lives quite literally *in spite* of human wishes: "And yet I quickly might arrive / Where my extended Soul is fixt, / But Fate does Iron wedges drive, / And alwaies crouds it self betwixt" (ll. 9–12).[21] In citing this passage even Hill is forced to recognize the Hobbesian aspects not only of Marvell's "Fate" but also of his original state of nature. As in "Upon Appleton House," the "World…first created" is not, as in *Paradise Lost*, simply tending to wild, but instead likened to the arena in which the Hobbesian war of all on all is conducted: "a Table rase and pure" like "the *Toril* / Ere the Bulls enter at Madril (ll. 445–48)."[22] Predictably, the culprit in this fable is the great Anarch and enemy, time, the enemy also of the original garden:

[The] state of perfection was dissolv'd in the first Instance, and was shorter-lived than Anarchy, scarce of one day's continuance…So that as God has hitherto, in stead of an Eternal Spring, a standing Serenity, and perpetual Sun-shine, subject Mankind to the dismal influence of Comets from above, to Thunder, and Lightning, and Tempest from the middle Region, and from the lower Surface, to the raging of the Seas, and the tottering of Earth quakes, beside all the other innumerable calamities to which humane life is exposed, he has in like manner distinguish'd the Government of the World by the intermitting seasons of Discord, War, and publick Disturbance. (*RT* 11: 231)

As in Eden, so ever after: mutability for Marvell is an unconditional curse rather than a Miltonic blessing. After cataclysmically canceling man's initial state of perfection in the beginning, time ever afterward serves only as a reminder that our earthly imperfection is ruled by iron laws of judgment, not the monist mercies of Milton's "one first matter" – at least until the end of time.

Obviously, then, for Marvell the arena of trial carries a largely negative rather than a positive Miltonic connotation. Imagined as a battleground or bullfight rather than the classical wrestling match Milton has in mind in the epigraph above, this arena hardly permits the gradual, immanent, yet inevitable "reforming of Reformation itself" (*CP* 11: 553) announced in *Areopagitica*.[23] For that apocalyptic unfolding the spiritual Calvinist must look to the Celestial City above, like the secular Calvinist awaiting a deferred "prize" while undergoing labors that are never their own reward. Marvell's religious verse regularly reveals both the deferral and the defensiveness required by this ethic, which values ceaseless vigilance far above a Miltonic process of natural error and correction. However, unlike Hobbes, Marvell is no Erastian, so his "Resolved Souls" remain ready and willing to do battle for Christian liberty in the Miltonic spirit. Yet they also significantly lack the Miltonic hope that they will thereby be rewarded in human time. While the Marvellian individual has a duty to soldier on through the relentless forces of historical progress, because the "world will not go the faster for our driving," his providential hopes are all too likely to be defeated.

Marvell himself was no stranger to such disappointments. Fervently affirming while Cromwell lived that "If these the Times, then this must be the Man" ("The First Anniversary," l. 144), after the Restoration he was willing to admit that the "Good Old Cause" was "too good to have been fought for," since "men may spare their pains where Nature is at work" (*RT* 1: 135). But this much-misunderstood remark is a product less of Marvell's cynicism than of his prevailing temporal pessimism. Though originally innocent and free, man and nature are now ruled by the rod of divine "Fate," which knows best, whether we do or not. In this world the garden is never enough, because by moving nature and Jupiter much closer to God and much further from man than Milton would, Marvell typically sees temporality through the lens of prospective loss rather than prospective gain. At best a surreal shadow of the New Jerusalem, his garden must be framed as a mere mental figment, fragment, or waking dream utterly unlike anything actually existing either in England or in the original Eden.

In sum, then, the difference between Milton's monist conception of apocalyptic redemption and Marvell's dualist conception of time and eternity produces two very different Protestant visions of history, progress, ethics, and eschatology. As opposed to Milton's providential "contractualism," Marvell's "profound theological nominalism" requires him to approach God only through a distant and fallen, not through an immediate or inspired, "Word" or language.[24] Although his nominalism is less extreme than that of Hobbes, Marvell seems to have read the "monster of Malmesbury" approvingly in his Royalist phase.[25] This influence is reflected in his similar belief that since "the time-bound nature of human intelligence ... renders it incapable of predicting occurrences and events with any certainty," man has no direct access to the providential design of future history.[26] Although Hobbes did accept the literal teachings of the prophets – there will be a resurrection of the saints – he also argued that because the age of prophecy has ceased, nothing definite can be known about this eventuality. Not only is human activity thereby segregated into two distinct spheres, natural and divine, but human knowledge of the divine realm is confined almost entirely to the prophetic past. Providential expectation is therefore restricted to a literal but largely atemporal hope concerning a future in no way coextensive with the present, which now affords the only proper sphere for human rationality or action. With direct communication between God and man rationally cut off, Christian conscience then becomes radically privatized and internalized as the sphere of moral and prudential rather than of broader social or spiritual considerations. In the service of politics, appeals to conscience are thus not only philosophically illegitimate but physically destructive because they bring about a return to the war of all upon all.[27]

Marvell's sympathy with these Hobbesian conclusions seems to stem from his similar suspicion of religious enthusiasm and his similar view of the irremediably fallen condition of language, nature, and time. This skepticism leads to a millennial "formalism" which, while following Protestant orthodoxy in placing the kingdom of Christ after, not before, the end of the world, rejects the Protestant millenarian conviction that human agency or faith can assist in bringing it about. This "Hobbesian" formalism also explains the somewhat different political sensibilities of Marvell and Milton. As J. G. A. Pocock shows, although Hobbes's history of prophetic authority still allows for an "eschatological future" which conserves the "messianic dimension" of politics, this dimension is "almost brutally political" in its concession to rational necessity and nationally expedient goals.[28] Marvell's satires suggest that while he personally deplores these rather regrettable concessions, he also accepts them as the price of not abandoning the world altogether. Ironically, these concessions to harsh necessity are not canceled but merely concealed in his pastoral world by repressive attempts to celebrate "sensuous pleasures supposed to be free from sensuality."[29] Because the "iron gates" of necessity are never invisible from even the shadiest nooks of the garden, its shepherds and shepherdesses self-consciously seek an enclosure within an enclosure, thereby setting up physical and emotional needs which end up repeating the restrictions of the "real" world even as they gratify sensuous needs.

The emotional effects of this dichotomizing can again be suggestively contrasted with those generated by Milton's iconoclastic attitude toward enclosures. With predictably monistic results this iconoclasm causes him to represent paradise and purgatorio, rapture and ravishment, as the opposite ends of a continuous and fundamentally reversible scale of value. This treatment of desire is in turn reflected in his representation of women, who are not dichotomized – like Marvell's completely innocent or all-too-experienced females – as either unworldly "nymphs" or classical temptresses/destroyers of paradise. Despite her traditional identification as *the* classical destroyer of paradise, Milton's Eve is thus no Juliana but a free agent capable of being either innocently or sinfully ravishing – or both, or neither. This emotional ambiguity demands a highly contextual representation of motives which takes into account not just her own desires but also those of her beholders. Hence only when she colludes with both Satan and Adam in narcissistically negative desire does this ambiguity collapse, causing Adam to echo the conviction of Marvell's gardener: "Two Paradises 'twere in one / To live in Paradise alone" ("The Garden," ll. 63–64). However, this definitively "fallen" perspective is soon reversed through Adam's "regenerative" understanding that the female principle – like time itself – remains a necessary ingredient in, not a real threat to, pastoral peace. For Milton, Eve's "wandering," like that of their "mazy" garden, "wild beyond rule or art," thus remains the true earthly counterpart of heaven's "grateful vicissitude" (*PL* 6.8) both before and after the Fall.

In contrast, as Carey rightly remarks, Marvell's "trepidation about sex is only part of that larger awareness of...reality as a restriction, a trap, [or]...thwarting" which follows from his belief that both post-lapsarian time and nature are "ruled by laws as immutable as those of mathematics."[30] In this relatively "tragic" conception of post-Edenic nature, there is virtually no reprieve from human ills except in the garden's all too temporary enclosures. Of course Milton similarly recognizes that because "we bring not innocence into the world, we bring impurity much rather," his "true warfaring" or "wayfaring" Christian must now race for the "immortal garland" in a dust and heat absent from Eden. Yet because Marvell never supposes that "that which purifies us is triall... by what is contrary," he cannot imagine that "youngling" virtue is not truly white or pure but merely "blank" if left untried or pastorally sequestered. Nor does he even remotely share Milton's suspicion that it may be "excrementall[y]" white in the same sense as the whitewashed sepulchers of Matthew 23:27: a pharisaical disguise hiding the inner corruption of dead men's bones (*CP* II: 515–16).

As poems such as "Young Love" and "Little T. C. in a Prospect of Flowers" indicate, Marvell's estimation of untouched or "youngling" innocence as a good in and of itself is precisely the opposite. Although no more Calvinistically "obsessed" with purity than Milton, Marvell's far greater investment in innocence can again be traced to his neo-Calvinist pessimism about the ravages of time and the frailty of the flesh.[31] Rather than being the immanent cure for what ails us, Marvell's time inhibits human wishes and directs them to their true remedy in eternity in ways which anticipate the attitude of eighteenth-century ironists such as Samuel Johnson and Alexander Pope. For he consistently believes that even if the virtuous or innocent player has a chance of discovering the "false dice" which will defeat his "Skill or good fortune," he is only more likely to be "drawn ever deeper" by the corrupt masters of the game, who when "it comes once to a great Stake, will Infallibly Sweep the Table."[32] This picture could hardly be more different from Milton's purification by trial: instead of inevitably winning, the "fairer Player" is almost inevitably overthrown by time, chance, and natural corruption, including his own vain desire to win against all odds. At once "star-crossed" and "hope-crossed," to use Geoffrey Hartman's apt phrase, Marvell's "youngling" player should stake his best chances of maintaining his virtue on avoiding the contest entirely.[33] For as he argues in refuting Samuel Parker's "Pelagian" belief "that we can merit salvation by our own unaided virtue," the presumption "that the superlative merit we see in ourselves will be recognized in heaven, is...mere pride."[34]

This position just as clearly distances Marvell from Milton's Arminian reliance on a rational "Spirit of Truth" (*PR* 1.461–63) to guide the faithful, who for Marvell can be entrusted only to a transcendent Spirit of irresistible grace. Thus "To render men capable of Salvation," he requires a "more extraordinary influence of Gods Spirit" than reason or faith alone: "For mine own part I have, I confess, some reason, perhaps particular to myself, to be diffident of mine own *Moral Accomplishments*, & therefore may be the more inclinable to think I have a necessity of some extraordinary assistance to sway the weakness of my belief, and to strengthen me in good duties" (*RT* 11: 267–68).

Of course Milton, too, trusts in divine grace, just as he stresses as well the folly of actively seeking out moral trials when we may not be as well-prepared as we think. His Eve clearly illustrates the folly of over-confidence in ourselves or in thoughtlessly "putting God to the test" by needlessly courting the path of danger, a course which the Son of *Paradise Regained* rightly rejects as a literally satanic temptation. Yet when confronting such temptations, Milton's spiritual heroes do not segregate their rational insights from their intuitive inspirations, much less their active from their passive reason. Instead, like his Samson, they struggle to achieve the synthesis modeled by the Son and the unfallen Adam and Eve, sinlessly putting divine principles to the test in the spirit of faith and freely questioning "without spot or blame" so long as their love of God remains "entire" (*PL* 5.117–19, 501–02) – that is, entirely free from vainglorious pride. The necessarily thin line between this attitude toward providence and "mere pride" is not nearly as troubling to a Milton who is both personally and philosophically far less diffident of his own moral accomplishments than Marvell, who prefers to see faith fencing or *containing* the "weakness of...belief" while *upholding* a proclivity to "good duties" perhaps otherwise ignored. Finally, because these proclivities wane rather than wax with our distance from original innocence, trials are reminders or tests of human weakness, not of human strength, which he believes is better invested in holding than in leading actions.

Milton scarcely slights original innocence, but since he cannot imagine it apart from growth, experimentation, and maturation, as Barbara Lewalski long ago pointed out, he regards postlapsarian experience as at worst a diminution and at best a continuation of an ever evolving "paradise within" *(PL* 12.587).[35] But since Marvell cannot imagine innocence coexisting with experience, his pastorals instead lament the inevitable loss of Edenic enclosure which Milton unbars from the beginning. This sentiment is especially marked in poems dealing with the threshold separating innocence and experience, the well-known theme of his "Nymph complaining for the death of her Faun." Yet, if anything, it is even more marked in prepubescent nymphs like his little T. C. For what the poet chiefly "admires" or wonders at in T. C. is the ironic contrast presented by his "picture" of her "in a prospect of flowers": the contrast between her Edenic innocence and the hidden sting unconsciously borne by this "virtuous Enemy of Man" (l. 16). While this "Nimph begin[ning] her golden daies" (ll. 1–2) for now innocently tames and names her flowers like Milton's unfallen Eve, unlike her she must play "only with the Roses" (l. 6). This queenly or "rosey" restriction serves subtly to reinforce her Diana-like ability to break love's bow and banners (l. 14), a quality which will "naturally" mature into her "sting," but which in the mature Eve augurs only thornless innocence. Foreseeing T. C.'s inevitable loss of innocence, the Marvellian observer can for now only "compound" (l. 17), mollify, or tame the stings of time before she has grown into her mature powers, an intervention possible only within the figurative enclosure of childhood and the literal "compound" where he is now "laid, / . . . [to] see thy Glories from some Shade" (ll. 23–24).

Although the sexual implications of the scene are no less evident than they are in Milton's Eden, the poet's "catechism" to his heroine is unlike anything learnt by Eve or any of Milton's virgin "Ladies." To "Reform the errours of the Spring" (l. 27), T. C. must retain the stasis of the golden age as long as possible. To do this she must not only elevate the scentless "Tulips" (which still are "sweet," since they are "fair," as Marvell puns, ll. 28–29) to the level of the dethorned roses (l. 30); but, above all, she must make the violets (classical symbols of innocence) "a longer Age endure" (l. 32). This ritual is necessary to reinforce her present stasis within a firmly demarcated garden "sealed" by a supplementary interdiction: if she in any way interferes with nature's course by hastening its "vegetable love" – that is, by willfully plucking "the Buds" instead of tamely receiving the "fruits and flow'rs" with which nature, personified as *Flora*, now actively "courts" this perfectly passive young goddess (ll. 34–36) – then she, too, will be "nipped" in the bud or "blossome" (l. 40) her beauty now bears. Of course no literal death threat is intended on the poet's part, nor need be, for the death threat is already there, fatally implanted in nature's "sting," which "spares" the buds only for so long as they tamely reside within their enclosed gardens.

Despite his strong compulsion to place both the garden and its female goddesses on virtually untouchable pedestals, Marvell's desire to find glimpses of original innocence or natural perfection in the postlapsarian world nevertheless exhibits some strong parallels to Milton's. The difference is that in order to deify the organic-as-innocent, Marvell must personally reenact the loss of paradise in the very act of recreating it. This process is most clearly charted in "The Garden," where after "the Mind, from pleasures less, / Withdraws into its happiness," it begins to lose itself in the mere "resemblance" of natural "kinds." Then, in the very act of "*Transcending*" these merely organic "kinds" by seeking out "Far other Worlds, and other Seas," it ends by "Annihilating all that's made / Into a green Thought in a green Shade" (ll. 41–48; my emphasis). In other words, by a mental withdrawal into a recreation of the eternal Edenic "now" of Augustinian tradition, fantasies of sinless sexuality such as those which surround little T. C. remain free to circulate; the "vegetable love" of the poet's inner garden successively "courts" him (like his T. C. and his Bermudans) with apples, grapes, nectarines, peaches, and melons, until at last seduced by this luxuriant "flesh," "I fall on Grass" (l. 40), the purest form of flesh. But the serious moral of this pastoral joke is simply that in this world the original paradise is accessible only in the mental passivity of daydreams, not in the truly active present of moral and/or temporal action. Whether in "the lost garden...[of] Eden or the Hesperides or England," Marvell must therefore always elevate and distance innocent nature even as he encloses it within the space of his mind, itself a prefiguration of the final enclosure of eternity.[36]

The distance of this transcendently enclosed nature from Milton's immanently and progressively purified nature further explains precisely how and why Marvell's New Eden/Jerusalem belongs to a distinctly different strain of Protestant millenarianism. For while Milton's apocalyptic imagination also demands strategies of projection and deferral, it typically moves in natural/horizontal rather than vertical/transcendental directions. In his sonnet on his twenty-third year, he defers taking stock of his disturbingly blossomless "late spring" by projecting his "ripeness" on to an immanently and organically maturing "Time" guided by "the will of Heav'n." Both forces harmoniously lead him in musical, apocalyptic measure toward his eventual blossoming in his "great task-Master's eye" – but only so long as he cooperatively exerts the "grace to use it so" in this life, which is here already continuous with eternal completion (sonnet 7, ll. 4, 10–14). After the defeat of the Commonwealth, when Milton's Areopagitican project of rebuilding the temple of Truth seems indefinitely if not permanently deferred, he still associates its cleansing with the gradual process of regeneration and the active destruction of false enclosures that his Samson completes at the Philistine temple. But by then Marvell's, not Milton's brand of millenarianism is more in step with a time weary of sectarian enthusiasm and the disastrous civil wars it was thought to provoke.[37] In their wake a full-scale retreat from the prospect of an immanent or actively participatory apocalypse was already well underway among Protestants who both theologically and politically began to reembrace the idea of the apocalypse as an Augustinian *nunc stans*, an eternal space/time of salvation outside of ordinary time altogether.[38]

The vertical/eternal orientation of Marvell's "Resolved Soul" clearly reflects this neotraditional stance. Firmly rejecting the "temptations" of both the natural horizon and the open "plain" of Miltonic combat, he sees the world as a purgatorial vale where the "greenness" of temptation thrives. Salvation thus means resigning himself to the hopelessness of his longings for the perfected or "enamelled" greenness of the transcendent garden – a renunciation essentially consistent with Marvell's secular pastorals. For in either case the inevitable recognition of the incompatibility of innocence and experience, past and future, reinforces his radical dichotomies between the *contemptus mundi* and *carpe diem* traditions – the very dichotomies erased in all of Milton's pastoral visions.[39] Ceaselessly torn between the impurity and uncertainty of the present as well as the incompatibility of body and soul, the "Resolved Soul" must accept the ceaseless conflict between them as the "trial" or price of his eternal reward. The libertine alternative but not the real solution to this dilemma is famously celebrated in "To His Coy Mistress," where once again the garden is clearly not enough. Faced with the inescapable transgression of the classically sacral threshold between field and garden, sun and shade, stream and fountain, Marvell's worldly speaker, like his self-mowing Mower, decides that he must forsake both past and future to live in the active "now" of time's inevitable ravages. This unequal opposite of the eternal now is ironically rejected by the Resolved Soul for equal but opposite reasons: because the ceaseless work of fencing oneself in or out of the gardens presents an inescapable duel inflicted by the unfortunately "dual" legacy of the old and the new Adam, the passive, prophetic past provides the only viable refuge from time.

This legacy decrees that since the body is now "built" in ironically "perfect" proportions for the unenameled greenness of sin to take root, the higher man can earn the perfectly enameled garden of the heavenly paradise only by consistently resisting the "clayey" pleasures of his earthly stopping places: "When the Creator's skill is priz'd, / The rest is all but Earth disguis'd" ("A Dialogue, between The Resolved Soul, and Created Pleasure," ll. 35–36). Obeying a similar ethic, Marvell's "Drop of Dew" remains true to its heavenly home by being "careless of its Mansion new," "scarce touching where it lyes, / But gazing back upon the Skies," and "Trembling lest it grow impure" before blissfully returning to heaven (ll. 4, 11–12, 17). In the meantime it must "shun...the sweet leaves and blossoms green" (l. 23), excluding the wider "World" and only "receiving in the Day" (ll. 29–30), the light of the Sun whose glories the dew "vocationally" reflects by "disdaining" the "dark beneath" in favor of the "bright above" (ll. 31–32). In this way remaining ideally "white, and intire, though congeal'd and chill" as manna, the dewy soul at last dissolves back into "the clear Fountain of Eternal Day" (l. 20), the "Almighty Sun" whose chief "glory" is to receive it. Like the sailors of the "Bermudas," the redeemed soul is thus a classically Puritan good steward, reflecting and dispensing God's gifts, but ready at any time to resign all, "girt and ready to ascend" (l. 35) upon the Son's return to earth or its return to him. Whether that cataclysmic event is the work of the Son himself or of potential delegates such as Cromwell, it descends vertically through the "thick Cloud" which "about that Morning lyes, / And intercepts the Beams of Mortall eyes" with its transcendent new order ("The First Anniversary," ll. 141–42).

While Milton, too, conceives of the light of the Almighty as both a fountain and an overpowering force "dark with excessive bright" (*PL* 3.380), he characteristically imagines redemption not as an external disso-lution but as an organic fruition. Unlike the purgative "re-creation" which Marvell's dew undergoes, Milton's glorious light "dawns" like the dazzling rays of planets which neither decrease nor distill but gradu-ally "*Combust*" or heighten at the "Masters second comming." Human eyesight is thus not violently "intercepted" but gradually accommodated to this overpowering but essentially natural vision, which is compared to

the normal combustion produced by planets and "stars of brightest mag-
nitude that rise and set with the sun, untill the opposite motion of their
orbs bring them to such a place in the firmament, where they may be seen
evening or morning." Rather than as a radically new heavens and new
earth, the apocalypse is imagined as the final "dawning" of the earthly
"light which we have gain'd," to "discover onward things more remote
from our knowledge" (*CP* 11: 549–50). Like Marvell's this vision is obviously indebted to St. Paul's description of the final moment when we will
no longer "see through a glass, darkly," but will know the divine image
"face to face" (1 Cor. 13:12), but Marvell's fateful "ray" remains as inor-
ganic and unimmanent as Jupiter's lightning bolt or Cromwell's sword.
Hence unlike the pilgrims actively perfecting their gardens in Milton's
Eden or his sonnets, Marvell's stewards only stand aside and await
"the mysterious Work, where none withstand" ("The First Anniversary,"
l. 137)

This un-Miltonic apocalypse is most fully explored in "The Coro-
net," where Marvell's shepherd-speaker laments his ineffectual temporal
"wandering" through the merely earthly and rapidly fading simulacra
of the true *hortus conclusus*. There he had gathered flowers from "every
Garden, every Mead" to adorn his "Shepherdesses head" (ll. 5, 8), but
the only result in "real" time (*sub specie aeternitatis*) is that these flowers (now
bearing his only "fruits") have acted as thorns in his savior's "crown." By
crowning the wrong "head," these fleshly "stings" have thus made "many
a piercing wound" (l. 2) in their rightful owner. At first the shepherd believes he can heal these wounds by retracing his path, summoning up
all his "store," and "Thinking (so I my self deceive) / So rich a Chaplet
thence to weave / As never yet the king of Glory wore" (ll. 9–12). But
because *no* earthly beauty or mortal design can escape the serpentine
taint of that first anarchical garden, he is in fact fooled: his wreath turns
into the original tree of that "Serpent old / That, twining in his speckled
breast, / About the flow'rs disguis'd does fold / With wreaths of Fame
and Interest" (ll. 13–16). Because the serpent's stains of "Fame and Interest" infect even the highest reaches of human humility and heavenly
praise, both prayer and praise here actually "debase" the true crown,
"Heavens Diadem" (l. 18), which can be worn by only one incomparable wearer: He who will at last untie the "slipp'ry knots" of body and
soul, serpent and wreath. Finally realizing that he has been only a false
shepherd gathering fading flowers, the poet therefore prays for the true
shepherd to "shatter" both the serpent and "my curious frame / And
let these wither, so that he may die, / Though set with Skil and chosen

out with Care" (ll. 20–24). For only in another, unearthly garden can the mortal "Spoils" on which the poet asks his savior to "tread" at least "crown [his] Feet, that could not crown thy head" (ll. 25–26).

Whereas Marvell's flowers can bloom only by being destroyed and trampled like the fabled grapes of wrath, Milton's final poems, like his earlier treatises, still imagine them immanently *growing* like the seeds of apocalyptic hope which gradually restore Samson's sight: "though blind of sight, / Despised and thought extinguish't quite / With inward eyes illuminated / His fiery virtue rous'd / From under ashes into sudden flame." Like a "combust" planet Samson finally kindles or "blooms" into a self-renewing Phoenix, symbol of inner and outer light (*SA*, 1687–91). This, added to the multitude of examples above, indicates why Milton's elect must actively work toward an immanent apocalypse, while Marvell's elect must remain passive witnesses of a transcendent providence. While not evading worldly action altogether, Marvellian "saints" must resign themselves to their ultimate inability to alter the unregenerate or in any way assist in bringing about the apocalypse. For while the salt still remains obligated to do its maximum leavening work in society, it will never "sweeten" the "putrified" in this world.[40] In accordance with mainline Calvinist doctrine, this "work" assures neither its own success nor the worker's final redemption, and even a good conscience is rarely its own reward: for "in this World a good Cause signifys little, unless it be well defended. A man may starve at the Feast of a good Conscience."[41]

For Marvell confronting the prospect of an indefinitely delayed kingdom of God therefore means recognizing that fallen nature will continue to "work" for whoever holds its reins, bad, good, or indifferent, until the "latest Day" ("The First Anniversary," l. 140). In the meantime the good steward will be willing to support "*Charles*" or any "prudent husbandman" who can sufficiently still "The idle tumult of his factious bees" until "The Insect Kingdome streight begins to thrive / And each work hony for the common Hive" (*Loyall Scott*, ll. 123, 127, 134–35). But while he may help to increase the store of "hony" by culling the "powdered Drones" (ll. 130–31), his final rest is up to God. The resigned, self-distancing dualism of this stance forms a strong if not complete contrast to the Miltonic dialectic between patience and heroic martyrdom alternately adopted by the "twinned" protagonists of his final poems. Simply by reasoning through which kind of heroism is required by their historical situations, Samson and the Son immediately profit from the actively self-rewarding ingredient(s) of their virtue in ways which make their victories strangely anticlimactic. But for the self-renouncing stewards of Marvell's gardens, climaxes like these can only constitute transcendent consummations most devoutly (and eternally) to be wished.

NOTES

1. Citations of Milton's poetry are from *John Milton, Complete Poems and Major Prose*, ed. Merritt Y. Hughes (New York, 1957).
2. Stylistic "temperament" can never be successfully isolated from philosophical or ideological "taste" for the simple reasons suggested by Ann E. Berthoff: "The *circulus methodicus* by which stylistic analysis proceeds – the expectation of matter being determined by an appreciation of manner, the manner judged in the light of what we take to be the matter – requires an attention not only to personality and the history of taste but to the philosophical implications of a characteristic use of language." See *The Resolved Soul: A Study of Marvell's Major Poems* (Princeton, 1970), p. 202.
3. Jane Brown, *The Pursuit of Paradise: A Social History of Gardens and Gardening* (New York, 2000), p. 51.
4. William Shakespeare, *The Tragedy of King Richard II*, I.iv.31, 42, 65–68, in Alfred Harbage (ed.), *William Shakespeare: The Complete Works* (New York, 1969), pp. 644–45. Interestingly, the speech contains all the elements listed by Brown: prophecy, philosophical debate, fertility (or the lack thereof), and intimations of death. The play's role in precipitating the English Revolution is of course debatable; but for the argument that plays like this one made the great rebellion "thinkable," see Franco Moretti, "The great eclipse: tragic form as the deconsecration of sovereignty," in John Drakakis (ed.), *Shakespearean Tragedy* (London, 1992), pp. 45–84.
5. Luther and Calvin are more ambiguous about the Book of Revelation than the English Reformers. Although it originally played only a small part in their theology, they later allowed for a loose identification of the Church of Rome with the whore of Babylon. Neither, however, deeply influences the English millenarian tradition.
6. Katharine R. Firth, *The Apocalyptic Tradition in Reformation Britain, 1530–1645* (Oxford, 1979), pp. 49, 103–06, 154, 174–75, 222–33. For a detailed account of Milton's debt to this tradition, see David Loewenstein, *Milton and the Drama of History: Historical Vision, Iconoclasm, and the Historical Imagination* (Cambridge, 1990). For Bacon's millennialism and Milton's Baconianism, see Charles Webster, *The Great Instauration: Science, Medicine, and Reform 1626–1660* (New York, 1976), pp. 1–6, 15–19, 30, 100–15, 133, 144, 190, 324–29.
7. Warren L. Chernaik, *The Poet's Time: Politics and Religion in the Work of Andrew Marvell* (Cambridge, 1983), pp. 100–01.
8. *Poems on Affairs of State: From The Time of Oliver Cromwell, to the Abdication of K. James the Second* (London, 1697), sig. A3–A5. See also Chernaik, *The Poet's Time*, pp. 63–101.

9. Christopher Hill, "Society and Andrew Marvell," in *Puritanism and Revolution: Studies in the Interpretation of the English Revolution of the Seventeenth Century* (New York, 1958), pp. 353, 362.

10. In *The Matter of Revolution: Science, Poetry, and Politics in the Age of Milton* (Ithaca, 1996), John Rogers subtly and ably sketches the vitalist immanence of Marvell's nature, which causes him to conclude that the transcendental stasis of "Bermudas" is "parodic" (p. 53). But for most readers the island clearly represents the final perfection of that immanence, as I argue in my article "Reversible Space, Linear Time: Andrew Marvell's 'Bermudas,'" *Comitatus* 27 (1990), pp. 72–89.

11. For a fuller exploration of these paradoxes along with a comparison of Milton's and Pascal's God, see my essay, "'Boundless the Deep': Milton, Pascal, and the Theology of Relative Space," *ELH* 63:1 (1996), pp. 45–78.

12. For a similar analysis of the open-ended covenant between divine and human sovereignty in both Milton's poetry and his prose, see Victoria Kahn, "The metaphorical contract in Milton's *Tenure of Kings and Magistrates*," in David Armitage, Armand Himy, and Quentin Skinner (eds.), *Milton and Republicanism* (Cambridge, 1995), pp. 82–105. Her contrasts between Milton and Hobbes are also instructive, especially in relation to my analysis of Marvell's Hobbesian view of time below.

13. For the revolutionary novelty of the idea of emergent revelation and, by implication, of the idea of an emergently free creativity in events and in nature, see Michael Fixler's discussion of the position of the Dissenting Brethren (with whom Milton was aligned) in the Westminster Assembly in *Milton and the Kingdoms of God* (London and Evanston, 1964), pp. 119–21.

14. "The Compendium" attached to *The Key of the Revelation*, trans. Richard More (London, 1643) fol. A5^v. Mede's *Clavis Apocalyptica* was published in three editions (1627, 1632, and 1642) and its translation was ordered by Parliament in 1643.

15. Many critics of this poem have interpreted Marvell as urging Cromwell to take the crown; if they are correct his politics, too, are more "transcendent" than Milton's, for the senior poet's sonnet to Cromwell (like his *Second Defence*) urges precisely the opposite: that unlike the deposed king (and perhaps unlike any human king whatsoever) the Lord Protector should safeguard the nation's spiritual liberties rather than augment his own powers. The main arguments for Marvell's politics as Royalist, monarchist, or at least conservative have been advanced by Joseph A. Mazzeo, "Cromwell as Davidic King," rptd. in Mazzeo, *Renaissance and Seventeenth-Century Studies* (New York, 1964), pp. 183–208, and John M. Wallace, *Destiny His Choice: The Loyalism of Andrew Marvell* (Cambridge, 1968), pp. 106–40. They have been countered both by Warren Chernaik in *The Poet's Time* and numerous articles, and by Annabel Patterson in *Marvell and the Civic Crown* (Princeton, 1978), pp. 70–84; see also ibid., pp. 50–51, n. 1–2, which contains a full review of the earlier criticism on the subject. For an update, see Patterson's *Early Modern Liberalism* (Cambridge, 1997); and for a concise treatment of Milton's place in the

classical republican tradition, see Quentin Skinner, *Liberty before Liberalism* (Cambridge, 1998) as well as the Armitage, Himy, and Skinner collection of essays, *Milton and Republicanism*, cited above. For Milton's consistent refusal to adopt a narrowly partisan view of the apocalypse, see Fixler, *Milton and the Kingdoms of God*. Finally, for Milton's intellectual affinities with Mede and their common historical background, see Ernest Lee Tuveson, *Millennium and Utopia: A Study in the Background of the Idea of Progress* (New York, 1964), pp. 76–92.

16. As Rogers observes in *Matter of Revolution*, the Cromwell poems seem to represent a resurgence of Marvell's belief that the "God of Calvinist theology" intervenes directly in nature and time, although he later returns to his enduring belief in nature "as a self-regulating agent of social change" divorced from divine agency (p. 61; see also p. 54). For a Calvinist reading of Marvell's pastoral lyric, see Marshall Grossman, "Authoring the Boundary: Allegory, Irony, and the Rebus in 'Upon Appleton House,'" in Claude Summers and Ted-Larry Pebworth (eds.), *The Muses Common-Weale: Poetry and Politics in the Seventeenth Century* (Columbia, Mo., 1988).

17. See Rosalie Colie, "Marvell's 'Bermudas' and the Puritan Paradise," *Renaissance News* 10:2 (1957), pp. 75–79, and Margarita Stocker, *Apocalyptic Marvell* (Sussex, 1986). However, Stocker's account suffers from an inaccurate conflation of chiliasm, millennialism, and apocalypticism.

18. Hill, *Puritanism and Revolution*, p. 365.

19. John Carey, "Reversals transposed: an aspect of Marvell's imagination," in C. A. Patrides (ed.), *Approaches to Marvell: The York Tercentenary Lectures* (London, 1978), p. 140.

20. Andrew Marvell, *The Rehearsal Transpros'd and The Rehearsal Transpros'd, The Second Part*, ed. D. I. B. Smith (Oxford, 1971), vol. II, p. 230 (hereafter cited in the text by part and page).

21. This and all subsequent citations are from *Andrew Marvell: The Complete Poems*, ed. George deF. Lord (New York, 1984).

22. Christopher Hill, "Milton and Marvell," in Patrides (ed.), *Approaches to Marvell*, pp. 16–17, 20.

23. For a very telling contrast between the immanently assembled or "discreet" building blocks of government in Milton's *Areopagitica* and the "almost supernatural power" by which the Cromwell of Marvell's "The First Anniversary" must quarry, cut, and forcibly join them, see R. I. V. Hodge, *Foreshortened Time: Andrew Marvell and Seventeenth-Century Revolutions* (Cambridge, 1978), pp. 14–15.

24. See Jon Parkin, "Liberty transpros'd: Marvell and Samuel Parker," in Warren Chernaik and Martin Dzelzainis (eds.), *Marvell and Liberty* (London, 1999), pp. 280–83. Parkin proposes an intriguing "revisionist" argument: that Marvell's greater knowledge of the "monster of Malmesbury" actually allows him to out-Hobbes Parker. This argument could be strengthened by noting that Marvell disagrees with the Erastianism of both Parker and Hobbes, but it does usefully point out that Marvell, like Hobbes, is

"wary of clerical claims to be able to interpret the will of an inscrutable God...in terms of religious doctrine, or of political theory." Milton is of course equally wary of granting these clerical claims, although unlike all of the above he believes that God continues to inform and instruct the individual conscience. For Milton's covenantal theology and contractural politics, see Kahn, "The metaphorical contract."

25. Hodge makes a convincing case for Marvell's intimate knowledge of and sympathy with Hobbes in Hodge, *Foreshortened Time*, pp. 18–22, 56–63, 104–8. See also Christopher Wortham, "Marvell's Cromwell poems: an accidental triptych," in C. Condren and A. D. Cousins (eds.), *The Political Identity of Andrew Marvell* (Aldershot, 1990), pp. 53–84, and Jon Parkin, "Liberty transpros'd."

26. J. G. A. Pocock, "Time, history, and eschatology in the thought of Thomas Hobbes," in *Politics, Language, and Time: Essays on Political Thought and History* (New York, 1971), pp. 156–57.

27. This paragraph briefly summarizes Pocock in "Time, history, and eschatology," pp. 157–72.

28. Pocock, "Time, history, and eschatology," pp. 173–74, 187.

29. Robert Ellrodt, "Marvell's mind and mystery," in Patrides (ed.), *Approaches to Marvell*, p. 219.

30. Carey, "Reversals transposed," p. 153.

31. For Marvell's lack of a deep sense of sinfulness, see Ellrodt, "Marvell's mind and mystery," p. 222.

32. Andrew Marvell, *An Account of the Growth of Popery, and Arbitrary Government in England* (Amsterdam, 1677), facsimile reprint, ed. Gamani Salgado (Farnsborough, 1971), p. 155.

33. Geoffrey Hartman, "Marvell, St Paul, and the body of hope," *ELH* 31 (1964), p. 182.

34. Chernaik, *The Poet's Time*, p. 74.

35. Barbara K. Lewalski, "Innocence and experience in Milton's Eden," in Thomas Kranidas (ed.), *New Essays on* Paradise Lost (Berkeley, 1971), pp. 86–117. Lewalski's reading of Milton's Eden can be usefully contrasted with Earl Miner's classic study of "The death of innocence in Marvell's 'Nymph complaining for the death of her Faun'"; see Michael Wilding (ed.), *Marvell, Modern Judgements* (London, 1969), pp. 273–84.

36. Joseph Summers, "Marvell's 'nature,'" in Wilding (ed.), *Marvell*, p. 144.

37. The "savagery" of *Samson Agonistes* has provoked a number of revisionist critics to regard Samson not as a regenerated but as a fallen antihero. I resist these claims by situating the tragedy in the context of Milton's rejection of the Hobbesian view of natural law as well as the generally Hobbesian tenor of the times. See my essay "The Phoenix and the Crocodile: Milton's Natural Law Debate with Hobbes Retried in the Tragic Forum of *Samson Agonistes*," in Claude Summers and Ted-Larry Pebworth (eds.), *The English Civil Wars in the Literary Imagination* (Columbia, Mo., 1999), pp. 242–70. The standard account of the Hobbesian climate of the Restoration is found

in Samuel Mintz, *The Hunting of Leviathan: Seventeenth-Century Reactions to the Materialism and Moral Philosophy of Thomas Hobbes* (Cambridge, 1962).

38. Pocock, "Time, history, and eschatology," p. 181. For Hobbes's demystification and "infinite" deferral of both the apocalypse and human redemption into a vague future time, see pp. 174–76; for Augustine, see p. 177.

39. For this tension in Marvell, see also Donald M. Friedman, *Marvell's Pastoral Art* (Berkeley, 1971), p. 49. Milton's *Lycidas* as well as his masque spectacularly erase these dichotomies in ways which anticipate the unenclosed pastoral landscapes of *Paradise Lost*.

40. Marvell, *An Account of the Growth of Popery*, p. 79.

41. Quoted from "To a Friend in Persia," in H. M. Margoliouth, *The Poems and Letters of Andrew Marvell*, 2 vols. (Oxford, 1927), vol. II, p. 309.

9

Matter and apocalyptic transformations in Paradise Lost

Juliet Cummins

Milton's depiction of the apocalypse in *Paradise Lost* is unusual in its insistent monism. Apocalyptic literature is typically dualistic, sharply distinguishing between this world and the next and between good and evil as substantial forces.[1] Milton does make use of dualistic concepts, as all monists must to some extent, but he also undercuts them through the presentation of matter and time in the poem. His portrayal of the material transformation of God's creatures at the apocalypse has not hitherto received much attention, but it creates important links between time and eternity.[2] I argue in this chapter that unfallen and regenerate human beings evolve toward a more materially and spiritually refined state on earth, anticipating their reformation at the end of time. Conversely, the unrepentant in *Paradise Lost* undergo a process of degradation which prefigures their eternal state of dissolution. At the apocalypse these contrary material processes are intensified, suggesting that being in this world anticipates being in the next.

Matter provides a connection between earthly and heavenly experience in *Paradise Lost*, creating synchronic continuities between the temporal, human world and the eternal heaven. Thus Raphael answers Adam's question – "what compare?" (5.467) – about angelic and human food by showing him that heavenly experience differs from earthly experience only in degree.[3] Created things consist of "one first matter all" (5.472), but are "more refin'd, more spiritous, and pure, / As neerer to him plac't or neerer tending" (5.475–76). The relationship between humankind and angel is manifested in the difference between their rational powers. Reason is, according to Raphael, "Discursive, or Intuitive; discourse / Is oftest yours, the latter most is ours, / Differing but in degree, of kind the same" (5.488–90). All created things are "of kind the same," but they differ in degree because of their different forms and levels of material purity. Raphael's revelation that there is a material relationship between human beings and angels provides a basis for Milton's construction of diachronic

continuities between this world and the eternal salvation promised to all
believers.

The transformation of the universe at the end of time to the "New
Heav'ns, new Earth" (12.549) is achieved in *Paradise Lost* through material
transmutation. In biblical accounts the new heavens and earth created
at the apocalypse have no necessary relation to the old (2 Pet. 3:13, Rev.
21:1). However, in *Paradise Lost* it appears that the new universe will
be a refined version of the matter of which the original universe was
comprised. Claude Stulting argues in this book that Milton foresees in
Paradise Lost "*another* heaven and earth discontinuous with the original."
He bases this argument on his view that, although Milton sometimes
"attributes to fire a purging effect," it "is also a means of destruction,"
and that the archangel Michael suggests in the epic that the new kingdom
of God "emerges from an apocalyptic destruction of the current order
and the institution of a *regnum Christi* which consists of an *inward* spiritual
reality."[4] The pause in Michael's discourse "Betwixt the world destroy'd
and world restor'd" (12.3) marks a break between the vision of the flood
and the renewed world and, as Stulting notes, it is "a powerful prolepsis
of the eschaton."[5] However, the prolepsis suggests that there *is* material
continuity between the existing world and the postapocalyptic world,
since matter remains constant before and after the flood. Furthermore,
when talking directly about the end of time, Michael tells Adam that,
on Judgment Day, "fire" will "purge all things new" (11.900) and later
that Christ shall "dissolve / *Satan* with his perverted World, then raise /
From the conflagrant mass, purg'd and refin'd, / New Heav'ns, new
Earth" (12.546–49). The words "dissolve," "purg'd," and "refin'd" have
alchemical currency. The word "dissolve" could mean to break into constituent parts, or to return to base matter, as I will discuss shortly. The
words "purg'd" and "refin'd" indicate that the apocalyptic process of
renewal involves a transmutation of base to refined matter. They suggest
that the natural alchemy by which created things are "sublim'd" (4.483)
is only intensified at the apocalypse when a purified world rises from the
"ashes" (3.334) of the fallen world.[6]

The renewal of the heavens and earth at the apocalypse in *Paradise
Lost* betrays the influence of contemporary alchemical theory. The question of whether the earth's matter would ultimately be destroyed was
controversial in the seventeenth century, and its resolution depended on
the applicability of alchemical principles. Alchemy suggested that material could not be destroyed, only altered. Rejecting such a position, the
Calvinist divine George Hakewill argued in 1635 that "the whole world

with all the parts and workes thereof (onely men and Angels, and Devils, and the third Heavens the mansion house of the Saints and blessed Angels, and the place and instruments appointed for the tormenting of the damned excepted) shall bee totally and finally dissolved and annihilated" at the apocalypse, his argument depending on the view that "As they were made out of nothing, so into nothing shall they re-turne againe."[7] However, in his 1605 translation of Joseph Du Chesne's *The Practise of Chymicall and Hermeticall Physicke, for the preservation of health*, Thomas Timme maintained:

> in the fulnesse & last period of time (which approacheth fast on) the 4. Elements (whereof al creatures consist) hauing in euery of thé 2. other Elements, the one putrifying and combustible, the other eternal & incombustible, as the heauen, shall by Gods *Halchymie* be metamorphosed and changed. For the combustible hauing in them a corrupt stinking feces, or drossie matter, which maketh thé subiect to corruption, shal in that great & generall refining day, be purged through fire: And then God wil make new Heauens and a new Earth, and bring all things to a christalline cleernes, & wil also make the 4. Elements perfect, simple, & fixed in themselues, that al things may be reduced to a *Quintessence of Eternitie*.[8]

Similarly David Pareus declared: "Now the *Heaven* and *the Earth* shall not bee new in Substance, but in Qualities, as puritie, brightnesse, and glory:... [Rev. 20.11] doth not signifie, that they should be brought to nothing, but that they are to be purified by fire from all present vanity and defilement." William Ames thought that "The elements shall not be taken away, but changed" and the Glaswegian minister James Durham was of the view that "fire melteth the elements and consumeth them not" and "out of this resulteth this new heaven and earth as a refined lump, from which the drosse is taken away."[9] In his *On Christian Doctrine*, Milton dismisses the question of whether the end of the world involves the "abolition of the world's substance, or only a change in its qualities" as one which "does not really concern us" (*CP* vi: 627). However, the alchemical principles endorsed in *Paradise Lost* suggest that, in the poetic context, the apocalypse effects a change in the world's qualities.

Milton clearly contemplates the continued existence of individuals in the state of eternal salvation, despite his reiteration of the scriptural promise that, at the end of time, God will be "all in all" (3.341, 6.732; 1 Cor. 15:28). Diana Treviño Benet considers that "'All in All'... hints at the erasure of separate identities," but the scriptural and textual contexts do not support this.[10] In the biblical chapter to which Milton alludes, St. Paul suggests that the individual identities of creatures will be preserved by comparing resurrected human beings to stars: "*There is one glory of the sun, and another glory of the moon, and another glory of the stars: for one star differeth from another star in glory. So also is the resurrection of the dead*" (1 Cor. 15:41–42; original italics). As Diane Kelsey McColley argues, Milton maintains "the possibility that those whom God shall be *in* are not reduced from an 'all' meaning a communicating congregation of lives to an 'All' that digests them, but may retain the distinctions that the process of creation proliferates."[11] I would argue that this is more than a possibility. God's declaration that "the just shall dwell" (3.335) in the new heaven and earth, reiterated by Michael (11.901), is unambiguous. The Son also contemplates that apocalyptic union will not preclude individuality when he tells the Father: "with me / All my redeemd may dwell in joy and bliss, / Made one with me as I with thee am one" (11.42–44). The syntax alone suggests that the redeemed are not conflated within the divine "all," and Milton's well-known insistence that the Son and Father are not one in essence, but are rather one in spirit, love, and glory, confirms that the identities of the redeemed will be preserved.[12] Furthermore, Milton's brief portrayal of prelapsarian heaven alludes to a unity with God which is consistent with individuality. Such unity is broken after the anointing of the Son – "All seemd well pleas'd, all seem'd, but were not all" (5.617) – in a line which may imply that Satan has shattered the "all in all" which originally obtained.

The use of organic imagery to describe ontological change in *Paradise Lost* provides continuity between unfallen, fallen, and regenerate states of being and suggests that all three are material. Ontological change manifests itself in material metamorphosis in *Paradise Lost*, either as evolution toward God or as devolution from God. Those who remain obedient to God undergo a natural alchemical process of purification and, correspondingly, their material substance is "by gradual scale sublim'd" (5.483) toward God.[13] This alchemical process occurs through digestion in human beings, as the "concoctive heate" (5.437) of the stomach "converts" (5.492) the "grosser" to the "purer" (5.416).[14] The conversion of food to spirits also effects the conversion of the gross body to the spiritual, Raphael suggesting that "from these corporal nutriments perhaps / Your bodies may at last all turn to Spirit, / ... If ye be found obedient" (5.496–97, 501).

After the Fall of Adam and Eve, such gradual sublimation is no longer possible, but there are indications in the poem that divine grace effects comparable, if limited, physical change. As I will argue below, the fallen are hardened physically and spiritually by sin in the epic. The narrative voice attributes Adam's and Eve's softening to "Prevenient Grace," which "had remov'd / The stonie from thir hearts, & made new flesh / Regenerate grow instead" (11.3–5). Grace functions to repair the damage done by the Fall by removing dead and hardened flesh and replacing it with new, vital body. Stulting argues that "paradise is to be an inward one, divested of any material aspect" and that the eschatological "fruits" of "Joy and eternal Bliss" (12.551) are "inward virtues, abstracted from the natural materiality of creation."[15] But Milton's choice of the richly evocative and sensuous word "fruit" to describe the state of bliss implies otherwise, as does the physical language he uses to depict the effects of grace. The "paradise within" (12.587) which Michael anticipates that Adam and Eve may attain is prefigured in the gift of "new flesh / Regenerate." Grace restores to Adam and Eve their prelapsarian potential to move toward God both physically and spiritually, even though such development is no longer so constant or so easy to maintain.

The change from the fallen, mortal state to a redeemed, immortal one is ontological, an exchange of death for "new life" (3.294) and corruption for incorruption. Recalling Raphael's analogy between gradual sublimation and a tree's metabolic processes, damnation and salvation are described in terms of gardening. The Son "root[s]" the reprobate angels "out of heaven" (6.855), leaving them without the capacity to grow. Eve, the "fairest unsupported Flour" (9.432) is "deflourd" (9.901) at the Fall, both in the sense of being violated (*Oxford English Dictionary*, senses 1, 2) and in the sense that she has been stripped of her identity as a flower (*OED*, sense 4). She is no longer an organic being with the capacity to grow toward God, but becomes like the "bountie of this vertuous Tree" (9.1033), "pluckt" (9.781) and severed from its source. And yet Milton depicts God and the Son as gardeners, repairing damaged plants. Faithful human beings "As from a second root, shall be restor'd" (3.288) by "implanted Grace" (11.23) and shall "live in [the Son] transplanted" (3.293).

Although such horticultural imagery has its origins in traditional Christian literature, in *Paradise Lost* it gains radical implications from its connection with Milton's materialist scale of being. The divine gift of "new life" (3.294) and the Son's "merit / Imputed" (3.290–91) raise human beings to an exalted state of being not achievable on earth. According to Milton's ontology such exaltation also involves material sublimation. Since the Son's "merit" is not merely spiritual but also physical, there is an inference that the faithful may literally partake of the Son's ethereal substance when they come to "live in" him. Milton's depiction of the angels as "pure / Intelligential substances" (5.407–8) provides a precedent for the physical state which human beings might achieve if they are "redeemd" (3.260).

Milton also portrays the physical and spiritual fate of "Bad men and Angels" (3.331) at Judgment Day as a continuation of the metamorphosis they experience in time. The ontological state of unrepentant sinners is depicted in terms of material and spiritual movement away from God and toward the chaotic state of prime matter. It has often been noted that sin causes physical deterioration in *Paradise Lost*, but the regression of creatures toward the "matter unformed and void" (7.233) of chaos has not been explicitly drawn out.[16] Stephen Fallon argues that "evil kicks creatures free on the ontological ladder" but it would be more accurate to say that they are doomed instead perpetually to descend it.[17] "[T]hough spirits of purest light," the falling angels become "gross by sinning grown" (6.660–61). They are "obdur'd" (6.785) both physically and spiritually, the "Deep scars of Thunder...intrencht" (1.601) on Satan's face testifying to "some loss of the essential ductility of angels; former tenuousness has hardened into rigidity."[18] The apostate angels forfeit the "perfect forms" (7.455) which God gave them and become deformed. When Satan arrives in hell, his "form [has] yet not lost / all her Original brightness" (1.591–92), but it becomes progressively distorted through the course of the poem. He comes to resemble his "sin and place of doom obscure and foule" (4.840), in a process of degeneration which culminates in his metamorphosis into "A monstrous Serpent on his belly prone" (10.514). The formal integrity of the faithful angels, which reflects the "lovly" shape of "Vertue" (4.848), becomes with sin "Distorted" and "Transform'd" (2.784–85), as Sin is herself.

The physical degeneration of sinners toward a chaotic state is the result of a loss of identity, as Milton portrays the threatening "deep" or "abyss" as a place of negation and nonbeing. Belial voices his anxiety about losing "this intellectual being" in chaos by being "swallowd up and lost / In the wide womb of uncreated night" (2.147, 149–50) and Satan claims that chaos "with utter loss of being / Threatens him" (2.440–41).[19] John Rumrich argues that "Milton carefully establishes the fallen angels as nonentities" and that "the amazing metamorphosis of the fallen angels signals their loss of identity in God's eyes."[20] The devils do undergo a loss of identity, their names "blotted out and ras'd / By thir Rebellion, from the Books of Life" (1.362–63). However, they do not become "nonentities," but rather acquire "new Names" (1.365) to describe their now corrupted natures. Satan describes himself in his Niphates speech as continually approaching but never reaching destruction, using images of hell and chaos:

> Which way I flie is Hell; my self am Hell;
> And in the lowest deep a lower deep
> Still threatning to devour me opens wide,
> To which the Hell I suffer seems a Heav'n.
>
> (4.75–78)

Satan's description of himself as hell identifies him with death, as hell is "A universe of death, which God by curse / Created evil, for evil only good / Where all life dies, death lives" (2.622–24). Death is the negation of being and identity, the poem's metaphysical evil.[21] However, Satan's is a living death, what Milton describes in *On Christian Doctrine* as the second death, consisting of both "the loss of the supreme good, that is, divine grace and protection and the beatific vision" and "eternal torment" (*CP* VI: 628). Satan's ontological hell is the movement toward chaos or the dissolution of identity, the "lower deep" within the "lowest deep" which threatens to devour him but never finally extinguishes him. It mirrors Jacob Boehme's description of the estate of the damned: "the deeper they desire to throw themselves, the deeper they fall, and yet they finde no end, or bottome."[22] The movement toward ontological chaos is also experienced by the fallen Adam, who complains that he is "from deep to deeper plung'd" into an "Abyss of fears" (10.844, 842). The unrepentant characters in the poem experience a continual loss of being due to their rejection of the source of being.

Adam and Eve also undergo material and formal dissolution as a result of sin, so descending the scale of being. The Father tells the Son that the fallen Adam and Eve must be expelled from paradise as a matter of natural law because:

> Those pure immortal Elements that know
> No gross, no unharmoneous mixture foule,
> Eject him tainted now, and purge him off
> As a distemper, gross to aire as gross,
> And mortal food, as may dispose him best
> For dissolution wrought by Sin, that first
> Distemperd all things, and of incorrupt
> Corrupted.   (11.50–57)

Milton's use of the word "dissolution" in this context is notable for its monistic reference to material, moral, and spiritual disintegration of the self as if they were commensurate (*OED*, sense 5, 1). The material nature of Adam's and Eve's dissolution is conveyed through the contrast between the "pure immortal Elements" of Eden and the "gross" nature of their "tainted" constitutions. The "mortal food" which they must now eat is appropriate to their gross mortal condition. They also undergo a formal disintegration experienced as a corruption of the rational soul which "is the form of man generically" (*The Art of Logic, CP* VII: 234). Just as "the whole man is the soul, and the soul the man" in *On Christian Doctrine* (*CP* VI: 318), the corruption of the soul in *Paradise Lost* is at once physical and spiritual. Sin dissolves and "distempers" the pair by upsetting their internal harmony, shaking "sore / Thir inward State of Mind, calm Region once / And full of Peace, now tost and turbulent" (9.1124–26). The imagery suggests that their souls have become chaotic in form, just as they have become materially closer to the impurity of chaotic matter. Sin also gives rise to a "distemperd brest" (9.1131), a physical condition according to contemporary medical theory. As Roy Flannagan notes: "To distemper is to disarrange the natural order of the four humors, so that a serious imbalance occurs in the human body."[23] This is apparent in the disturbance of the soul's faculties. When Adam and Eve sin, they allow "sensual Appetite" to "Usurp[] over sovran Reason" (9.1129, 1130), and so upset the natural order in the soul where "many lesser Faculties . . . serve / Reason as chief" (5.101–2). The corruption of the incorrupt self through the unnatural decision to sin reverses the process of purification ordained by God, and substitutes a contrary process of ontological decay.

Michael alludes to the apocalyptic fate of the fallen in language evocative of their temporal decline when he prophesies that the Son will come again to "dissolve / *Satan* with his perverted World" (12.546–47). Many scholars have suggested that the word "dissolve" indicates that Satan and his world will be annihilated.[24] An alternative interpretation, put forward by Leonora Leet Brodwin, is that the word argues that Satan, the perverted world, and presumably "bad men" will be "return[ed] to the state of primordial chaos" at Judgment Day and their identities destroyed.[25] Recalling that chaos is "perhaps [nature's] Grave" (2.911), Brodwin argues that "the final hurling of '*Grave*' through '*Chaos*' [10.635–36] means that the conflagration of the world will reduce it to its original 'dark materials' [2.916]." This, she contends, is consistent with Milton's materialist view expressed in *On Christian Doctrine* that "no created thing can be finally annihilated." The "New Heav'ns, new Earth" (12.549) will then be created "from the same chaos to which the old polluted world had been reduced."[26] Brodwin's construction of Milton's eschatology is attractive as it is consistent with Milton's materialism, whereas the annihilationist theory is not. However, it begs the question of how the identities of the redeemed will be preserved in the final conflagration, and it is contrary to many indications in the text that the damned will experience eternal torture in hell.

There is much evidence in the poem for the continued existence and suffering of the unrepentant after Judgment Day. The "immortal" (1.53) fallen angels are "condemn'd / For ever now to have thir lot in pain" (1.607–8), Satan contemplates "endless pain" (2.30) and "eternal woe" (4.70), Death tells Satan that he and the fallen angels "are here con-demn'd / To waste Eternal dayes in woe and pain" (2.693–95), and Raphael tells Adam and Eve that Satan is plotting to make them "par-take / His punishment, Eternal miserie" (6.903–4). Milton's God adds the weight of his authority to such perceptions. He declares: "Bad men and Angels . . . arraignd shall sink / Beneath [the Son's] Sentence, Hell her numbers full, / Thenceforth shall be for ever shut" (3.331–33). Then, when Sin and Death are "cramm'd and gorg'd," the Son will "obstruct the mouth of Hell / For ever, and seal up his ravenous Jawes" (10.632, 636–37). As Brodwin acknowledges: "The orthodox suggestion of these lines is that . . . the shutting of hell . . . would consign [evil creatures] to an eternity of torment." Brodwin argues that the lines do not necessarily imply "the perpetuation of hell" and that the shutting of hell is consistent with its perishing in the final conflagration.[27] However, the interpreta-tion is strained and inconsistent with other statements in the poem about the eternal punishment of the damned and the eternal existence of hell. Milton's God proclaims that the disobedient angel will be "Cast out from God and blessed vision" and fall "Into utter darkness, deep ingulft, his place / Ordaind without redemption, without end" (5.613–15). Consid-ering these lines Brodwin acknowledges that hell is elsewhere described as a place of "utter darkness" (2.72), but maintains that the "utter darkness" of the apostate angels signifies their "reduction to [chaos's] 'dark mate-rials' (II, 916)."[28] Yet God does not speak of two falls, one into hell and a later one into oblivion, and the "utter darkness" of hell is clearly Satan's initial destination. Furthermore, the word "place" seems to imply that Satan's eternal doom is both a physical location and a spiritual state.[29]

Michael's prophesy that Christ will "dissolve / *Satan* with his perverted World," which is the key source of both the annihilationist theory and the return-to-chaos theory, probably refers not to the dissolution of Satan himself, but rather to the dissolution of Satan's power. Reading the pas-sage in 1695, Patrick Hume annotated it as follows:

XII.547 To dissolve Satan with his perverted world. To destroy the Kingdom of
Satan, When the judgment of this world shall be, and the Prince of this world
shall be cast out John 12.31. When the Prince of this world shall be judged, John
16.11.[30]

This interpretation is, as Hume points out, consistent with the Gospel
according to John, and it also gains strength from 2 Peter 3, to which
Milton alludes with the word "dissolve":

10. But the day of the Lord will come as a thief in the night; in the which the
heavens shall pass away with a great noise, and the elements shall melt with
fervent heat, the earth also and the works that are therein shall be burned up.
    11. *Seeing* then *that* all these things shall be dissolved, what manner *of persons*
ought ye to be in *all* holy conversation and godliness,
    12. Looking for and hasting unto the coming of the day of God, where the
heavens being on fire shall be dissolved, and the elements shall melt with fervent
heat?

The dissolution of "*Satan* with his perverted World" in Milton's poem is
equivalent to "the earth also and the works that are therein" being burnt
in the scriptural account. It is, as Michael has just pointed out, "Not
by destroying *Satan*, but his works / In thee and thy Seed" (12.393–95),
that the Son brings salvation to humanity. Milton appears to consider
that while perverted works will dissolved with the earth itself, the creatures will not be involved in such dissolution. As Michael explains, the
Son:

>   shall come,
> When this worlds disolution shall be ripe,
> With glory and power to judge both quick and dead,
> To judge th' unfaithful dead, but to reward
> His faithful, and receave them into bliss,
> Whether in Heav'n or Earth.   (12.458–63)

The "unfaithful dead" and the "faithful" are punished or rewarded, but
are not destroyed in the final conflagration. The unfaithful are sent to
hell before its closure, and before the new heaven and earth rise from
the ashes of the old world:

>   Hell, her numbers full,
> Thenceforth shall be for ever shut. Mean while
> The World shall burn, and from her ashes spring
> New Heav'n and Earth, wherein the just shall dwell
>   (3.332–35)

The dissolution of "*Satan* with his perverted World," then, does not signal the destruction of Satan himself, but rather the end of his role as God's adversary, his identity as the "Prince of aire" (12.454).

There is a sense in which the damned in hell are condemned to dissolution, as they continue to experience the spiritual and physical degeneration anticipated in time. Milton portrays sin as its own punishment, because it corrupts the body and soul. In *Comus* the Elder Brother describes evil as eternally self-destructive, a kind of chaos of "eternal restless change":

> But evil on it self shall back recoyl,
> And mix no more with goodness, when at last
> Gather'd like scum, and settl'd to itself
> It shall be in eternal restless change
> Self-fed, and self-consum'd.   (ll. 593–97)

In this image unadulterated evil at once feeds on and consumes itself without destroying itself. Such "eternal restless change" is the nature of the punishment of the damned. The spiritual hell Satan articulates is to continue indefinitely, as his punishment is "Eternal miserie" (6.903). His discovery of a lower deep in the lowest deep is repeated throughout eternity, a movement toward a destruction which is never reached. The identities of the fallen continue to disintegrate chaotically, but are never extinguished. The devils' thoughts of "sweet / Compulsion" (9.472–73) shall "wander through Eternity" (2.147), in realization of evil's endless circularity. Sin's hellhounds, which return into the womb to "howle and gnaw / [Her] Bowels" (2.799–800) before "bursting forth / Afresh" (2.800–01), symbolize such destructive and compulsive repetition, as does the image of the devils eating ash which appears to be "Frutage fair" (10.561), then falling "Into the same Illusion" and eating it again (10.570). Such self-deception and self-enthrallment are the eternal fate of those divorced for ever from God.

This spiritual state of the damned has its physical expression in Milton's allusions to the eternally self-consuming fires which they endure. As John Rumrich argues, "the hot Hell that alwayes in [Satan] burns" (9.467) is both physical and spiritual. Rumrich notes that in the Renaissance anger was commonly thought to be a burning of spirits around the heart, and proposes that "Milton depicts a Satan whose insides have in fact caught fire because of this congregation of inflammatory spirits."[31] The devils, then, suffer both internal inflammation and the "great Furnace" (1.62) of hell, the "fiery Deluge, fed / With ever-burning Sulphur unconsum'd"

(1.68–69). The idea of eternal fires which do not consume their object was well-established. St. Augustine maintained that bodies could remain unconsumed and alive in fire eternally and gave the example of the salamander living in fire.[32] Similarly George Sandys held that the fire of hell "ever feeds on the bodies of the damned; which suffer no diminution; but afford unconsumable nourishment."[33] These fires which always consume but never annihilate the damned must contribute to eternal, physical "dissolution wrought by Sin" (11.55), bodily degeneration which is neverending.

Another image of the perpetual punishment of the damned in *Paradise Lost* evokes their eternal burning by association. As Raphael explains to Adam and Eve, in order to end the War in Heaven the Son determines to "rid heav'n of these rebell'd, / To thir prepar'd ill Mansion driven down / To chains of darkness, and th' undying Worm" (6.737–39). Alistair Fowler notes that "At *Mark* ix 44 hell is 'where their worm dieth not'."[34] This passage in Mark itself refers to Isaiah 66:24, where the Lord says that the faithful shall one day "look upon the carcasses of the men that have transgressed against me: for their worm shall not die, neither shall their fire be quenched." According to the *Oxford English Dictionary*, "worm" could refer to a maggot or an earthworm which was supposed to eat dead bodies in the grave (sense 6a), and was used figuratively to refer to the pains of hell (sense 6b). Although the *OED* records Milton's usage of the word in this context as figurative, the materialist imagery in the poem suggests it might also be literal. Satan is described by Adam as a "false worm" (10.1068), the word here being used in the sense of a serpent or snake (*OED*, sense 1). Just as Satan becomes the burning hell which tortures him but is never "quenched," so, too, he may be eternally eaten by the worm he has become, but never consumed. These images suggest that the eternal punishment of the damned is a continuation of the dissolution experienced before the apocalypse, a dissolution brought on by sin itself.

Milton's insistence on the continuities between pre- and postapocalyptic states of being supports what Walter Schmithals calls a "dualism of decision," as it indicates that salvation is partly in the control of the individual.[35] Consistent with Milton's Arminianism, ontological change in *Paradise Lost* is caused by a creature's exercise of free will. Obedience to God ensures one's elevation on the scale of being, just as the decision to rebel against God ensures one's descent. At the apocalypse the faithful and the damned are effectively polarized on the ontological scale. The faithful are exalted to a state of being close to that of the Son, while the damned experience a near chaotic dissolution of body and spirit. This perspective allows Milton to emphasize the importance of faith and "Deeds to [one's] knowledge answerable" (12.582) in the present, as faith and works substantially change the individual. Just as the "Hell" and "lowest deep" (4.75–76) within the unrepentant become more intensely experienced in eternity, the "paradise within" (12.587) in the temporal world provides an anticipation of the final paradise, when matter and spirit are in harmony with each other and with God. Since the apocalypse intensifies the contrary processes of metamorphosis experienced by the faithful and by the unrepentant, free choices on earth determine the nature of human beings' fate at the end of time.

NOTES

1. For the typical dualism of apocalyptic literature, see Walter Schmithals, *The Apocalyptic Movement: Introduction and Interpretation*, trans. John E. Steely (Nashville, 1975), pp. 22–23. See also John T. Shawcross's chapter in this book.
2. Discussions of the apocalypse by Leland Ryken, C. A. Patrides, Michael Fixler, Austin C. Dobbins, and Helen Wilcox barely mention the connection between matter and apocalyptic transformation. See Ryken, *The Apocalyptic Vision in* Paradise Lost (Ithaca, 1970); Patrides, "'Something like Prophetick strain': apocalyptic configurations in Milton," in C. A. Patrides and Joseph Wittreich (eds.), *The Apocalypse in English Renaissance Thought and Literature: Patterns, Antecedents and Repercussions* (Manchester, 1984); Fixler, "The Apocalypse within *Paradise Lost*," in Thomas Kranidas (ed.), *New Essays on* Paradise Lost (Berkeley and Los Angeles, 1969), pp. 131–78; Dobbins, *Milton and the Book of Revelation: The Heavenly Cycle* (University, Alabama, 1975); and Wilcox, "'Is this the end of this new glorious world?': *Paradise Lost* and the beginning of the end," *Essays and Studies* 48 (1995), pp. 1–15. Ryken examines Milton's monism, but because "The traditional concept of futurity... is not part of [his] definition" of "apocalyptic," but rather it means for him "an ideal state which is infinitely desirable" (p. 3), he discusses monism only in relation to the scale of being and Milton's presentation of light in *Paradise Lost* (pp. 34–41). Nor is the relationship between matter and the apocalypse discussed in any detail in studies of Milton's materialism such as William Kerrigan's *The Sacred Complex: On the Psychogenesis of* Paradise Lost (Cambridge, Mass., and London, 1983), Stephen M. Fallon's *Milton Among the Philosophers: Poetry and Materialism in Seventeenth-Century England* (Ithaca, 1991); John Rogers's *The Matter of Revolution: Science, Poetry, and Politics in the Age of Milton* (Ithaca, 1996); and John Rumrich's *Matter of Glory: A New Preface to* Paradise Lost (Pittsburgh, 1987).
3. All citations of Milton's poetry are from Roy Flannagan (ed.), *The Riverside Milton* (Boston, 1998).
4. See chapter 10, pp. 197, 194, 196, 197 (original italics).
5. Ibid., p. 194.

6. On alchemy in *Paradise Lost*, see note 13 below.

7. George Hakewill, *An Apologie or Declaration of the Power and Providence of God In the Gouernment of the WORLD* (3rd edn., London, 1635), p. 565.

8. Joseph Du Chesne, *The Practise of Chymicall and Hermeticall Physicke, for the preservation of health*, trans. Thomas Timme (London, 1605), rptd. (Amsterdam, 1975), A2.

9. David Pareus, *A Commentary Upon the Divine Revelation of the Apostle and Evangelist John*, trans. Elias Arnold (Amsterdam, 1644), p. 550; William Ames, *The Marrow of Sacred Divinity, Drawne Out of the Holy Scriptures, and the Interpreters thereof, and brought into Method*, trans. from Latin (London, 1642), p. 189; and James Durham, *A Commentarie Upon the Book of Revelation* (London, 1658), p. 747.

10. Diana Treviño Benet, "'All in All': The Threat of Bliss," in Charles W. Durham and Kristin A. Pruitt (eds.), *"All in All": Unity, Diversity and the Miltonic Perspective* (Selinsgrove and London, 1999), pp. 48–66, especially p. 48.

11. Diane Kelsey McColley, "'All in All': The Individuality of Creatures in *Paradise Lost*," in Durham and Pruitt (eds.), *"All in All,"* pp. 21–47, especially pp. 24–25 (original italics).

12. In his *On Christian Doctrine*, Milton maintains that the Son and the Father "are one in that they speak and act as one" and that they "are one in the same way as we are one with him: that is, not in essence but in love, in communion, in agreement, in charity, in spirit, and finally in glory" (*CP* VI: 220). He also observes that it "appears that each man will rise with the same identity as he had before" and then notes that we "learn of the transformation of the living in I Cor. xv. 51, 52" (*CP* VI: 620–21). For the controversy over Milton's authorship of the treatise, see the chapters by William Hunter and John Shawcross in this book.

13. For the alchemical basis for Milton's scale of nature, see Lyndy Abraham, "Milton's *Paradise Lost* and 'the sounding alchymie'," *Renaissance Studies* 12 (1998), pp. 261–76, especially pp. 270–71; Kerrigan, *The Sacred Complex*, pp. 221–23; and Stulting's chapter in this book, pp. 189–90.

14. Kerrigan, *The Sacred Complex*, pp. 219–20.

15. See Stulting's chapter in this book, pp. 197, 193.

16. See Kerrigan, *The Sacred Complex*, p. 242; Fallon, *Milton Among the Philosophers*, pp. 208–9, 213; and Rumrich, *Matter of Glory*, pp. 84–86.

17. Fallon, *Milton Among the Philosophers*, p. 186. Fallon also associates "downward ontological movement" with evil (p. 209), but does not identify this movement as a physical and spiritual journey toward chaos.

18. Ibid., p. 208. John Rumrich argues that "Milton . . . presents the fallen angels, like the matter of hell, being metamorphosed by burning sulphur into darker, more solid, almost metallic, substances." See *Matter of Glory*, p. 86.

19. For the loss of identity in chaos, see Michael Lieb, *The Dialectics of Creation: Patterns of Birth and Regeneration in "Paradise Lost"* (Amherst, 1970), pp. 21–5, 49, 88–9.

20. Rumrich, *Matter of Glory*, pp. 88–89.
21. Fallon, *Milton Among the Philosophers*, p. 185.
22. Jacob Behmen [Boehme], *XL Questions Concerning the Soule Propounded by Dr Balthasar Walter and answered by Jacob Behmen, written in the German language 1620* (London, 1647), p. 134.
23. Flannagan (ed.), *The Riverside Milton*, p. 661n.
24. Critical suggestions that Satan will be annihilated are made in *The Complete Poems of John Milton*, ed. John Carey and Alistair Fowler (London, 1968), p. 1054n; Robert M. Myers, "'God Shall be All in All': The Erasure of Hell in *Paradise Lost*," *Seventeenth Century* 5 (1990), pp. 43–53, especially p. 50; and Flannagan (ed.), *The Riverside Milton*, p. 706n. Albert C. Labriola also maintains that "the Second Coming is described as a condition of total destruction, followed by a process of judgment whereby the damned are consumed but the faithful saved": "The Medieval View of Christian History in *Paradise Lost*," in John Mulryan (ed.), *Milton and the Middle Ages* (Lewisburg, 1982), pp. 115–32, especially p. 125.
25. Leonora Leet Brodwin, "The Dissolution of Satan in *Paradise Lost*: A Study of Milton's Heretical Eschatology," *Milton Studies* 8 (1975), pp. 165–207, especially pp. 167, 173.
26. Ibid., p. 173.
27. Ibid., p. 170.
28. Ibid., p. 182.
29. My interpretation of these lines also provides support for Milton's authorship of *On Christian Doctrine*, as it suggests that the two are consistent. The author of *On Christian Doctrine* is of the view that the damned will suffer "eternal torment" and that hell, the place of eternal torment, will not be destroyed at the apocalypse (*CP* vi: 628, 630).
30. Patrick Hume, *Annotations on Milton's* Paradise Lost (London, 1695).
31. Rumrich, *Matter of Glory*, p. 85.
32. Augustine, *The City of God against the Pagans*, ed. and trans. R.W. Dyson (Cambridge, 1998), p. 1048.
33. George Sandys, *Ovid's Metamorphosis Englished*, ed. Karl H. Hulley and Stanley Vandersall (Lincoln, 1970), p. 211, cited in Rumrich, *Matter of Glory*, p. 85.
34. Carey and Fowler (eds.), *The Poems of John Milton*, p. 762n.
35. Schmithals, *The Apocalyptic Movement*, p. 160.

10

"New Heav'ns, new Earth": apocalypse and the loss of sacramentality in the postlapsarian Books of Paradise Lost

Claude N. Stulting, Jr.

In *De Doctrina Christiana* Milton describes the glorification of humankind in terms that suggest a richly tangible and material environment: "Our glorification," he writes, "will be accompanied by the renovation of, and our possession of, heaven and earth and all those creatures in both which may be useful or delightful to us" (*CP* VI: 632). So, too, in *Paradise Lost* there are some intriguing intimations that the redemption of humankind – and ultimately the eschatological restoration of the entire creation – will reproduce the material conditions of prelapsarian existence. In the "Argument" to Book 10, for example, Milton describes how God foresees the victory over Sin and Death and the "renewing of all things." When God speaks to the heavenly host on these matters, he declares that when Sin and Death will finally "obstruct the mouth of hell," "Then heaven and earth renewed shall be made pure / To sanctity that shall receive no stain" (10.636, 638–39). And the joyful choral response to God's proclamations affirms the Son as the "Destined restorer of mankind, by whom / New heaven and earth shall to the ages rise, / Or down from heaven descend" (10.646–48). Some commentators see in such passages an equivalence between beginning and end, a congruence between humankind's prelapsarian life and postlapsarian destiny. Michael Fixler, for one, writes that "Milton apparently regarded the conditions of the beginning and the end as essentially identical, with history cyclically returning upon itself, so to speak, once man was to be absolutely restored to beatitude." This identity is, for Fixler, as for Milton, the key to the epic's theodicy; it is "that fulfillment which ultimately best justifies the ways of God to Man."[1] Indeed, as the heavenly choir sings in response to God's intentions to renew heaven and earth, "Just are thy ways, / Righteous are thy decrees on all thy works; / Who can extenuate thee?" (10.643–45). More recently Diane Kelsey McColley, in her cogent defense of the integrity of individual identities in *Paradise Lost* – human, animal, and angel – when God shall be "All in all," has described Milton's eschatological cosmos as one that is replete with materiality.[2] And in this book Juliet Cummins argues that Milton's apocalyptic universe is a transfiguration of the matter of ordinary existence. She writes that the "material transformation of God's creatures at the apocalypse" results in a "material continuity between the existing world and the postapocalyptic world."[3]

What I want to argue in this essay is that the possibilities intimated by both *Paradise Lost* and *De Doctrina Christiana* are not fully realized in the epic. A closer look at humankind's prelapsarian and apocalyptic conditions in *Paradise Lost* reveals their discontinuity, one which not only dilutes the epic's rich sacramentality but also undercuts the success of Milton's theodicy.

PRELAPSARIAN SACRAMENTALITY

In the prelapsarian books of Milton's *Paradise Lost*, there is a rich sacramental vision of nature. This is to say two things about the natural world as it functions in *Paradise Lost* before the Fall. First, nature – not history – is the means by which God is present in the world; nature is that in and through which God is immanent in creation. Second, therefore, nature is the means by which Adam and Eve come to live in communion with God – what Eastern Christianity calls *theosis*, or deification. In *Paradise Lost* this sacramental vision finds its focus in the act of eating, specifically through Adam's and Eve's sharing of a proto-eucharistic meal with Raphael (Book 5). Milton's eucharistic sense here suggests a sacramental vision of nature which reiterates the theological vision of the early Greek Fathers, especially Gregory of Nyssa and St. John of Damascus, whose writings, among other Eastern Fathers, Milton had read.

Gregory of Nyssa expounds his eucharistic theology in the *Catechetical Oration*. Commenting first on the physiology of nutrition, he points out that eating effects a transformation of the elements of food into our bodily nature. "In me," Gregory writes, "[bread and wine] become blood and flesh, since . . . the food is changed by the power of assimilation into the form of the body."[4] Developing his views from Aristotle's concept of hylomorphism, Gregory argues that the elements (*stoicheia*) which constitute the form (*eidos*) of bread and wine are rearranged and assume a different bodily form of flesh and blood.[5] The elements themselves remain the same, but their altered relation (form) endows them with a different power which is appropriated by the human body.[6] What is true universally of all persons was also true of the incarnate Word; Christ, too, needed to eat in order to live. But Christ's body was transformed by

God into glory: "by the indwelling of God the Word," Gregory writes, "that body was raised to divine dignity." So the bread and wine which Christ's body transfigures through eating *themselves* acquire the divine property of immortality. The elements of bread and wine become not merely mortal flesh and blood but *sanctified* flesh and blood.[7]

The same process occurs in the Eucharist. Just as God's Word sanctified Christ's body which was bread, so in the Eucharist the elements of bread and wine are sanctified by the same consecrating power of the Word. The only difference is that the process of assimilation for Christ was gradual, whereas the eucharistic change is immediate. In both cases, however, the elements which constitute bread and wine receive a new form. When the consecrated bread and wine are eaten by believers, God unites himself with humankind so that it, too, "by its union with what is immortal, may share in incorruptibility." Through the power of the blessing, God changes (*metastoicheiosas*) the visible elements of the sacrament into immortal body which becomes a means of humankind's deification.[8]

Gregory's eucharistic theology is duplicated by St. John of Damascus in his *On the Orthodox Faith*.[9] But what is unique in St. John's account is his extensive use of images of fire and heat to portray the interaction between humankind and the elements of the Eucharist. "Let us draw near to it," he writes:

> with an ardent desire, . . . and let us apply our eyes and lips and brows and partake of the divine coal, in order that the fire of the longing, that is in us, with the additional heat derived from the coal may utterly consume our sins and illumine our hearts, and that we may be inflamed and deified by the participation in the divine fire.[10]

The images of fire assume a more specifically alchemical flavor, as they do in Milton. The Eucharist, he writes, is a "*purging* from all uncleanness: should one receive base gold, . . . [the alchemists] *purify* it by the critical *burning* lest in the future we be condemned with this world."[11]

For both Gregory of Nyssa and St. John of Damascus, it is in the Eucharist that humankind's dual vocations as sovereign and priest of creation converge; liturgically articulating and summing up those two roles, the Eucharist confers upon them their fullest and most focused expression. The two elements of the sacrament constitute this focus. Because humankind is the sovereign of creation, it does not harvest the grain of the field or the grapes of the vine and take them in their natural state to the eucharistic table; rather, humankind first transforms the products of nature by imparting to them a new form. The blessings of God in nature are given a new shape. So grain is made into bread, and grapes are made into wine; humankind reconfigures the constituent elements of grain and grape and gives each a new *eidos*. Only then does humankind offer up the elements in the Eucharist. This defines what it means to be priest – to return one's blessings to God in thanksgiving. In the Eucharist humankind sacramentally articulates its gratitude in giving back to God the transfigured fruits of the earth; in this the whole world is restored as gift and blessing. Such a sanctification of nature through the Eucharist renews the world and makes it into a sacrament, into communion with God.

In Milton's *Paradise Lost* Adam and Eve also find their *telos* as the priests of creation. As with the Greek Fathers, Milton's Adam and Eve regard creation as a blessing; not just the food with which they are provided but *all* of creation is for them, as Chrysostom puts it, a "lavish table," and, as Gregory of Nazianzus says, an "abundant banquet." Both Adam and Eve live in awareness of what Satan, ironically, tells Eve in his temptation of her, that "all things [are] thine / By gift" (9.539–40). In response to this apprehension of creation as blessing, Adam and Eve articulate a profound sense of gratitude.

Adam is created to be a creature who, as Raphael declares, is "grateful to acknowledge whence his good / Descends" (7.511–12). Milton creates Adam and Eve *homo adorans*, worshiping beings, who offer thanks to God for His blessings. As Eve acknowledges to Adam: "For we to him indeed all praises owe, / And daily thanks" (4.444–45). It is through such worship that Adam and Eve embody the prelapsarian possibility of humankind's sacramental relation to nature as sovereign and priest of creation.

But the eucharistic dimension of their worship is most evident in those scenes involving food. After Satan lands in paradise, he observes Adam and Eve at the conclusion of their "sweet gardening labor": "They sat them down, . . . and made ease / More easy, wholesome thirst and appetite / More grateful, to their supper fruits they fell" (4.327–31). And later, in Book 5, when Raphael first approaches Adam and Eve, Adam comments:

> well we may afford
> Our givers their own gifts, and large bestow
> From large bestowed, where nature multiplies
> Her fertile growth, and disburdening grows
> More fruitful, which instructs us not to spare.
> (5.316–20)

The eucharistic impulse to offer back to God the very bounty he has provided is also heard in Eve's response to Adam (5.326–30) and is evidenced in the subsequent "haste" with which she prepares the meal.[12]

Eve's work is perhaps most illuminating for the eucharistic impulse as it relates to her sovereign role. Eve considers carefully "What choice to choose for delicacy best" and "What order, so contrived as not to mix / Tastes, not well joined, inelegant, but bring / Taste after taste upheld with kindliest change" (5.331–36). In choosing only the most delectable foods and deciding upon the best order for them, Eve creates beauty, a pleasing and harmonious form, in a way reminiscent of God's adorning of the cosmos. Similarly, when preparing the meal, Eve "crushes" the grape for drink; she "presses" "sweet kernels" with which she "tempers" "dulcet creams"; and she "strews the ground / With rose and odours" (5.344–49). Not simply offering the food to Raphael as it is found in the garden, Eve takes what is given to her by nature and transforms it into something else. The preparation of the meal, in short, is an exercise in sovereignty, in the creation of form amid nature's bounty.

More significantly, however, it is in an act of worship that Eve gathers and prepares for Raphael the food which is a "tribute large" (5.343–45). The meal is created as an offering to God, an expression of thanksgiving, a returning to God of what he has already provided. In short it is a eucharistic meal. When Adam invites Raphael to eat, he offers "These bounties which our nourisher, from whom / All perfect good unmeasured out, descends, / To us for food" (5.398–400). As sovereigns of creation Adam and Eve creatively provide form to the earth; as priests of creation they eucharistically offer back to God that transfigured creation.

These various sacramental impulses are eloquently, if ironically, summed up on the morning of Adam's and Eve's Fall, when flowers and "all things that breathe, / From the earth's great altar send up silent praise / To the creator," in the form of "morning incense," just as Adam and Eve offer him "vocal worship" (9.194–98). The earth is an altar – not indeed some Protestant postlapsarian sacrificial altar upon which to make offerings to "satisfy" an offended god – but an altar upon which Adam and Eve eucharistically return to God the gift of creation. This is the altar upon which sacrifice is to be understood not as expiation but as the expression of thanksgiving which defines the nature of humankind as priest.[13]

Thus is the blessing of nature for Adam and Eve a sacrament of God's presence. Through their sovereign and priestly vocations, Adam and Eve transfigure creation and make it into a means of communion with God. Nature itself becomes the very means of worshiping God and participating in his presence.[14] These sacramental impulses clearly resonate with the eucharistic sensibility of the Greek Fathers.[15]

But Adam's and Eve's sacramental relation to nature also extends to the very act of eating, which for Milton, obviously, bears a significance that resonates throughout the poem. In the meal which Adam and Raphael share, and in their accompanying discourse, we see how food is transfigured in other ways. It is, first, transfigured physiologically in the act of eating. In being assimilated by the body, food becomes something else. This physiological process, in turn, becomes the means to yet another transfiguration. The transfigured and eucharistically proffered food *as eaten* becomes itself a means of communion with God, that is, the means of attaining a kind of *theosis* or deification. This also echoes the mind of the early Greek Fathers.

In response to Adam's query concerning the diet of angels, Raphael reassures Adam that angels, just as humans, need sustenance: "food alike those pure / Intelligential substances require, / As doth your rational" (5.407–09). Angels are endowed with all the senses – sight, smell, hearing, touch, and, most importantly, taste – by which they "concoct, digest, assimilate, / *And corporeal to incorporeal turn*" (5.412–13; my emphasis). "For know," Raphael assures Adam, "whatever was created, needs / To be sustained and fed" (5.414–16). So angels only instance a larger cosmic exchange in the scale of nature wherein the lower feeds the higher and the "grosser feeds the purer" (5.416). All creation, Raphael points out, feeds on – and transfigures – what is heavier than itself: earth feeds the sea, earth and sea feed the air, the air feeds the moon and "fires / Ethereal," and the moon the "higher orbs" (5.416–26). The transfiguration from body to spirit defines the heart of this process.

The specific dynamics of this transformation emerge more clearly when Adam and Raphael proceed to eat, the angel employing "concoctive heat / To transubstantiate" his food (5.437–38). The term transubstantiate calls to mind the Roman Catholic doctrine of the Eucharist in which the "accidents" of the bread and wine apprehended by the senses remain the same; and in which the substance of the elements – their underlying, inner reality – apprehended by the mind becomes the Body and Blood of Christ.[16] But this is not the process Milton has in mind here. What he describes approaches more nearly Gregory of Nyssa's eucharistic theology.[17]

As we saw earlier, Gregory describes the Eucharist in hylomorphic terms, terms which differentiate it from transubstantiation. So, too, is it in Milton's account of eating. For Milton, a materialist, all things are made of the same substance, the same primary matter; it is the *form* of that substance which provides it with a unique identity vis-à-vis any other object.[18] So in the process of eating, the heat of digestion transmutes matter into different (and higher) forms. The *stoicheia* of food are rearranged into a different order so that they assume another *eidos*. It is a microcosmic variant of the macrocosmic process which Raphael describes.

Milton's analogy between physiological and alchemical processes (5.439–43) suggests this. Alchemy, too, is a process which involves the lower feeding the higher, or, perhaps better, the higher purging and transforming the lower through the heat of fire. It is the alchemical fire which refines matter and drives away impurities, just as the heat of digestion effects a hierarchical purification of food. One of the basic convictions of Hellenistic and medieval alchemy, one which carried over into the Renaissance, was that all created things derive from a primal matter. From the transmutation through fire of this single primal matter, all other substances could be produced. In such a transformation the underlying substance remains the same; it is the form which is transfigured.[19] Milton's analogy with alchemy thus suggests, as it does with St. John of Damascus, that the material purification of ores is kin to the spiritual purification effected through eating.[20]

The implicit significance of Milton's use of the term transubstantiation, then, is that, just as with Gregory of Nyssa's and St. John of Damascus's postlapsarian sinner, so it is with Milton's prelapsarian Adam and Eve, that is, that by eating they have the prospect of living in communion with God. Adam and Eve, before the Fall, retain their mobility and possess the possibility of ascending in the hierarchical scale of being. And if they had not fallen, their communion with God would have increased as they rose up the *scala natura*. The result would have been something approximating to *theosis*. This is suggested by Raphael's so-called "ontological speech" in which he declares "time may come when men / With angels may participate, ... / And from these corporeal nutriments perhaps / Your bodies may at last turn all to spirit" (5.471–72, 474–75). Raphael's speech situates the Miltonic act of eating in the context of Adam's and Eve's cosmic destiny, which can, I think, be understood as a kind of deification, a possibility grounded in the sacramentality of nature.

POSTLAPSARIAN REDEMPTION

What, then, becomes of Adam's and Eve's sacramental relation to nature – and hence the possibility of their deification – in their postlapsarian redemption? If Milton does indeed view creation as a sacrament in the prelapsarian life of humankind, and if that sacramentality is lost at the Fall, one might well expect its recovery in the restoration of fallen humankind; paradise lost shall be paradise regained. But this is not the case – at least not unambiguously. In the postlapsarian sections of *Paradise Lost*, Milton fails to sustain the sacramental vision of nature in the redemption of creation and humankind; he fails to envision the salvation of humankind as a restoration of its prelapsarian sacramental relation to creation. Nature is divested of any role in the salvific destiny of humankind, which now undergoes two radical shifts: rather than being grounded externally in the materiality of the created order, Adam's and Eve's relation to God becomes radically interiorized; and rather than being located in nature, Adam's and Eve's relation to God becomes situated in history.

There are numerous indications of this, Adam's and Eve's repentance after the Fall being one of the most explicit. The two begin by confessing their faults and begging pardon, with "tears / Watering the ground" (10.1090–91, 1101). But rather than moving humankind toward a restored relation to the material creation, as is suggested by this phrase, we find that their relation to the earth will assume a different character. This is borne out by the Son, who speaks to the Father concerning Adam's and Eve's repentance:

> See Father, what first fruits on earth are sprung
> From thy implanted grace in man, these sighs
> And prayers, which in this golden censer, mixed
> With incense, I thy priest before thee bring,
> *Fruits of more pleasing savour from thy seed*
> *Sown with contrition in his heart, than those*
> *Which his own hand manuring all the trees*
> *Of Paradise could have produced, ere fallen*
> *From innocence.*   (11.22–30; my emphasis)

The material fruits of the earth are replaced by the spiritual fruits of inward repentance. The natural sacramentality which characterized Adam's and Eve's prelapsarian relation to creation and which enabled their communion with God is supplanted by an inner, immaterial means of communion. So it is not altogether unexpected when Michael reassures Adam that he "wilt . . . not be loath / To leave this Paradise, but shalt possess / A *paradise within thee*, happier far" (12.585–87; my emphasis). Paradise becomes an inward, spiritual condition, quite independent of the materiality of creation.

Perhaps most revealing is Adam's response at the conclusion of Michael's speeches: "Henceforth I learn, that to obey is best, / And love

with fear the only God, to walk/*As* in his presence, ever to observe/
His providence, and on him sole depend" (12.561–64; my emphasis).
With the comparative "as" Milton reduces the literalness and sacramental materiality of God's prelapsarian immanence to a metaphoric,
immaterial, postlapsarian transcendence. When Adam worries that his
expulsion from the garden would deprive him of God's "blessed countenance," Michael reassures him that he will find "of his presence
many a sign," "his face/Express, and of his steps the track divine"
(11.316–17, 351, 353–54). But while God's immanence in creation before the Fall had assumed a material character, with the "signs" of his
presence not only pointing to but also embodying that presence in nature, in the postlapsarian world God is abstracted from his presence
in and through the material creation. Adam can only walk "as" in the
divine presence. Indeed Michael wants to teach Adam that "God attributes to place/No sanctity" (11.836–37). Paradise is no longer an actual place of sacramental communion with God but an inward spiritual
condition.

Also striking here is not so much what is said but what is omitted:
the recovery of Eucharist. Adam was created to be a creature who, as
Raphael puts it, is "grateful to acknowledge whence his good / Descends"
(7.511–12). Milton makes Adam and Eve worshiping beings who praise
and offer thanks to God for his blessings; they are, in short, created *homo
adorans*. As Eve says to Adam: "For we to him indeed all praises owe, /
And daily thanks" (4.444–45). It is through such eucharistic worship
that Adam and Eve embody the prelapsarian possibility of their sacramental relation to nature and the prospect of their deification. But after
the Fall this *gratus animus* which so pervasively defines their prelapsarian
relation to God as priest of creation no longer constitutes the primary
way in which humankind is to exist vis-à-vis God and creation. Expressions of gratitude give way to "faith and faithful works" and to "prayer,
repentance, and obedience" (11.64, 3.191).

This move away from the sacramentality of the world also occurs in
the shift from nature to history. Most notably, the series of visions which
Michael reveals to a fallen Adam (Book 11) and Michael's narration of
Israel's history from Abraham to the Restoration, and of Christ's birth,
death, and resurrection (Book 12) bespeak the relocation of Milton's focus
from nature to history. Michael comes to comfort Adam, to show "what
shall come in future days" (11.357), but the drama here is exclusively
historical, and it amounts to a kind of *Heilsgeschichte*, a salvation history,
in which nature finds no place.

Indeed Michael's revelations to Adam betray the absence of sacramentality. The "new heaven and earth" which will arise at the end of time, God declares to the Son, will "See golden days, fruitful of golden deeds, / With joy and love triumphing, and fair truth" (3.335–38). Michael reiterates this at the end when he says to Adam that the "New Heav'ns, new Earth" will be "Founded in righteousness and peace and love / To bring forth fruits Joy and eternal Bliss" (12.549–51). The food imagery remains, but it no longer signifies a sacramental role in the life of humankind. The "fruits" are inward virtues, abstracted from the natural materiality of creation.

William Madsen identifies well this tendency in Milton's epic. "There is," he says:

a systematic progression in the epic from the material to the spiritual, from the literal to the metaphoric: from the abstract-made-concrete of Hell to the concrete-made-abstract of Heaven; from the literal seeds of the Garden to the metaphoric seeds of Grace; from the literal fruit of the Garden to the metaphoric fruits of Joy and Love in Heaven; from the earthly Paradise itself to the metaphoric Paradise within.[21]

All of these transformations in the epic describe the movement from pre- to postlapsarian humankind, and they represent a shift from a cosmic Greek patristic sacramentality to an interiorized Protestant spirituality.

The disruption in Milton's sensibility is perhaps clearest in how he speaks of the final apocalyptic fate of all creation, the heavens and earth, and how he understands the place of matter therein. Milton's fundamental conviction is that there will be a new heaven and earth but that first this fallen – and material – world will be subject to destruction by fire, a theme that stands as the alpha and omega of God's presence in the epic.[22] It is announced early in Book 3 when God decrees to the Son that at the end of time: "The world shall burn, and from her ashes spring / New heaven and earth wherein the just shall dwell" (3.334–35). And in Book 11 Michael reassures Adam that after the flood (revealed to Adam in the final of the six visions) all the world and nature, "day and night, / Seed time and harvest," shall remain regular "till fire purge all things new, / Both heaven and earth, wherein the just shall dwell" (11.898–901).

Significantly, these are the last lines of Book 11, and the break here between Books 11 and 12 reflects a pause in Michael's discourse to Adam.[23] But the opening of Book 12, describing Michael, continues the same apocalyptic focus: "As one who in his journey baits at noon, / Though bent on speed, so here the archangel pauses / Betwixt the world destroy'd and world restor'd." Then, referring to the vision of the flood which he has just shown to Adam, but also in a powerful prolepsis of the eschaton, Michael remarks to Adam: "Thou hast seen one world begin and end" (12.1–3, 6).

Finally, in Book 12, Michael, relating to Adam the events of the eschaton itself, declares that after the Son destroys the Serpent and returns to the Father's right hand, "When this world's dissolution shall be ripe," he will come "to judge both quick and dead" (12.459–60). Michael's very last words to Adam emphasize once again God's final judgment:

> Last in the clouds from heaven to be revealed
> In glory of the Father, to dissolve
> *Satan* with his perverted world, then raise
> From the conflagrant mass, purg'd and refin'd,
> New Heav'ns, new Earth, ages of endless date
> Founded in righteousness and peace and love
> To bring forth fruits, Joy and Eternal bliss.
>
> (12.545–51)

There is no doubt that Milton believes in the cosmic destruction of the world by fire at the end of time.[24] In this he reflects the widespread outlook of his time. Thinkers of the Renaissance generally believed in a cosmic conflagration of the universe, in which, as John Harvey states it, there will be "burning flames, and brimstone from heauen, utterly consuming, and wasting euerie part, and parcell thereof."[25]

But what is the nature of the new heaven and earth in *Paradise Lost*? What is the status of matter therein? What is the character of this fiery apocalypse, this cosmic conflagration that brings about the new creation? How does fire function in this apocalyptic scenario? Fire certainly destroys, but it is not, at least in *Paradise Lost*, unequivocally destructive. Milton also attributes to fire a purging effect (11.898–901, 12.545–51), and this serves to cleanse and refine, which, as we have seen, is precisely its function in alchemical theory and in the sacramental theology of the Greek Fathers. What, then, are the implications of this for how we are to understand the nature of Milton's apocalyptic "new heaven and earth"? This question can be clarified, I think, by letting the contours of Greek patristic eschatology set in relief the widespread Protestant vision of apocalypse.

Although they do not speculate in detail about eschatological matters, the Greek Fathers generally eschew the dire apocalyptic perspective which predominates in the West, and understand the "new" in "new heaven and earth" to mean renewed. In other words, while the Latin West affirms that the new heaven and earth are discontinuous from the old, the Greek East holds that this very heaven and earth which we now inhabit are renewed, with the result that the new heaven and earth are continuous with the old. The East affirms that the cosmos is not destroyed but *restored* to its original wholeness, a wholeness in which the sacramentality of this world is revitalized and recovered; it is a transfiguration, not a destruction, of the whole creation.

That the end of time will bring about "the final restoration of the perfect status of God's original creation" is the general outlook of the Cappadocian Fathers, especially of Gregory of Nyssa.[26] All of them describe the purpose of the incarnation as ultimately enabling "the regeneration and renewal of the whole world which has grown old under its sin," as Basil the Great describes.[27] But it is in Gregory of Nyssa's writings that we find the clearest and most forceful articulation of cosmic restoration. Gregory's opinion is that matter is not subject to destruction. Affirming that "substance is the essence of the will," Gregory states that:

when the divine will wishes it, a thing comes into being and the divine wish is realized and, once this has occurred, the divine will never revokes what it has wisely and skillfully effected.[28]

The consummation of the kingdom of God, therefore, will bring about "the restoration of the universe."[29] There will be not only personal salvation but also a cosmic restoration. "None of the beauties we now see," Gregory writes, "not only in men, but also in plants and animals, will be destroyed in the life to come."[30] Kallistos Ware cites St. Irenaeus: "Neither the structure nor the substance of creation is destroyed. It is only the 'outward form of this world' (1 Cor. 7:31) that passes away – that is to say, the conditions produced by the fall."[31]

In this eschatological consummation as described by Gregory, images of fire abound. Just as fire has a central role in the Protestant apocalyptic vision, so for Gregory it plays an essential part in the regeneration of the cosmos. Contrary to the way fire functions in Protestantism, however, fire for Gregory has a propaedeutic purpose; it is for discipline, not for destruction, and so has a purifying function. In his *On the Soul*, Gregory describes the pain which those who are being drawn to God suffer. God does not inflict punishment simply because he wishes to punish those who have sinned; rather, Gregory feels:

He, who is the source of all blessedness, draws them to Himself for a higher purpose. The feeling of pain comes of necessity to those who are being drawn up. Just as those who, by means of fire, purify gold mixed with matter, not only melt the impure matter, but also melt the pure gold along with the counterfeit, and when the counterfeit portion is consumed, the pure gold remains; so, also, when evil is being consumed by purifying fire, it is entirely necessary for the soul immersed in the evil to be in the fire until the alien and earthly and counterfeit elements scattered through it are destroyed.[32]

In Gregory's eschatology matter is not to be destroyed; like gold, it is to be refined.[33] In his vision of the "last things," it is not just souls but the entire material creation which will ultimately be sanctified. And in his most daring theological stance – *apokatastasis*, or universal restoration – Gregory claims that even Satan will be redeemed.

How does the Eastern Christian eschatological tradition help us sort out what Milton means by "new heaven and earth" in *Paradise Lost*? On the one hand, it is true that Milton's diction does at times suggest that he sees the new heaven and earth as a material restoration of the old, as a renewed heaven and earth. In this context Milton speaks of the purging, refining function of fire in this process (11.900, 12.548). And insofar as Milton's monism remains intact, Cummins is right to argue for the "continuities between pre- and postapocalyptic states of being" in *Paradise Lost*.[34] But Milton's diction is not consistent, as we have seen; fire is also a means of destruction. Such inconsistency, taken together with the general loss of sacramentality in Milton's postlapsarian world which we have noted, suggests that the dominant tone falls on the disjunction between the "world destroy'd and world restor'd."

It is interesting to note that the equivocal nature of Milton's apocalyptic vision is reflected in *De Doctrina Christiana*. In the chapter on creation, Milton reveals that one consequence of his belief in creation *ex deo* is that "no created thing can be utterly annihilated" (Book I, chapter 7; *CP* vi: 310). Indeed, given his belief in creation *ex deo*, one would expect Milton to affirm unambiguously that matter cannot be destroyed. But he does not follow through with this conclusion in his discussion of eschatological matters. He fails to appropriate fully the import of his belief in creation *ex deo*. Matter, in the final analysis, is only to be annihilated.[35] Not only does Milton fail to resolve the discrepancy, he also becomes "much less certain and interested" about the indestructibility of matter (*CP* vi: 630, n. 38). He writes: "Whether this end means the actual abolition of the world's substance, or only a change in its qualities, is uncertain, and does not really concern us" (*CP* vi: 627).

In *Paradise Lost* Milton's vision of the "ends of time" lacks that clear material, sacramental character which we find in the Eastern

Christian tradition. His apocalyptic thinking follows more closely the general Protestant view that the "new heaven and earth" are to be understood as a *new*, that is, *another* heaven and earth discontinuous with the original. In the Western Christian tradition, this "new heaven and earth," the eschatologically realized kingdom of God, emerges from an apocalyptic destruction of the current order and the institution of a *regnum Christi* which consists of an *inward* spiritual reality. The archangel Michael says as much. In the new age, he tells Adam, "Whether in heaven or earth, for then the earth / Shall all be paradise, far happier place / Than this of Eden, and far happier days," paradise is to be an inward one, divested of any material aspect; the "paradise within thee" is to be "happier far" (12.463–65, 587). Madsen rightly observes that "Milton's 'faith in matter' is much less evident than his desire 'to transcend physical limitations'"; and he surmises that Milton's "unrelenting Protestantism ... triumphed over his abstract belief in 'the inherent goodness of matter.'"[36] If, as Cummins argues, Milton does sustain the philosophical basis for the apocalyptic transformation of matter, his poetic realization of such a possibility does not bespeak the same unequivocal confidence in the ability of matter to function as a sacrament which we find in the epic's prelapsarian books. Milton's apocalyptic vision perhaps acknowledges matter, but it refuses sacrament.

It would thus seem that Milton's poetic vision in *Paradise Lost* remains fundamentally ambivalent. If Milton accomplishes for prelapsarian humankind a sacramental vision that affirms the participation of the entire material creation in the divine nature, for postlapsarian humankind no such sacramental vision of creation is realized, at least confidently. If Milton himself is, as John Rumrich puts it, a Janus figure, simultaneously looking back to his classical, medieval, and Renaissance heritage and forward to his Enlightenment prospects, then *Paradise Lost* represents a specific instance of that twofold gaze, at once creating a richly sacramental cosmos and then rending that universe into impalpable and ethereal abstractions which betray the materiality of the incarnation.[37] Malcolm Ross writes that:

> while Milton comes at the end of the universal Christian culture and preserves much from the mediaeval heritage ..., it is also true that he projects into the secular culture which succeeds him values and techniques which already in his most characteristic work contradict and repudiate significant aspects of the traditional Christian aesthetic.[38]

Ross complains that Milton is unable to take seriously the sacramental meaning of the incarnation as expressed in traditional Catholic and

Anglican eucharistic symbols. In *De Doctrina Christiana* and in Book 12 of *Paradise Lost*, it is especially evident, he observes, how extensively Milton abstracts his symbolization of Christ "from understood techniques of communion and participation." The result is an inability to establish a bond of union between the visible, material creation and the salvation of the individual, a salvation which, as envisioned by Milton, becomes radically inward, invisible, and solipsistic. What is lost is the "corporate Christ" in whom, by means of the Eucharist, all of creation in its very materiality is joined and united.[39]

More significantly, however, Ross discerns a difference between the pre- and postlapsarian poetics of *Paradise Lost*. Only before the Fall of Adam and Eve do we find a cosmos erected by sacramental symbol. It is, he writes, "only in the Garden and before the Fall that nature is seen to rise on an analogical ladder to the divine . . . Only in the Garden, the prelapsarian Garden, could man know with surety by analogy."[40] Before the Fall Adam and Eve live in a harmonious world of hierarchical order, and this enables them to live and know creation analogically. But the Fall disrupted this *analogia entis*. The consequence is that "Nature and history are cut adrift and in themselves are unredeemably lost." They are not reunited. Milton's rejection of postlapsarian eucharistic symbol means that Christ cannot redeem time and nature. Christ may be for Milton the "second Adam," but what Christ enables is the possibility of the individual's salvation, *sola fide*, through the grace of Christ's righteousness; Christ does not recover what was lost in the Fall – the sacrament of creation.[41]

Despite what both God and the Son say, that at the end of time "God shall be all in all" (3.341, 6.732), the redemption of the entire creation is not a clear possibility in *Paradise Lost*. Not only do Satan, the fallen angels, and the wicked remain outside the realm of the blessed, but the created order, the material world of nature, does also.[42] Milton's failed sacramentality undercuts the poetic fulfillment of an eschatological reality which we can fairly describe as material. And insofar as Milton's theodicy depends upon the apocalyptic renewal of what was originally created – that is, matter – Milton's epic disappoints.

NOTES

1. Michael Fixler, *Milton and the Kingdoms of God* (London and Evanston, 1964), pp. 229, 227, 13.
2. Diane Kelsey McColley, "'All in all': The Individuality of Creatures in *Paradise Lost*," in Charles W. Durham and Kristin A. Pruitt (eds.), *"All in All":*

Unity, Diversity, and the Miltonic Perspective (Selinsgrove and London, 1999), pp. 21–38.

3. See chapter 9, pp. 169, 170.
4. Edward R. Hardy (ed.), *Christology of the Later Fathers* (Philadelphia, 1954), p. 319. Hereafter cited as *CLF*.
5. Hylomorphism (*hule*, "matter," plus *morphe*, "form") holds that objects are made up of primary matter and substantial form. In any change what remains as a principle of continuity is primary matter; what alters is the substantial form, that which determines an object's particular identity. See W. Norris Clarke, SJ, "Form and Matter," in J. A. Komonchak, M. Collins, and D. A. Lane (eds.), *New Dictionary of Theology* (Wilmington, Del., 1987), pp. 398–404. See also, for example, Aristotle's *Physics*, Book 2, and *On the Soul*, Book 2, chapter 4.
6. Cyril C. Richardson, "Introduction to Gregory of Nyssa," in *CLF*, p. 248.
7. Nyssa, *Catechetical Oration*, in *CLF*, p. 320.
8. Ibid, p. 321. What Gregory adumbrates is not a version of Latin Christianity's doctrine of transubstantiation, which holds that the underlying substance of the bread and wine (the *materia*) are altered but their outward appearances ("accidents") remain the same. The Latin doctrine presupposes that the identity of something is a result not of its form but of its substance. See Richardson, "Introduction to Gregory of Nyssa," p. 249.
9. Book IV, chapter 13, in Philip Schaff and Henry Wace (eds.), *A Select Library of Nicene and Post-Nicene Fathers*, Second Series (New York, 1890–1900), vol. IX, p. 82. Hereafter cited as *NPNF*, 2.
10. *NPNF*, 2, vol. IX, p. 83.
11. Ibid., vol. IX, p. 84; my emphasis.
12. The frequent use of the word "haste" in conjunction with Adam's and Eve's labor in the garden is striking. It suggests the urgency of work, not so much for the sake of efficiency, but for the sake of worship. See Genesis 18:6, where Abraham urges haste in preparing for the arrival of the angels.
13. This is, according to Alexander Schmemann, the fundamental impulse behind the liturgy of the Eucharist. See *For the Life of the World: Sacraments and Orthodoxy* (Crestwood, N.Y., 1973), pp. 23–46.
14. Alastair Fowler remarks that in view of 9.195–97, "commune" could mean "take communion." See *Paradise Lost*, ed. Alastair Fowler (Essex, 1971), 9.201n.
15. The liturgical nature of *Paradise Lost* has also been noted by Michael Fixler. See "The Apocalypse within *Paradise Lost*," in Thomas Kranidas (ed.), *New Essays on* Paradise Lost (Berkeley and Los Angeles, 1969), p. 131.
16. In transubstantiation the change is not an actual physical alteration but a *meta*physical change which is perceived not by the senses but by the mind of the believer during the Eucharist. See Joseph Martos, *Doors to the Sacred: A Historical Introduction to Sacraments in the Catholic Church* (Tarrytown, N.Y., 1991), pp. 235–36.

17. John King has a very different reading of Adam's and Eve's communion meal in *Milton and Religious Controversy: Satire and Polemic in* Paradise Lost (Cambridge, 2000). He sees an antipapal sentiment (pp. 133–52).

18. Matter is the first principle of Milton's ontology, and forms the first principle of his metaphysics. It is form which constitutes various objects in space and time and confers upon them a distinctive identity. See John Rumrich, *Matter of Glory: A New Preface to* Paradise Lost (Pittsburgh, 1987), pp. 57, 65–66; and Raphael's "ontological speech" (*PL* 5.469ff.).

19. Henry Kahane and Renee Kahane, "Alchemy: Hellenistic and Medieval Alchemy," in Mircea Eliade (ed.), *The Encyclopedia of Religion* (New York, 1987), p. 193. See also Eliade, "Alchemy: An Overview," in ibid., p. 185.

20. The alchemist understood that matter, too, was amenable to a similar change from "corporeal to incorporeal," as Milton puts it. The alchemist "identified this escalation [of ores into gold] with the renewal of man, to which he assigned the same chain of transmutations to reach the goal of redemption". See Kahane and Kahane, "Alchemy," p. 193. Rumrich, too, notes the kinship between Milton and the alchemists on the question of digestive and spiritual metamorphosis.

21. William G. Madsen, "The Idea of Nature in Milton's Poetry," in Richard B. Young (ed.), *Three Studies in the Renaissance: Sidney, Jonson, Milton* (New Haven, 1958), p. 233.

22. Milton's principal biblical texts here are 2 Peter 3:7–13 and Revelation 21:1.

23. Books 11 and 12 were joined in the first edition of the poem (1667). In 1674 the books were separated as they are now precisely at this point. See C. A. Patrides, *Milton and the Christian Tradition* (Oxford, 1966), p. 277.

24. Patrides identifies Milton as the "most distinguished English expositor of the literalistic belief in the conflagration of the universe" (*Milton*, p. 277). In *De Doctrina Christiana* Milton states that the "whole world must eventually be destroyed by fire" (Book I, chapter 33; *CP* VI: 630).

25. John Harvey, *A Discoursive Problem* (1588); quoted in Patrides, *Milton*, p. 277.

26. Werner Jaeger, *Early Christianity and Greek Paideia* (New York, 1961), p. 89. This is, Jaeger points out, a reaffirmation of the fundamental belief in the goodness of nature, humankind, and the entire material cosmos.

27. Basil the Great, "Homily 15" ("On Psalm 32"), in *Fathers of the Church: A New Translation*, trans. Agnes Clare Way (Washington, D.C., 1947–), 46:231. Hereafter cited as *FOC*.

28. Gregory of Nyssa, *On the Soul and the Resurrection*, in *FOC*, 58:253.

29. Ibid., 58:226.

30. Ibid., 58:270. Kallistos Ware explains contemporary Eastern Orthodox eschatology. The "new heaven and a new earth" means that humankind is "not saved *from* the material world but *with* it." See Ware, *The Orthodox Way* (Crestwood, N.Y., 1986), p. 183.

31. Ibid., p. 183.

32. Gregory of Nyssa, *On the Soul*, in *FOC* 58:241. See also 58:242, 267, 271–72.

33. William Moore and Henry Austin Wilson, "The Life and Writings of Gregory of Nyssa," in *NPNF*, 2, vol. V; and D. S. Wallace-Hadrill, *The Patristic View of Nature* (Manchester, 1968), p. 17. Gregory of Nazianzus holds similar views about the function of fire in eschatological matters. In *Oration XXXIX (Oration on the Holy Lights)*, §19, Nazianzus speaks of a purifying fire which will cleanse those who are not baptized in Christ. It is, he says, "more painful and longer... and consumes the stubble of every evil" (*NPNF*, 2, vol. VII, p. 359).

34. See chapter 9, p. 180.

35. See M. H. Abrams's discussion of apocalypse and Milton in Abrams, *Natural Supernaturalism: Tradition and Revolution in Romantic Literature* (New York, 1971), pp. 37–42.

36. Madsen, "Idea of Nature," pp. 233, 231.

37. See Rumrich, *Matter of Glory*, p. 72.

38. Malcolm Ross, *Poetry and Dogma: The Transformation of Eucharist Symbols in Seventeenth-Century England* (New Brunswick, N.J., 1954), p. 183.

39. Ibid., pp. 188–89.

40. Ibid., pp. 220–21. Michael Lieb takes issue with Ross's estimation of Milton's poetics, but, unlike Ross, Lieb fails to appreciate the radical difference between the pre- and postlapsarian sections of the epic. See Lieb, *Poetics of the Holy: A Reading of Paradise Lost* (Chapel Hill, 1981).

41. Ross, *Poetry*, pp. 220–21.

42. See *Paradise Lost* 3.330–33; 12.546–47; and Harry F. Robins, *If This Be Heresy: A Study of Milton and Origen* (Urbana, 1963), p. 54.

The apocalypse in Paradise Regained

Ken Simpson

According to Frederic Jameson, *Paradise Regained* is marked "very explicitly by the emphasis on personal, private salvation and the repudiation of millenarianism," both of which express the "failure of hope following upon the failure of revolution."[1] Similarly, Andrew Milner maintains that the theme of quietism in *Paradise Regained* "is itself an indication of a general fatigue in the revolutionary movement" even if Milton's quietism is "tactical" as he prepares for "that future time when 'doing' rather than 'suffering' will be the order of the day."[2] More recently, however, this interpretation has been questioned for omitting what it claims to value most – historical contextuality. These readers, rather than placing *Paradise Regained* in an abstract narrative of emergent capitalism, discuss the context of religious dissent and nonconformity in which the poem was written. The result is a more radical Milton consistent with the polemicist of the 1640s and 1650s, but one whose voice has been modified by conditions of censorship and the generic demands of the brief epic. Gary Hamilton presents Jesus as a "nonconformist hero" whose interiority provides an example for persecuted dissenters exiled to worship in private houses by the Conventicle Act of 1664 and 1670.[3] Ashraf Rushdy concludes that *Paradise Regained* is a "stridently anti-monarchist tract," while Laura Knoppers suggests that "the construction of the self-disciplined subject is a model for dissenters of the 1660s and 1670s."[4] In addition, I will argue that in scriptural and astrological references to the apocalypse in *Paradise Regained*, Milton continues his critique of the English Reformation and its failure to recognize Christ's spiritual rule of the church and, therefore, the separation of church and state.[5] As Milton argued in *On Christian Doctrine*, Antichrist arose within the church, thriving during Constantine's reign and persevering well into the Restoration.[6] In Jesus' rejection of Satan, then, is an implicit denunciation of the Church of England and encouragement for persecuted nonconformists of the 1670s.

As several scholars have shown, significant developments in English apocalyptic thought were introduced during the seventeenth century.[7] For most sixteenth-century reformers, history was seen through the lens of The Revelation (Apocalypse) of St. John the Divine, the last book of the Protestant Bible. This resulted in a conviction that Antichrist – the pope and the doctrines of Roman Catholicism – would soon be defeated, eventually leading to the Second Coming of Christ, the Last Judgment, and the new heaven and earth. Seventeenth-century Puritans were less enthusiastic about this reading of Revelation and contemporary events, however, since many traces of Catholicism remained in the doctrine and especially the discipline of the English church. Antichrist for Puritans included the English church, making them more open to a reading that emphasized the progressive nature of the apocalypse. Despite the differences between the Anglicans' opponents which would surface later in the century, as the nation approached Civil War, and especially after the fall of Laud and the bishops in the early 1640s, many felt that the Second Coming was imminent in the newly reformed church; but a new emphasis in English apocalyptic thought on the literal reign of Christ and his saints derived from Revelation 20:1–10 and the interpretations of Joseph Mede, Johann Heinrich Alsted, and others, particularly Independents and a group later called Fifth Monarchists, began to emerge as well. Unlike Anglicans and Presbyterians, these radicals envisioned the beginning of a literal thousand-year period of peace ruled by Christ and his saints after years of persecution by Antichrist, even though not all millenarians, and not even all Fifth Monarchists, advocated the use of force to create the conditions for Christ's millennial reign. These expectations of Christ's return, whether spiritual or literal, turned to bitter disappointment when first the Presbyterians, then the Independents, and finally the return of Charles II and the Anglican hierarchy made it clear that a state church would continue to delay the apocalypse. Many turned to the armor of patience and scripture to sustain them during the continuing battle with Antichrist. While belief in a future millennial kingdom persisted among nonconformists after the Restoration, Christ's return no longer seemed imminent as the saints entered a new era of persecution. Passive or quietist millenarianism was certainly for some one response to these new conditions, but for others, including Milton, standing and waiting – and especially writing – were defiant acts of resistance, as they continued to perceive Antichrist in their reading of scriptural and astrological signs.

Throughout his career Milton's political hopes were linked to the Second Coming of Christ to defeat Antichrist and reign with the saints in judgment.[8] The identifying mark of Antichrist is consistent, too. As Milton suggests in *Of Reformation* (1641), "Antichrist began first to put forth his horne" during Constantine's reign because he encouraged the confusion of civil and religious authority, leading to the church's accumulation of wealth, its use of force in religious matters, and its alliance with the state (*CP* I: 551). In *On Christian Doctrine*, assembled throughout Milton's career but probably reaching the state in which we have it in the late 1650s, the pope is identified as Antichrist for the same reasons the English church was in the antiepiscopal tracts: arising within the church, Antichrist uses civil power to compel individuals in religious matters (*CP* VI: 604, 797–98). What changes in Milton's apocalyptic thought is the timing of Christ's return. Whereas in 1641 Christ's return seemed imminent, in the decade after the Restoration the continuing spiritual struggle with Antichrist is emphasized. The turn to inwardness in the last stage of Milton's apocalyptic thought should not be confused with passivity, quietism, or indifference about the apocalypse, however. Vigorous spiritual preparedness is never absent from Milton's early hope for a literal reign of Christ, but here it receives special emphasis in the Restoration wilderness of persecution suffered by nonconformists, republicans, and the hero of *Paradise Regained*.

The presence of apocalyptic imagery in a temptation narrative would not have surprised Milton's readers because the setting of Jesus' battle with Satan in the wilderness would bring to mind not only the struggles between Israel and Egypt in the Old Testament but also the apocalyptic struggles of the end times.[9] In his opening speech in *Paradise Regained*, Satan boasts about ruling "th' affairs of Earth" but also reminds his colleagues of the "dread attending when that fatal wound / Shall be inflicted by the Seed of Eve / Upon my head" (*PR* 1.53–55). Satan refers here to the *protoevangelium* of Genesis 3:15 which was commonly read as a prophecy of the last battle between Christ and Satan. John Diodati, for example, suggests that this verse prophesies Satan's "continual war" with the church in which Christ and "his elect through his Spirit, shall destroy all... [Satan's] kingdom, power, and works by a compleat and everlasting victory."[10] Interestingly, in his misuse of Scripture on the spire of the Temple in Book 4, Satan fails to refer to this prophecy in his citation of Psalm 91. He omits the second clause of verse 11 – "to keep thee in thy ways" – and ignores references to the apocalypse in verse 13 which refer to the Messiah who will "Tread upon the lion and the adder: the young lion and the dragon shalt thou trample under feet" (Psalm 91:13). At the end of the poem, as the angelic chorus reminds us, Satan's fall from the pinnacle prefigures his more permanent over-throw when he "like an Autumnal Star / Or lightning shalt fall from Heav'n trod down / Under his feet" (*PR* 4.619–21). This reference con-flates the Son's defeat of Satan in heaven, Jesus' defeat of Satan on the spire, and the Son's final defeat of Satan in Revelation 20. Isaiah 14:12 ("How art thou fallen from heaven, O Lucifer, son of the morning!") and Jesus' own report in Luke 10:18 ("I beheld Satan as lightning fall from heaven"), and especially Revelation 12:4, 9, when Satan is defeated and thrown to earth, were all read as evidence of the War in Heaven but also as prophecies of the time when, according to the angels in the poem, Satan will receive his "last and deadliest wound" (*PR* 4.622). Finally, the purpose for which Jesus has been sent to defeat Satan is announced in apocalyptic terms as well, this time in the reference to the Old Testament apocalypse of Daniel (2:34–35).[11] Christ's kingdom, imperfectly shad-owed in the earthly church, will have no end and "shall to pieces dash / All Monarchies besides throughout the world" (*PR* 4.149–50), without force of arms. At a time when the church was referred to as Christ's kingdom and when a monarchy was restored which did not hesitate to use force in spiritual matters, this strident prophecy is anything but quietist. Milton's readers probably expected these allusions and recognized in the temptations not just an ethical trial of a solitary individual but an ongoing combat of the whole church against Satan which epitomized not only their own struggles but also the last battle between the Son and Satan.

If Milton's readers could have expected this eschatological context, neither would they have found surprising, as I have suggested, the asso-ciation of the temptation narrative with the church. A long line of com-mentary on Revelation 12 shows that this association was quite common. In his exegesis of Revelation 12 in 1548, John Bale identifies the woman clothed with the sun as the church, her crown as the twelve apostles and "all other godly ministers of the word," her child as faithful Christians of all times, the dragon as Antichrist, and the flight of the woman as the persecuted church fleeing Rome. Even during the apostolic period, the church had to flee persecution, seeking God "in the solitary heart" and hiding in the wilderness where she was "fed with the scriptures." Bale also links Revelation 12 with the temptations: "He that will live godly in Christ, and be a patient sufferer; he that will stand in Gods fear and prepare himself to temptation ... let him give himself wholly to this prophecy."[12] Bale's advice was even more poignant 120 years later when the nonconformist churches were suffering for their beliefs.

David Pareus, whose exegesis of Revelation Milton clearly knew, continued this tradition. The visions of St. John touch on "the present conflicts of the Christian Church, which already were in John's time." The battle in which Michael overthrows Satan is also explicitly linked to the temptation narratives of Luke and Matthew. "The first conflict," Pareus writes, "consisted in Satans temptations, the which Christ did often most stronglie sustaine and suppresse." The battle, however, does not end there. Verse 13 refers to "the 300 years from Constantine until the rising of the Antichrist" when "the true church fled into the wilderness."[13] For Pareus Revelation 12 unfolds the persecution of the true church throughout history by the Roman Antichrist, and, by extension, for English Puritans, by the unreformed English church. Such persecution also offered hope, however, because it was a sign of the coming apocalypse and the final defeat of Satan by the Son, whether this defeat would bring about an imminent, earthly kingdom or not.

The historical interpretation of Revelation 12 became more and more specific in the years which followed. John Diodati identifies Michael with Jesus, the angels with "the Pastors and Ministers of his Word" and the dragon's angels with "the Ministers of Satan, namely antichrist and his adherents."[14] For the Westminster Divines the persecuted church in the wilderness refers to the Waldenses, the small Christian community which Milton believed had preserved apostolic Christianity in the isolated valleys of the French Alps.[15] Mary Cary also connects Daniel 7:26 and Revelation 12:14, implying that Charles I, the little horn which subdues three kings in Daniel 7:24, forced the church into the wilderness, but the persecution "is very neer come to a period," for once the kingdom of the beast is diminished, as it had been with the regicide, the saints can "go on in their work of breaking down the strength of the beast, and bringing it to nothing, that the Lord Christ may be all."[16] In Christ's temptation in the wilderness, then, Milton's readers would also have seen, with varying degrees of specificity, the persecution of the true church by Antichrist in the Roman or English church. For some the persecution was held to have begun as early as the apostolic period but certainly after Constantine's reign, reaching its height during the period of papal supremacy before the beginning of the end during the Reformation, when the true church, the kingdom of Christ, began to emerge. When that kingdom failed to appear, however, especially after the Restoration, the timetable of the battle with Antichrist needed to be revised as nonconformists like Milton realized that the church would be in a state of militancy and persecution for an indefinite period. The identity of Antichrist had to change as well when it became clear that the kingdom of Christ was not being realized. The Antichrist was, at different times, Satan himself, or, more often, one of his agents, including the pope, the Roman church and its government and ceremonies, the vestiges of the Roman church in the English church, Charles I, Cromwell, or the spiritual attributes which made such obstacles to Christ's kingdom possible.[17]

Milton identified the apocalyptic vision of Revelation 12 with the trials of the church in his prose as well. In 1641 he describes the dragon's "traine of error" sweeping "the Starres out of the Firmament of the Church" while the militant Protestant church scorns "the fiery rage of the old red Dragon" (*CP* 1: 524–25). In *The Reason of Church Government*, he declares that "Christ by those visions of S. John foreshewes the reformation of his Church" (*CP* 1: 760). He cites the "general apostasy that was foretold and the Churches flight into the wildernes" (*CP* 1: 827) and claims in *Animadversions upon the Remonstrant's Defence against SMECTYMNUUS* that the church has been in "this our wildernesse since Reformation began" (*CP* 1: 703). In *On Christian Doctrine* he describes Antichrist as "the great enemy of the church" which "arises from the church itself," and also notes that "the revealing of antichrist" is a sign of Christ's Second Coming, as are persecutions, false prophets, and "an almost universal apostasy" (*CP* VI: 604, 617, 616).

In *The Tenure of Kings and Magistrates* (1649), Milton is more specific: Satan's offer of worldly power to Jesus in Luke 4 is linked to the dragon's empowering of the beast in Revelation 13 and marks tyrannical monarchy as satanic government (*CP* III: 210). Milton shared with many radical Puritans the view that the Antichrist worked not only through Rome or the pope, but also through any religious hierarchy or practice, including the Church of England's, which confused civil and spiritual jurisdictions or violated the freedom of individuals to understand God's will through the Word and Spirit. This is particularly important because dissenters, often persecuted during the Restoration for claiming precisely this religious freedom, defined themselves as "sufferers for truth in the wilderness" at the same time as Milton was composing *Paradise Regained*.[18]

The association of the temptation narrative with the apocalypse, and both with the church in a state of persecution, would have had a special and precise resonance for Milton and the dissenting churches of the Restoration. The Cavalier Parliament (May, 1661) set the tone for the 1660s and 1670s: the Solemn League and Covenant was burnt, MPs received the Eucharist by the order of the *Book of Common Prayer*, the Act of 1641 excluding the bishops from the upper house was repealed, and the definition of treason was expanded to include writing and speaking. To commemorate Charles I's execution, on 30 January 1661 the bodies of Bradshaw, Cromwell, and Ireton were disinterred, hung at Tyburn, and decapitated.[19] On 24 August 1662 more than a thousand nonconformist ministers were ejected from their churches for failing to give "unfeigned assent" to the Act of Uniformity which prescribed the *Book of Common Prayer* and the Thirty-Nine Articles throughout the realm, forced members of the clergy to swear not to subvert church or state, and compelled all clergy to be ordained by a bishop – all impossible conditions for nonconformists. The Licensing Act of the same year made it nearly impossible for dissent to be heard, for it required the "censorship of all printed works by a panel of the most important government ministers and churchmen."[20]

The king was not altogether against some kind of reconciliation with the nonconformists, but despite his attempts to adopt a policy of toleration – a policy designed for Roman Catholics, but including dissenters by default – events such as Venner's Fifth Monarchist uprising of 1661 and the Yorkshire Plot of 1663, as harmless to the state as they were in themselves, gave hardliners in Parliament more evidence to support their view that harsh legislation against nonconformists was necessary. A royal proclamation against all "seditious sectaries and other disloyal persons" was developed further in the Conventicle Act of 1664, culminating in the Second Conventicle Act of 1670. The 1664 Act threatened with deportation ministers who presided at prayer meetings of more than five people, and gave sweeping powers to officials for the arrest of conventiclers, while the 1670 Act levied stiffer fines and held church wardens and court officials more accountable than previously if they failed to administer the Act.[21] For a man who had fought for liberty of conscience and the spiritual kingdom of Christ's church for decades, this atmosphere of fear and persecution must have been oppressive to say the least. The Anglican church, in its support of the Conventicle Act and in its antitolerationist campaign, supported the use of civil power to enforce conformity throughout the early Restoration period and stands boldly condemned in *Paradise Regained*, its position on the relationship between church and state reflected in Satan's persecution of Jesus.

In *Paradise Regained*, then, Jesus' apocalyptic battle is also a Restoration one and his arguments reflect Milton's earlier radicalism. In *A Treatise of Civil Power in Ecclesiastical Causes* (1659), Milton argues that Christ's spiritual reign "show[s] us the divine excellence of [Jesus'] spiritual kingdom able without worldly force to subdue all the powers and kingdoms of this world" (*CP* VII: 255). In Jesus' defeat of Satan by patience, argument, and exegesis, Milton illustrates how Christ's kingdom will come about, condemning in the process the intrusion of the state in the church in legislation like the Conventicle Act, the state's persecution of dissenters, and the idolatry implied in works such as Samuel Parker's preface to *Bishop Bramhall's Vindication of Himself and the Episcopal Clergy, from the Presbyterian Charge of Popery* (1672). Parker, a former acquaintance of Milton and now bishop of London, claims that God, priest, and king are so interwoven that one cannot be rejected without rejecting the others.[22] In addition, by emphasizing Jesus' refusal to act before his time, let alone speculate about the time of his kingdom's arrival, Milton distances himself from those Fifth Monarchists who advocated the use of force to bring about the thousand-year reign of the saints described in Revelation 20:1–10. Although Milton still seems to expect the coming of Christ in judgment, this part of the apocalypse is no longer as imminent as it was for him in the 1640s. The nature of the kingdom which Jesus will proclaim and for which he is being prepared by the temptations is identical to the one Milton had been advancing at least since *A Treatise of Civil Power* was published in 1659: the church is a religious society ruled by Christ through scripture, not a civil society ruled by the king through force. It will suffer persecution in its struggle against Antichrist, and will ultimately prevail as the temptation narrative and Revelation disclose, but no one, not even Jesus, knows when this victory will occur. In propounding such a view, Milton rejects the Restoration Settlement, radical Fifth Monarchism, the Independents, and the Presbyterians, all of whom, at one time or another, used force to persecute Protestants who attempted to derive the principles of their churches from scripture alone.

Milton's *Considerations Touching the Likeliest Means to Remove Hirelings Out of the Church* (1659) was published only months after *A Treatise of Civil Power*. Here Milton argues that the ordained clergy, especially in their insistence on the necessity of tithes and a university education, are implicated in this corruption of the church by civil power. This concern is continued in *Paradise Regained* as well. Milton first presents Satan disguised in "rural weeds" following "a stray Ewe" – feigning a conventional figure of the minister, his pastoral care for his flock, and his duty to persuade and discipline lost sheep back into the fold of the church through "winning words."[23] The whole passage recalls Matthew 18:11–18, the prooftext commonly cited in the Protestant tradition for its scheme of pastoral discipline (*PR* 1.314–34). The "Son of Man" comes to save lost sheep, not false priests; he comes in preaching, not in miracles. If we are led astray, we should "tell it to the church" not to the "Town or Village" of the "heathen man and [a] publican." Finally, when the church binds or loosens on earth it does so to open or close the doors of the kingdom of heaven rather than to increase the fame of a member or to satisfy those who "curious are to hear" (*PR* 1.333). Satan's abuse of scripture throughout the poem also marks him as a false teacher, one of the signs of the Second Coming of Christ mentioned in *On Christian Doctrine* (*CP* vi: 616).

Not only is Satan a false priest, unwittingly identifying himself with the lying spirit that inspired the false prophets of Ahab's court (*PR* 1.371–77, 1 Kings 22:13–23), but his advice to Jesus is clearly unsound as well. If Jesus is, as Satan suggests, a lost sheep "far from path or road of men," Satan should put him on the right path, not toward "Town or Village" to gain fame (*PR* 1.322, 332). Jesus' answer confirms this. Instead of accepting the mediation of a false priest, he acknowledges "no other Guide" but the Spirit, and no other food but the "Word / Proceeding from the mouth of God" (1.336, 349–50). Moreover, Christ's willingness to be fed by the Word echoes the Protestant explanation of how the church is sustained in the wilderness from the time of apostasy until the beginning of the apocalypse. According to John Bale the church is to be "fed with the scriptures" in the wilderness. Satan's temptation of Jesus to distrust God's providence – to provide his own food by turning stones into bread, fearing that God has abandoned him to starve – is also a temptation to distrust God's spiritual kingdom founded on the Word alone and to submit to the temporal, carnal power offered by Satan.

Similar arguments were used by Milton against the state church in *Hirelings* twelve years earlier. Milton claims that the clergy turn Christ's "heavenly kingdom into a kingdom of this world, a kingdom of force and rapin," transforming the church into "a beast of many heads and many horns" when they distrust providence by taking tithes and insisting on a university education (*CP* vii: 313, 308). Tithes are "tempting baits" that lure unfit ministers into the church; instead, clergy should "trust in God and the promise of Christ for thir maintenance" (*CP* vii: 300, 303). The argument that tithes are necessary to support a university-educated clergy is equally distrustful of God's providence, Milton argues, since "the providence of God and the guidance of the Holy Spirit" are sufficient to sustain the church just as they are sufficient to sustain Jesus in *Paradise Regained* (*CP* vii: 304, *PR* 1.335–36). Jesus depends on the "inward Oracle" and the "Light from above," just as whatever "makes a fit minister, the scripture can best informe us to be only from above" (*PR* 1.463, 289,

CP VII: 316). By tempting Jesus to turn stones to bread, Satan is also tempting him to turn the church into a worldly kingdom. Milton, unlike the defenders of the Restoration Act of Uniformity, continues to insist that religious and civil jurisdictions should be separate.

The temptation of the kingdoms is more explicitly linked to the church. This time Satan appears in courtly guise, chiding the Son for his harsh, otherworldly purity, just as members of Charles II's court and the religious establishment ridiculed nonconformists for their unrealistic and hypocritical saintliness (*PR* 2.300, 324–36).[24] Although several specific temptations are included under the heading of the kingdom here, ranging from the temptations to "worth, [of] honour, glory, and popular praise" (2.227) to the political kingdom of Rome and the intellectual kingdom of Greece, they are all temptations to idolatry, to worship the ruler of the kingdoms of the world as a ruler of the kingdom of God. The banquet scene, for example, could depict what Milton called the "paganisme of sensuall idolatry" in *Of Reformation* (*CP* I: 520) – the external, worldly, carnal, and ceremonial aspects of worship introduced by Archbishop Laud and renewed during the Restoration.[25] The banquet, according to Satan, is a "thing indifferent," something Jesus can enjoy and use without endangering his salvation. He claims that Jesus has a "right to all Created things," just as Christians are not bound by dietary laws because of Christian liberty.

Jesus answers as Puritans had argued since the sixteenth century: outward ceremonies, like the banquet, are not indifferent when they imperil the spiritual condition of Christ's kingdom; therefore, Jesus asks rhetorically, "who withholds my pow'r that right to use?" (*PR* 2.324, 380). In other words, who withholds his power of choice in things indifferent and uses civil power in the church but Satan himself? If things of the created world are indifferent, as Satan suggests, Christ can freely reject them as his conscience sees fit. Milton's audience, familiar with the arguments about discipline and ceremonies, would identify with Christ's choice not to participate in the banquet because ceremonies which are not scriptural cannot be forced on the individual by the leader of the state or church, "unless," as Milton argues in *On Christian Doctrine*, "he wants to be called antichrist as the Pope, chiefly for this reason, is" (*CP* VI: 797–98).

When the sacramental imagery of the banquet is considered, the meal is anything but indifferent. When Jesus replies that he would eat if he liked "the giver," he rejects – as many Protestant theologians, including Milton, did – a principle of sacramental theology which maintains the efficacy of the sacrament regardless of the spiritual condition of the priest who administers it. In addition, Satan's table resembles the altar of the Roman and English churches; it is "richly spread, in regal mode" (*PR* 2.340). The table's luxuriance, but also the corruption of ceremony by the state implied in the word "regal" make it clear that this is not an indifferent ceremony but a spiritually perilous one. To eat the meal is to worship Satan; therefore, Jesus is justified in refusing to participate in the meal, even though, in itself, it is a "thing indifferent."

After Satan falls from the pinnacle of the Temple, Jesus is presented with a celestial meal prepared by the angels, a meal which foreshadows the eternal kingdom after the apocalypse when all the faithful will sit at the Lord's table in God's presence. Jesus, as a worthy communicant who has demonstrated his faith, sits down at a celestial banquet, a banquet which symbolizes communion in the nonconformist tradition and prefigures the everlasting kingdom at the end of time.[26] It was this communal, eschatological sense of the Lord's Supper which often prevailed in nonconformist churches and in the sacramental theologies they developed. The Westminster *Directory for the Public Worship of God* (1645), even though too prescriptive for many nonconformists, including Milton, still anticipates this view in its directive "that the communicants may orderly sit about it, or at it" [the Lord's table] in anticipation of the time when we "are admitted to eat and drink at his own Table."[27] The food imagery of *Paradise Regained*, then, develops the theme of the kingdom. Whereas Satan offers a demonic sacramental meal associated with the churches of England and Rome, Christ's victory over Satan on the pinnacle and the celebration of that victory in the celestial meal which follows it is associated with the persecuted nonconformist church and foreshadows the revelation of Christ's everlasting kingdom of glory in which the church is called "unto the marriage supper of the Lamb" (Rev. 19:9).

Before Jesus returns to his "Mother's house private" (*PR* 4.639) to begin the process of regaining paradise and forming his kingdom, the angelic choir provides a glimpse of another feature of the apocalypse – the judgment of Satan and his followers. After he has fallen from the spire of the Temple, the choir proclaims that Satan will again "Rule in the clouds," but "not long": "like an Autumnal Star / Or Lightning thou shalt fall from Heav'n trod down / Under his feet" (*PR* 4.618–21).

I have already alluded to the biblical texts which illuminate Satan's fall from the pinnacle – Isaiah 14:12 and Luke 10:18 in particular – but verses which depict Satan or his adherents falling from the sky or being thrown down – such as Revelation 12:4, 9, 19:20, 20:3, and 20:10 – are important in establishing the apocalyptic context of these lines as well. To these should be added passages such as Matthew 24:29, Mark 13:25, and Luke 21:25 in which signs in the heavens and stars falling to the earth are associated with the effects of Satan's influence or signs of the approaching Last Judgment. Since Satan will fall like an "Autumnal Star," well-known images of judgment as a harvest of God's wrath might be recalled, too. Like weeds at harvest time and the tares that he has sown (Matt. 13:38–40), Satan will be harvested and thrown in the fire at the end of the world; he and his followers will be reaped with a sharp sickle and thrown "into the great winepress of the wrath of God" (Rev. 14:19). The reference to the winepress in *Paradise Regained* (4.15–16), then, is more menacing than might appear at first glance: Satan, returning to his assault on Jesus like a mindless fly to a winepress "in vintage time," does not recall this image of judgment even though he is more than capable of quoting scripture. Similarly, he is unable to read the signs of Jesus' baptism or understand the sense in which Jesus is the Son of God. Readers, on the other hand, understand that this image is proleptic; it anticipates the apocalyptic, autumnal harvest of Satan as well as his fall from the pinnacle of the Temple.

Milton must also have known that autumnal stars were associated with comets in handbooks of astronomy and astrology. Although the debate about the origins of comets and their significance was still ongoing and would not be settled until Halley and others proved that comets had their own orbits, most seventeenth-century readers of the stars believed that comets were generated when hot, dry vapors coagulated in the upper atmosphere during the autumn. As John Gadbury, an important astrologer of the 1660s, explains: "although the Comets that appeared in the years 1618 and 1652 and now in 1664 with us, have bin in the Winterseason; yet are divers Astronomers and Philosophers of opinion, that they are generated in Autumn or Summer but mostly in Autumne."[28] Gadbury goes on to note with some skepticism that spring has too much moisture and too little heat, while winter has too little heat and summer too much to account for the appearance of comets; therefore, autumn, with the right combination of heat and dryness, is the only season in which comets could be produced.

Milton's "Autumnal Star" simile, then, is one of his most extraordinary; it condenses the charged, dramatic context of the apocalypse and the visual power of the comet while reinforcing the contrast in the poem between Jesus, "our Morning Star then in his rise" (*PR* 1.294, Rev. 22:16) who stands on the spire, and Satan, the "Autumnal Star," or comet who falls from it. But Milton refers here not only to the scriptural apocalypse and its signs; he also refers to astrological signs of the end times.[29] Astrological tracts and almanacs were still very popular in the seventeenth century and contributed to Protestant eschatology becoming "an amalgamation of Christian and astrological speculation."[30] John Bainbridge, Oxford professor of astronomy, considered the comet of 1618 a sign of the fall of Antichrist and a portent of the Second Coming.[31] John Booker, republican licenser of almanacs and mathematics texts during the Civil War, linked the prophecies of John Napier to contemporary events, noting "strange wonders in the Ayre" and proclaiming the downfall of monarchy, the defeat of Antichrist, and the spread of Christ's kingdom.[32] William Lilly, "Parliament's unabashed apologist," argued that eclipses, comets, and conjunctions proclaimed God's displeasure with "Monarchicall Pomp" and "Popery" and associated the appearance of the 1618 comet in Scorpio with the scorpions of Revelation 19 and the "legates of the Pope."[33] Black Monday – the solar eclipse of 29 March 1652 – created the biggest stir, primarily because of its closeness to 1656, the date many chose for the defeat of Antichrist and the beginning of the end.[34] For Nicholas Culpeper the eclipse and the comet which appeared after it seemed to confirm the justice of the fall of monarchy and to portend that "the Fifth Monarchy of the world is coming," while John Durant, in *A Set Time for Judgement* (1656), clearly identifies the signs of apocalypse with the natural phenomena observed by astrologers: "by the signs that shall appear in Heaven as the darkening of the Sun, obscuring the moon, and shaking or falling of stars, I understand the debasing, dethrowning and destroying of the Kings, Princes, and powers of this world."[35] Milton, then, could have counted on his readers to recognize allusions to comets, the fall of monarchy, and the apocalypse in his description of Satan as an "Autumnal Star."[36]

Before the Restoration countless almanacs and astrological tracts routinely associated comets with contemporary events, especially the fall of Charles I. Several even cite Du Bartas's *Divine Weekes and Workes* (1592) where comets portend "To Princes death, to Kingdomes many crosses."[37] After the king's return, however, it became more difficult for nonconformists and republicans to make these associations openly. Many turned from domestic politics to foreign policy – especially the Dutch wars – in their predictions about comets as they resigned themselves to monarchy and episcopacy.[38] But tales of comets, fiery dragons, prodigies, wonders, and judgments upon enemies of nonconformists persisted in works such as Henry Jessey's *The Lords Loud Call to England* (1660), *Mirabilis Annus* (1661) and *Mirabilis Annus Secundus* (1662). These narratives of signs and wonders "encourage[d] the Godly, to hope and rejoyce in the Lord," for they were "praeludiums to that signal and last revelation which makes way for the new Heavens and the new Earth."[39] Through the Licensing Act the government quickly censored this popular genre because of its support of "the Good Old Cause" but also, more generally, because it was thought that a prophecy could influence the course of events, whether it was true or not. As Thomas suggests, the Stuart government sensed that the predictions were self-fulfilling to some extent because "nothing is more likely to bring about the success of an enterprise than the conviction of those who undertake it that they are predestined to succeed."[40]

Interpretations of comets were especially suspect because a long tradition of commentary associated them with "unusual calamities [such] as the death or deposition of princes, &c. Destruction and Ruine of Kingdomes, Empires, States, and Governments."[41] The return of monarchy and the failure of earlier prophecies did not deter later republicans and nonconformists from reading the comets of November to December 1664, and those of January and March to April 1665, as signs of God's displeasure and the approaching fall of monarchy. Many post-Restoration references are vague, however, leaving open the possibility that if monarchy did not fall immediately, it would eventually. In 1668 William Lilly commented on the connection between comets and the death of princes, reminding his readers of "some dreadful matter at hand," but "a prediction of the fall of kings and tyrants" was removed from a draft of his 1670 almanac by Roger L'Estrange.[42]

Once monarchy was restored some astrologers looked to 1666 as the date of the defeat of Antichrist, even though Lilly seemed to backtrack on his earlier apocalyptic predictions for the year.[43] Thomas Trigge was a royalist but still hoped to avoid "the many vials of wrath, threatened to be poured upon them, by the apparition of these Celestial Ministers, the Comets."[44] But when that date passed, it became clear that the battle with Antichrist was to last much longer than expected. After quoting Matthew 24:7 one author urged his readers to "see that you be not troubled (saith our blessed Saviour) for all these [signs] must come to pass, but the End is not yet. There will doubtless, after these grand revolutions, be a time of tranquility and peace, but it cannot yet be expected."[45]

Most royalists refuted the traditional association of comets with the death of kings and the ruin of kingdoms, though, claiming that the signs were far too indeterminate in meaning to be read accurately, but offering their own readings anyway. As if to refute Culpeper and others, one author suggests that the comet of 1652 was a sign of Charles II's return: "this Comet...hath a signification of a great man to arise, and this man is King Charles." He will be "a man deprived of all his just rights," yet "guided by God's speciall providence."[46] John Gadbury supports Charles II by rewriting the discourse of comets, asserting that "this Comet had a principle signification of his said Majesty King Charles, and [that] he is that Man, who shall act his part on the stage of Europe with so much divine assistance, that it will not be in the power of any Prince, King, or Nation to resist him."[47] After noting that the comet of 1652 could be read in at least two contradictory ways, the author of *The Blazing Star: or, A Discourse of Comets* points out that "a sign signifieth; and what signifieth is known and how little understood or known any Meteor, Exhalation, Comet, Apparition is." He finds "in reason no ground" for "political effects that are ascribed to...[comets] by those that would arouse and deceive the World," but goes on to suggest that the comet of 1664 portends "that a Kingdom or Dominion shall remain a long time" and that the king will "be active, and freely forward in good things."[48] Another tract of the same title condemns those who associate the comet of 1664 with "the grand Revelation of the world [in] the Year 1666, wherein they expect the down-fall of the Pope, and other strange and wonderful businesses."[49] John Spencer's sustained attack on the nonconformist discourse of prodigies, including comets, particularly in the *Mirabilis Annus* tracts, reduces all prophetic discourses to party interests: "each party superstitiously interprets all accidents in favour of it self." If God "intended these portentous occurences as his trumpets to alarm a drowsy world," he asks, why are they so obscure that no one can understand them? Comets are not signs of evil, nor do they portend the deaths of princes, argues Spencer. The deaths of many princes have not been accompanied by comets, while malignant influences have not followed when they have appeared:

Almost four years and an half are past from us, since the Nation was first alarm'd with the dreadful news of strange Sights in Heaven and Earth, and yet (with all due thankfulnes to God be it spoken) never did those three National Felicities, Peace, Health, Plenty, more bless our habitations.[50]

Milton appears to share Spencer's skepticism, since Jesus rejects "false portents" in *Paradise Regained* and Satan remarks that "turbulencies" in the air "*seem* to point" [my emphasis] to the "affairs of men" (4.491, 462, 463, 462). It is, admittedly, difficult to infer an author's specific beliefs or ideas from literary works, but we can assume that Milton would have rejected the signs in *Mirabilis Annus* of beasts, monsters, toads and frogs, apparitions of armies in battle and fields of corn being reaped in the air, people dying in remarkable ways after cursing nonconformists, and many other stories which parallel too conveniently nonconformist interpretations of contemporary events or enact thinly disguised revenge fantasies.[51] In fact, critics of judicial or predictive astrology often claimed that prophecies of the future based on the stars and other natural signs were "heathen" at best and ultimately the "work of the devil," reminding readers of texts such as Matthew 24:24 which cite false prophets and signs.[52] Milton, too, must have been skeptical about natural signs or prodigies which had no scriptural basis, but as the defenders of astrology pointed out, numerous verses could be read as justifying astrology, especially Matthew's account of the nativity and the earthquakes, comets, and eclipses of the apocalypse. As one defender of astrology argued:

> though Comets...do not *make* [my emphasis] future events uncontroulably legible, yet when they are placed in Conjunction with Sacred Script, they are not without their proper Instruction, but foretell singular things provided the word of God (who is the creator of Comets) be the rule of that Interpretation.[53]

A similar, conservative acceptance of natural signs based on scripture seems to inform the richly ambiguous lines of *Paradise Regained* in which Jesus rejects "false portents." He rejects them because they are sent from Satan, have no basis in scripture, and imply a belief in fate rather than God (*PR* 4.489, 491). Satan reads in the stars what fate has in store for Jesus and, ironically, he is right: Jesus will suffer violence and "cruel death," but Satan is unable to understand the importance of suffering for Christ's kingdom to come, is unable to distinguish between the real and figurative characteristics of the kingdom, and is reduced to feeble puns about the nature of the kingdom's eternal presence. Since his reading of the stars is based on fatalism – Satan is the only character to use the word "dismal" with its connotations of astrological determinism (1.101, 4.452) – the meaning of the stars is beyond his grasp. No date is "prefixt" in the "Starry Rubric" for the beginning of the kingdom, leaving Satan perplexed about what is meant by "eternal" and "without end" (4.382–93). Satan then sends storms, thunder, lightning, and dreams as signs of that cruel, uncertain future to frighten Jesus into submission and to urge him to begin his kingdom before the time set by God. Such signs "seem to point" to "turbulencies in the affairs of men" and again Satan is partly right, but to accept Satan's reading of the storms is to accept

Satan himself rather than scripture. Instead Jesus asserts his freedom of choice. Refusing to be compelled by the signs and prodigies which "oft fore-signify and threaten ill" (4.482, 464), Jesus rejects the "portents" not because signs are inherently false but because they are "not sent from God." He remains steadfast in his belief in his Father's eternal kingdom as it has been revealed to him in scripture.

More importantly, Milton counters the royalist reading of comets and signs with his apocalyptic one, prophesying the fall of monarchy and its anti-Christian reign. Regardless of the truth or falsity of the reports of lightning striking conformist churches, of meteors in the shape of fiery dragons falling to the ground, or of comets portending the fall of princes, Milton could be certain that the apocalyptic tenor and meaning of his "Autumnal Star" would be recognized. The natural portents interpreted by astrologers confirmed the visions of judgment cited in scripture which everyone would have known, whether or not they believed that comets or any other prodigies were true signs. By using this simile Milton could draw on both scriptural and astrological discourses, creating a powerful image which conveys once again his continuing commitment to reformation in England. Knowing that comets were associated with the fall of princes, he associates both with Satan's apocalyptic downfall in order to condemn the Stuart monarchy, especially its confusion of spiritual and civil authority and its use of civil power to force free consciences. By condemning Satan's astrological predictions (4.382–93) as "false portents" and rejecting his interpretation of the storm's significance (4.462–64), as well as refusing the temptation to name the precise date of his kingdom's inception, Jesus also indirectly condemns both the Anglican settlement and Fifth Monarchist radicalism.

Royalists often compared Charles II to Christ, turning the star that appeared on the day of Charles's birth into a sign of the messianic Restoration of 1660.[54] By placing Jesus, not Charles II, on "David's throne" and having Satan fall like a comet to the earth, Milton emphasizes the authority of scripture and Christ's spiritual kingdom, both of which were corrupted by Satan in the poem and the Stuart regime in Restoration England. By having Jesus refuse to act before his time or to name the date of his Second Coming, Milton also distances himself from enthusiasts like Thomas Venner and his congregation of Fifth Monarchists who attempted to usher in Christ's kingdom on earth by seizing political power in January 1661, not to mention from many of his own suggestions of an imminent apocalypse in the 1640s. Not force of arms but patience and scriptural combat will lead to Christ's kingdom.

The "battle of the Book," the "hermeneutic contest" between Satan and Jesus throughout *Paradise Regained*, then, prefigures the apocalyptic battle at the end of history and is informed by both scriptural and astrological imagery.[55] By associating with Satan views of corrupt religious and, therefore, political life which he had fought against earlier in his career and continued to fight against during the Restoration, Milton shows his readers what must be accomplished before Satan is defeated for ever and Christ's kingdom can begin. The sources of corruption are the same in 1671 as they were in 1641: the confusion of religious and civil authority, the persecution of those who seek God's will through the Word and Spirit alone, and the idolatry which both of these views imply. That Milton would engage in such a polemic against Anglicanism in the 1660s and 1670s when the persecution of nonconformists was at its height speaks clearly, albeit quietly and figuratively, of his ongoing commitment to this embattled minority community. Despair, quietism, and conformity may have been possibilities for some defenders of "the Good Old Cause" after the failure of the revolution, as they have been for other failed revolutionaries, but not for Milton. He created a hero whose patience, endurance, and faith were the conditions for nonconformity's survival in the Restoration wilderness, giving it a strategy for resistance and a hope for renewal until the apocalypse finally arrived.

NOTES

1. Frederic Jameson, "Religion and Ideology: A Political Reading of *Paradise Lost*," in Francis Barker et al. (eds.), *Literature, Politics, and Theory* (London, 1986), pp. 37, 50. See also Joan Bennett's more detailed analysis in *Reviving Liberty: Radical Christian Humanism in Milton's Great Poems* (Cambridge, Mass., 1989), pp. 2–6.
2. Andrew Milner, *John Milton and the English Revolution* (London, 1981), pp. 168, 174.
3. Gary Hamilton, "*Paradise Regained* and the Private Houses," in P. G. Stanwood (ed.), *Of Poetry and Politics: New Essays on Milton and His World* (Binghamton, N.Y., 1995), pp. 248, 240.
4. Ashraf Rushdy, *The Empty Garden: The Subject of Late Milton* (Pittsburgh and London, 1992), p. 118, and Laura Knoppers, *Historicizing Milton: Spectacle, Power, and Poetry in Restoration England* (Athens, Ga., 1994), p. 141.
5. Parenthetical references to Milton's poetry in my text are to *John Milton, Complete Poems and Major Prose*, ed. Merritt Y. Hughes (New York, 1957). Biblical references are to The Holy Bible, King James Version (Nashville, 1984). Throughout this paper "apocalypse" refers primarily to the allegories, visions, and signs about the end of the world and the beginning of a new heaven and

earth outlined in The Revelation of St. John the Divine 4–20 and the "little" apocalypses of Matthew 24, Mark 13, and Luke 21, but the Bible refers to many different examples of the apocalyptic genre, including Daniel 7–12, several apocryphal works, and many other texts such as 2 Thessalonians 2 which include apocalyptic features. I use "apocalyptic" rather than "millennial" or "millenarian" to refer to Milton's views of the end of the world for reasons outlined by John Shawcross in this book. Essentially, Milton held a broadly apocalyptic view of history throughout his career and continued to refer to a literal Second Coming and reign of Christ even when Christ's imminence was unlikely, but remained circumspect about a thousand-year reign of Christ and the saints preceding or separate from the Last Judgment.

6. I assume that *On Christian Doctrine* is Milton's unfinished work. See Gordon Campbell, Thomas N. Corns, John K. Hale, David I. Holmes, and Fiona J. Tweedie, "The Provenance of *De Doctrina Christiana*," *Milton Quarterly* 31 (1997), p. 110.

7. My brief synopsis is based on the following: Bryan W. Ball, *A Great Expectation: Eschatological Thought in English Protestantism to 1660* (Leiden, 1975); B. S. Capp, "The Political Dimension of Apocalyptic Thought," in C. A. Patrides and Joseph Wittreich (eds.), *The Apocalypse in English Renaissance Thought and Literature: Patterns, Antecedents and Repercussions* (Manchester 1984), pp. 93–124; Norman Cohn, *Cosmos, Chaos and the World to Come: The Ancient Roots of Apocalyptic Faith* (New Haven and London, 1993); Katharine R. Firth, *The Apocalyptic Tradition in Reformation Britain, 1530–1645* (Oxford, 1979); Christopher Hill, *Antichrist in Seventeenth-Century England* (London, 1971); and W. R. Owens, "John Bunyan and English Millenarianism," in David Gay et al. (eds.), *Awakening Words: John Bunyan and the Language of Community* (Newark, 2000), pp. 81–96. Stella Revard's chapter in this book has also been especially useful.

8. See Stella Revard's acute analysis in this book of the link between politics and the apocalypse throughout Milton's career.

9. For further discussion of the wilderness image in Puritan texts, see Christopher Hill, *The Experience of Defeat: Milton and Some Contemporaries* (London, 1984), pp. 47, 72, 77, 122–23, 300–03, 359, and William Haller, *The Rise of Puritanism* (New York, 1938), p. 131. See also Samuel Smith, " 'Christ's Victorie Over the Dragon': The Apocalypse in *Paradise Regained*," in *Milton Studies* 29 (1993), pp. 59–82. According to Smith *Paradise Regained* and Thomas Taylor's *Christs Victorie Over the Dragon or Satans Downfall* (1633) share the apocalyptic subtext of the temptation and wilderness narrative, but the immediate political and religious context of the poem is not discussed.

10. John Diodati, *Pious Annotations Upon the Holy Bible* (3rd edn., London, 1651), D2.

11. See Stella Revard's analysis of references to Daniel in *Paradise Regained* in this book.

12. John Bale, *The Image of Both Churches, Being an Exposition of the Most Wonderful Book of Revelation*, in *Select Works of John Bale* (Cambridge, 1849), pp. 401–10, 252.

13. David Pareus, *A Commentary upon the Divine Revelation of the Apostle and Evangelist John*, trans. Elias Arnold (Amsterdam, 1644), pp. 16, 266, 272, 275.
14. Diodati, *Pious Annotations*, Xxx4.
15. John Downame et al., *Annotations Upon All the Books of the New and Old Testament* (2nd edn., London, 1651), Rev. 12:14–17. For Milton's references to the Waldenses as the true church hidden in the wilderness, see *The Tenure of Kings and Magistrates* (*CP* III: 227), *Eikonoklastes* (*CP* III: 514), and *Considerations Touching the Likeliest Means to Remove Hirelings Out of the Church* (*CP* VII: 291, 306, 308, 311).
16. Mary Cary, *The Little Horns Doom and Downfall* (London, 1651), pp. 8, 39–41, 171.
17. Hill, *Antichrist*.
18. See Mark Goldie, "The Theory of Religious Intolerance in Restoration England," in O. P. Gell, J. I. Israel, and N. Tyacke (eds.), *From Persecution to Toleration* (Oxford, 1991), p. 332, and J. R. Knott, Jr., "'Suffering for Truth's Sake': Milton and Martyrdom," in David Loewenstein and James Grantham Turner (eds.), *Politics, Poetics, and Hermeneutics in Milton's Prose* (Cambridge, 1990), pp. 153–70.
19. See Knoppers, *Historicizing Milton*, pp. 110–15.
20. Ronald Hutton, *The Restoration* (Oxford, 1985), p. 156. See also John Spurr, *The Restoration Church of England, 1646–1689* (New Haven, 1991), pp. 39–72.
21. Hamilton, "*Paradise Regained* and the Private Houses," p. 241.
22. Samuel Parker, "Preface" to *Bishop Bramhall's Vindication of Himself and the Episcopal Clergy, from the Presbyterian Charge of Popery* (London, 1672), e2.
23. Howard Schultz, "Christ and Antichrist in *Paradise Regained*," *PMLA* 67 (1952), p. 797. I am generally indebted to Schultz throughout this section on the ecclesiastical context of *Paradise Regained*. The source of the shepherd/flock image is, of course, biblical, but see also Richard Baxter, *The Reformed Pastor*, ed. Hugh Martin (London, 1956), pp. 50, 57, 61–71. Baxter emphasizes that "every minister should be a man that hath much insight into the Tempter's wiles."
24. See Simon Patrick, *A Friendly Debate between a Conformist and a Nonconformist* (London, 1669), and Samuel Butler, *Hudibras* (London, 1663), part 1, canto 1, lines 221–28. See also Schultz, "Christ and Antichrist," 798.
25. Schultz, "Christ and Antichrist," p. 799.
26. The eschatological dimension of the Eucharist is based on Luke 14:15–24, 13:29, Matthew 8:11, Mark 14:25, and other texts, including several parables of the kingdom. For further discussion, see William R. Crockett, *Eucharist: Symbol of Transformation* (New York, 1989), pp. 5–8, 206, and Horton Davies, *Worship and Theology in England: From Andrewes to Baxter and Fox, 1603–1690* (Princeton, 1975), pp. 13, 208, 323, 415.
27. Bard Thompson, *Liturgies of the Western Church* (Cleveland, 1961), pp. 369–70.
28. John Gadbury, *De Cometis* (London, 1665), p. 13.
29. For astrological signs of the end times in *Paradise Lost*, see Malabika Sarkar's chapter in this book.

30. B. S. Capp, *Astrology and the Popular Press* (London, 1979), p. 170. For the popularity of almanacs, see Keith Thomas, *Religion and the Decline of Magic* (Harmondsworth, 1971), pp. 360–61.

31. Cited in Capp, *Astrology*, p. 168. For a discussion of John Bainbridge's views about the 1618 comet, see Malabika Sarkar's chapter in this book, pp. 86–87.

32. John Booker, *The Bloudy Almanack, for this present Jubilee* (London, 1647), frontispiece, p. 3. For Napier's views, see Stella Revard's chapter in this book.

33. Ann Geneva, *Astrology and the Seventeenth-Century Mind: William Lilly and the Language of the Stars* (Manchester, 1995), p. 56, and William Lilly, *England's Propheticall Merlin* (London, 1644), pp. 25, 44.

34. Capp, *Astrology*, pp. 164–65.

35. Nicholas Culpeper, *Catastrophe Magnatum: or, The Fall of Monarchie* (London, 1652), pp. 68, 40, and John Durant, *A Set Time for Judgement* (London, 1656), cited in Ball, *A Great Expectation*, p. 110.

36. In addition to remembering the comets of 1660, 1664, 1665, and 1667, some readers perhaps recalled a "fiery dragon," a type of meteor or comet known to be especially menacing because of its long tail, seen 15/16 November 1656. See [n.a.], *Miraculum Signum Coeleste: A Discourse of Those Miraculous Prodigies that have been seen since the Birth of our blessed Lord and Saviour Jesus Christ* (London, 1658), pp. 24–25. See also *Samson Agonistes*, line 1692, for a similar image of scriptural and astrological judgment.

37. Cited in *Miraculum Signum Coeleste*, p. 23; John Gadbury, *Natura Prodigiorum: or, A Discourse Touching the Nature of Prodigies* (London, 1665), p. 38; and Samuel Danforth, *An Astronomical Description of the Late Comet or Blazing Star* (London, 1666), frontispiece v.

38. [n.a.], *Mr Lillyes Prognostications of 1667* (London, 1667), Vincent Wing, *An Almanack and Prognostication for the Year of Our Lord, 1670* (London, 1669), C2; [n.a.], *The Bloody Almanack For the Year, 1666. And the Fiery Trigon* (London, 1666), p. 4–5; and William Lilly, *Astrological Judgements for the Year 1668* (London, 1667), A3–A4.

39. [n.a.], *Mirabilis Annus, or The Year of Prodigies and Wonders* (London, 1661), A4ᵛ.

40. Thomas, *Religion and the Decline of Magic*, pp. 409, 471.

41. Gadbury, *De Cometis*, p. 18.

42. Lilly, *Astrological Judgements*, A3, and Capp, *Astrology*, p. 48.

43. Capp, *Astrology*, pp. 173–74.

44. Thomas Trigge, *Calendarium Astrologicum: or, an Almanack For . . . 1666* (London, 1666), C2.

45. [n.a.], *The Bloody Almanack*, p. 4.

46. [n.a.], *King Charles his Starre* (London, 1654), pp. 4, 35, 36.

47. John Gadbury, *Britains Royal Star* (London, 1660), p. 41.

48. [n.a.], *The Blazing Star: or, A Discourse of Comets* (London, 1665), pp. 12–13, 42.

49. Ibid., p. 5.

50. John Spencer, *A Discourse of Prodigies* (Cambridge, 1665), pp. 16, 102.

51. [n.a.], *Mirabilis Annus*, pp. 26, 37, 16, 18, 69.

52. See John Allen, *Cases of Conscience Concerning Astrologie* (London, 1659), p. 8, and Spencer, *A Discourse of Prodigies*, p. 20.

53. Christopher Ness, *A Full and True Account of the Late Blazing Star* (London, 1680), p. 7.

54. David Gay's paper at the 1997 Rocky Mountain Medieval and Renaissance Association Conference, "'The Starry Rubric': Renaissance Astrology and Political Wisdom in Milton's *Paradise Regained*," triggered my interest in the language of comets and the apocalypse, even though he was primarily interested in a different astrological phenomenon – the appearance of "Charles Wain" at the birth of Charles II and its use by royalists as the sign of a messianic Restoration. See Gay's "Astrology and Iconoclasm in Milton's *Paradise Regained*," *Studies in English Literature* 41 (2001), p. 175.

55. Georgia Christopher, "The Secret Agent in *Paradise Regained*," *Modern Language Quarterly* 41 (1980), p. 131, and Mary Ann Radzinowicz, *Milton's Epics and the Book of Psalms* (Princeton, 1989), p. 26.

Inspiration and melancholy in Samson Agonistes

Karen L. Edwards

Milton deftly connects satanic "inspiration" and flatulence when in *Paradise Lost*, Book 4, Satan is discovered attempting "if, inspiring venom, he might...raise [in Eve]...inordinate desires / Blown up with high conceits" (4.804, 806, 808–09).[1] Upon being touched with Ithuriel's spear, Satan himself is "blown up" in a different sense:

> up he starts
> Discoverd and surpriz'd. As when a spark
> Lights on a heap of nitrous Powder, laid
> Fit for the Tun som Magazin to store
> Against a rumord Warr, the Smuttie graine
> With sudden blaze diffus'd, inflames the Aire:
> So started up in his own shape the Fiend.
>
> (*PL* 4.813–19)

John Guillory has commented on this passage that "[t]he impulse to literalize is in a hidden sense apocalyptic, and Ithuriel's spear, as it touches off Satan's explosive return to 'his own likeness' is a small rehearsal for the final conflagration out of which New Heaven and New Earth will arise."[2] Guillory's comment lets us understand Satan as a failed phoenix. He will not arise from ashes, his own or the world's, to embody the new creation, but will endlessly revert to "his own shape."

Inspiration, apocalyptic violence, and the phoenix meet again in *Samson Agonistes*. But the poetic context, like the historical moment, has changed.[3] The line between true inspiration and false, so clearly demarcated and maintained in *Paradise Lost*, is blurred in the ambiguous "rouzing motions" (*SA* 1382) Samson begins to feel. The epic represents a controlled explosion that demolishes satanic pretense and lays bare the truth; the dramatic poem offers a mediated and "distract" view of offstage destruction. Whereas *Paradise Lost* shows Satan to be incapable of phoenixlike regeneration, *Samson Agonistes* subtly questions the usefulness of the phoenix as a figure for resurrection. Interpretive certainty recedes in *Samson Agonistes*. Yet the apocalyptic final scene of the play is shown crucially to derive from the interpretive act of its hero. If Samson has been allowed a revelation, readers have not – and *if* precisely locates the problem. Near the end of the poem, Samson's offstage body, as described by the Messenger, signifies that he is thinking: "with head a while enclin'd, / And eyes fast fixt he stood, as one who pray'd, / Or some great matter in his mind revolv'd" (1636–38). But this is to see him through a glass, darkly: our view of Samson is mediated by a messenger who himself is uncertain of what he has seen, leaving us unavoidably aware that we are engaged in an act of interpreting Samson's mental processes. *That* he is thinking is uncertain; *what* he is thinking is withheld – but not *simply* withheld. The play encourages us to understand Samson as a melancholic, and in so doing it authorizes incompatible readings of the interpretive process we attribute to him. Samson's thinking may be illuminated by divine inspiration; but, equally, it may be darkened by self-delusion. Melancholy, terrible and glorious, allows either possibility.

It is a daring representational strategy. Lodged at the center of the increasingly secular cultural politics of the Restoration, melancholy is the weapon of Milton's enemies. In *Samson Agonistes* he wrests it from them. Boldly reshaping the conventional typology of Samson as a Christ figure, he represents rather the experience of the believer awaiting apocalypse, an apocalypse no longer "shortly-expected."[4] This essay will argue that by rendering unstable our judgment of Samson's final act, the play instructs us how to wait for the Last Judgment.

"Enthusiasme is nothing else but a misconceit of being inspired," Henry More declares in *Enthusiasmus Triumphatus*, first published in 1656.[5] From its earliest use in English, the word "enthusiasm" encompassed both secular imagination (or fancy) and the claim to divine inspiration.[6] More's treatise draws hostile attention to the claim, representing it as delusion. What permits this treatment and makes it distinctive is More's fusion of traditional and emerging medical theories about melancholy. Enthusiasm, as understood by the Renaissance, was the child of mixed classical parentage, born from the union of the creative, melancholic temperament described in Aristotle's *Rhetoric* and the poetic furor described in Plato's *Ion* and *Symposium*.[7] Melancholy itself, in Renaissance humoral theory, could denote an unhealthy imbalance of the humors as well as the temperament associated with creativity.[8] Intertwined and malleable concepts, melancholy and enthusiasm were vulnerable to the reforming tendencies of the seventeenth century. Robert Burton's contribution is decisive. In *The Anatomy of Melancholy* (1621), he argues that enthusiasm is a symptom of religious melancholy.[9] His argument represents a departure from what had become by his day the conventional Establishment criticism of enthusiasm, that is, that enthusiasts are hypocritical charlatans who merely pretend to be inspired by the Holy Spirit. No, says Burton: they are ill, "farre gone with melancholy, if not quite mad, and have more need of Physicke, then many a man that keepes his bed, more need of Hellebor, then those that are in Bedlam."[10]

More's innovatory treatment of enthusiasm owes a great deal to Burton. With devastating satirical effect, however, More reclassifies it, so that it appears in *Enthusiasmus Triumphatus* not as a symptom of religious melancholy (a category of disease, Burton admits, which is of his own invention), but as a symptom of hypochondriacal melancholy, fast becoming the era's most fashionable disease.[11] Humoral theory held that any distempered part of the body could cause melancholy.[12] Accordingly hypochondriacal melancholy was attributed to distempered hypochondria, viscera such as the spleen, liver, and gall-bladder.[13] Burton regards this "*Hipocondricall* or flatuous Melancholy" as "the most grievous and frequent" kind.[14] More's treatise is devoid of Burton's compassionate concern and exploits for satirical purposes a growing preoccupation with "vapours" (rather than imbalanced humors) as the cause of disease.[15] The satire culminates in More's claim that inspiration is identical to the symptom for which "windy melancholy" is named:

The spirit then that wings the Enthusiast in such a wonderful manner, is nothing else but that flatulency which is in the melancholy complexion, & rises out of the *Hypochondriacal* humour upon some occasionall heat, as winde out of an *Æeolipila* applied to the fire.[16]

More's equation of flatulence and *inflatus* at one stroke debases melancholy's long association with divine and poetic *enthusiasmos*, deriding their once venerated claims to prophecy, fluency, and vision. The equation not only ridicules enthusiasm and renders suspect any assertion of being inspired; it also provides a means, seized upon at the Restoration, for enforcing conservative political control. After 1660 religious and political dissent, identified with enthusiasm, becomes increasingly defined as the expression of mental pathology.[17]

Most vulnerable to ridicule was enthusiasm's claim to illumination, its claim to have access to the future. Seizing upon More's argument, Joseph Glanvill identifies as an infallible sign of the enthusiast's disturbed mind a preoccupation with "last things." In *A Loyal Tear Dropt on the Vault of Our Late Martyred Sovereign* (1667), he condemns the "publick Spirit of *Phrensie*

& mischief in the World" that has recently prevailed (and still threatens), when religion was torn from its association with virtue and "placed in *emotions, raptures,* and *swelling words* of *Vanity*":

> And when these had *kindled* the *imagination,* and sent the *phansie* into the *Clouds* to flutter there in *mystical non-sense*: and when it was mounted on the *Wings* of the *Wind*, and got into the *Revelations* to *loosen* the *seals, pour* out the *vials,* and *phantastically* to interpret the *fates* of *Kingdoms*; when it flew into the *Tongue* in an *extravagant ramble,* and abused the Name and Word of God, mingling it with *canting, unintelligible* babble. I say, when the *diseasd* and *disturbed phansie* thus *variously displayed* it self, many mad themselves believe that they were *acted* by the *Spirit,* and that those *wild agitations* of *sick Imagination,* were *divine motions.*[18]

"*Wings* of the *Wind*" (echoing More's "spirit then that wings the Enthusiast") signals the nature of the illness that so distorts the imagination. In his conclusion Glanvill is explicit: "When *heated Melancholy* had kindled the busie and *active phansie,* the *Enthusiast* talks of *Illuminations, New Lights, Revelations,* and many *wonderful fine things.*"[19]

The charge continued to be made for the next two decades, becoming so familiar that the briefest of references to the apocalypse suffices for George Rust in *Discourse of the Use of Reason in Matters of Religion* (1683):

> [I]t is very well known what an Innumerable company of Men there have been, who upon such like grounds have very pertinaciously affirmed themselves to be compounded of Glass, or Butter, to be Dogs, Cats, Kings, Emperors, Popes, the Paraclete, the Messiah, the last and greatest Prophet, the Judge of Quick and Dead, nay, even God himself. And we find most of these to have been actuated with an Excess of Joy, and transported with a seemingly Divine Fervor. And which Effects are so far from the Inspiration of the Holy Spirit, that they are no better then Frenzies and Symptoms of Melancholy, and derive their Original from no higher Principle then the undue Fermentation of the Blood and Spirits, and chiefly from that Melancholy which above all other disposes the Minds of Men to fancy Divine Influxes and Illuminations.[20]

The "*strange sights, voices,* and wonderful *discoveries*" that enthusiasts dream, Glanvill asserts, are "nothing but the unquiet agitations of their own disordered brains." For the advocates of rational religion, it is the enthusiasts' claims to have discovered, or uncovered, the mysteries of the future, and specifically of the apocalypse, which are most offensive – and which can most easily be construed as a symptom of hypochondriacal melancholy.

Samson is not called "melancholy" in *Samson Agonistes*, a fact the significance of which we will need to consider. The term appears, however, in "Of that sort of Dramatic Poem which is call'd Tragedy," Milton's prefatory note to the poem. There "melancholic" appears along with "salt" and "sowr," where it is used to illustrate the concept of homeopathic purging: "Nor is Nature wanting in her own effects to make good his [i.e., Aristotle's] assertion: for so in Physic things of melancholic hue and quality are us'd against melancholy, sowr against sowr, salt to remove salt humours." In one of the few sustained studies of melancholy in *Samson Agonistes*, Raymond Waddington argued some years ago that Milton's preface informs us that the action of the dramatic poem is to be the homeopathic purging of destructive passions. The purging occurs, Waddington explains, when Samson encounters three parodic versions of himself in Manoa, Dalila, and Harapha.[21] But melancholy is not a passion and is thus not comprehended in "pity and fear, or terror . . . and such like passions." Rather, Milton adduces melancholy as a confirming example: as medicine acts upon the patient's humors in the physical realm, so tragedy acts upon the reader's passions in the emotional one. This does not mean, however, that melancholy is merely an example, or that as an example it has only one function. On the contrary, the prominent mention of melancholy in the preface introduces it into the field of expectations that readers bring to the play. It guides us to recognize in Samson the signs of melancholy. But Samson's is not the hypochondriacal melancholy of conservative Restoration writers. Nor is it the medicalized melancholy of contemporary physicians.

The medical community of Milton's day did not engage in Henry More's politically motivated pathologizing of melancholy. In *De Anima Brutorum* (1672), the prominent physician Thomas Willis displays compassion for and appreciation of the complex ravages of melancholic disease, observing at the outset of his discussion that "it is a complicated Distemper of the Brain and Heart."[22] For many aspects of his discussion of melancholy, Willis is dependent on Burton, as are most writers on melancholy in the late seventeenth and eighteenth centuries. Only in exploring the cause of melancholy does Willis significantly depart from Burton. Rather than the dozens of causes Burton assigns to melancholy, beginning with "*God* and *his Angells*, or *by Gods permission from the Divell*, and his Ministers," Willis offers a single cause.[23] When an "evilly affected" spleen is involved, it is properly called "Hypochondriack," Willis states; but it is not a disease of the humors.[24] Rather, its cause must be sought in irregularities of the animal spirits and their differential effects upon "Brain and Heart."[25] Willis explains:

as *Melancholick* people talk idly, it proceeds from the vice or fault of the Brain, and the inordination of the Animal Spirits dwelling in it; but as they become very sad and fearful, this is deservedly attributed to the Passion of the Heart.[26]

We recognize in Willis's attribution of different traits to brain and heart the traditional poles of melancholy, what the nineteenth century would call "high" and "low" states. The state Willis labels "idle talking" had only recently, and well within political memory, been called "inspiration," "prophecy," "illumination," and "revelation."

Borrowing from Burton, Willis offers a general definition of melancholy which embraces the two poles: it is "a raving without a Feavour or fury, joined with fear and sadness."[27] Although melancholy has "manifold Delirious *Symptoms*," he observes, its distortions of thinking are its "*primary* Phænomena":

1. That the distemper'd are almost continually busied in thinking, that their *Phantasie* is scarce ever idle or at quiet. 2. In their thinking they comprehend in their mind fewer things than before they were wont, that oftentimes they roll about in their mind day and night the same thing, never thinking of other things that are sometimes of far greater moment. 3. The *Ideas* of objects or conceptions appear often deformed, and like hobgoblins, but are still represented in a larger kind or form; so that all small things seem to them great and difficult.[28]

We name melancholy according to what its obsession centers on, Willis explains, that is, "as it is employed about diverse things, to wit, either Sacred, or Magical, or Humane...the chief of which...are Religious, Amorous, and Jealous *Melancholy*."[29]

The "new" medicine of the seventeenth century – though admirable in its recognition of the range and severity of melancholy's symptoms, its compassion for sufferers, and its commitment to finding a cure – offers no comfort to the melancholic who would claim divine inspiration. For Willis and his contemporaries, melancholy is strictly an illness; claiming divine inspiration falls under the medical category of "ravings," to rehearse which "would be a prodigious work, and almost an endless task," Willis declares.[30] It is this disavowal of any possibility of inspiration which makes the new medicalizing of melancholy as unacceptable to Milton as More's politicizing of it is. To represent melancholy as it was traditionally understood, Milton cannot call Samson a melancholic. The term had become, for Milton's purposes, unspeakable. The brave new discourse of the Restoration had stripped melancholy of its ancient grandeur; melancholic *enthusiasmos* cannot be taken seriously after 1660. The poet who had hailed "divinest Melancholy" in his youth is able to make use of the traditional concept for the hero of *Samson Agonistes* only by withholding the name.[31] Why he should want to make use of melancholy is what we must consider next.

When we turn to Samson's suffering in *Samson Agonistes*, we find depicted not an obsession with "objects or conceptions" but Samson's horrified awareness that he can no longer marshal or control his thoughts. His sufferings are terrible, but this is not the suffering that Willis and his colleagues describe. This is, rather, a tormented inwardness, a painful consciousness of his thoughts *as thoughts*. At the outset of the play, although he can find some slight ease for his enslaved and overworked body, Samson laments that he can find no ease:

> From restless thoughts, that like a deadly swarm
> Of Hornets arm'd, no sooner found alone,
> But rush upon me thronging, and present
> Times past, what once I was, and what am now.
>
> (*SA* 19–22)

Waddington observes that the swarm of hornets "possibly has a basis in the iconography of melancholy."[32] In a more direct allusion to melancholy, Manoa warns his son to leave the despairing "suggestions which proceed / From anguish of the mind and humours black" (599–600). But leaving such suggestions is precisely what a melancholic cannot do. Samson confirms his father's diagnosis by ignoring his advice to "be calm" (604):

> O that torment should not be confin'd
> To the bodies wounds and sores
> With maladies innumerable
> In heart, head, brest, and reins;
> But must secret passage find
> To th' inmost mind,
> There exercise all his fierce accidents,
> And on her purest spirits prey,
> As on entrails, joints, and limbs,
> With answerable pains, but more intense,
> Though void of corporal sense.
>
> (*SA* 606–16)

The intensity of the pain described here suggests that hornets are not adequate as a simile for the thoughts Samson cannot leave.

As Samson's anatomizing of his suffering continues, the increasing intensity of his language, and particularly the likening of his thoughts to "deadly stings," suggests the grievous harm which scorpions were thought to inflict:

> My griefs not only pain me
> As a lingring disease,
> But finding no redress, ferment and rage,
> Nor less then wounds immedicable
> Ranckle, and fester, and gangrene,
> To black mortification.
> Thoughts my Tormentors arm'd with deadly stings
> Mangle my apprehensive tenderest parts,
> Exasperate, exulcerate, and raise
> Dire inflammation which no cooling herb
> Or medcinal liquor can asswage,
> Nor breath of Vernal Air from snowy *Alp*.
> Sleep hath forsook and giv'n me o're
> To deaths benumming Opium as my only cure.
> Thence faintings, swounings of despair,
> And sense of Heav'ns desertion. 　　(*SA* 617–32)

As the natural historian Edward Topsell explains: "in short space the [scorpion's] poyson disperseth it self within the skin, and runneth all over the body, never ceasing untill it come to possesse some predominant or principall vitall part, and then followeth death."[33] Or the desire for death, in Samson's case. The implicit reference to scorpions makes of Samson's lament an elaboration and demonstration of Macbeth's cry, "O, full of scorpions is my mind" (itself a response to Lady's Macbeth's warning, "You must leave this").[34] It would perhaps be difficult to find an apter figure for the anguish produced by melancholy's sad and fearful aspect. But the sting of scorpions hints, too, at melancholy's prophetic aspect, an aspect expressing itself, in the seventeenth century, in intimations of apocalypse. The reinforcing of "torment" by "Tormentors" in Samson's lament evokes Revelation 9:5, describing the torture inflicted by locusts: "And to them it was given that they should not kill them, but that they should be tormented five months: and their torment *was* as the torment of a scorpion, when he striketh a man."

　The hint of apocalypse makes even more pointed the absence of any explicit reference to the future in Samson's complaint, which painfully juxtaposes or even reverses past and present ("present / Times past": *SA* 21–22). Melancholic disease erases the future by transforming the present into a prospect of unrelieved, indefinitely extended pain. This despair, a loss of hope which amounts to loss of the future, often drives the melancholic to suicide, so that "deaths benumming Opium" comes to seem the "only cure." As Burton observes, "it proceeds many times, that [melancholics] are weary of their lives, and ferall thoughts to offer violence to their owne persons, come into their mindes."[35] Such despair is a symptom of melancholy and may be regarded as the most extreme expression of a sufferer's characteristic anguish of mind. Those scholars who have written about Samson's melancholy have tended, however, to *equate* his melancholy with despair – despair in its specific, theological significance, the loss of faith in one's salvation. Defining Samson's melancholy in this way makes it possible to argue that he is cured by the end of the play, a reading established fifty years ago with the publication of D. C. Allen's *The Harmonious Vision*.[36] In this influential study Allen argued that the play traces Samson's step-by-step regeneration from despair as he overcomes the different temptations offered by Manoa, Dalila, and Harapha.

Such regenerationist readings (as John Carey has named them) cannot, except by recourse to typology, reconcile Samson's recovery from despair with the poem's apocalyptic elements.[37] These burst into the poem in the messenger's description of Samson's final act:

> As with the force of winds and waters pent,
> When Mountains tremble, those two massie Pillars
> With horrible convulsion to and fro,
> He tugg'd, he shook, till down they came and drew
> The whole roof after them, with burst of thunder.
>
> *(SA* 1647–51)

In the face of the Restoration's repudiation of eschatological concerns, the unmistakable references to apocalypse in the Messenger's description are highly polemical (and, in the reference to "two massie Pillars," horribly amplified for twenty-first-century readers). Such references suggest not that Samson's melancholy has been "cured" but that, manifesting itself in its full grandeur and terror, it has been transformed into its prophetic aspect. If we recall that Samson's despair is but a symptom of melancholy, we will be less optimistic about the possibility of a twenty-four-hour cure.[38] Milton's contemporaries did not underestimate the tenacity of melancholy, regarding it as one of the most distressing features of the illness. Spenser represents this feature in the Redcrosse Knight's encounter with Despair in *The Faerie Queene*. As Harold Skulsky observes: "To Una's 'great perplexitie,' Redcrosse persists in 'Disdeining life, desiring leave to die' even after such feelings have outlived the function of godly sorrow by prompting him to learn how to take 'assured hold' on hope's anchor (x.22)."[39] Melancholy *can* be cured, Burton assures his readers, but not easily, and indeed the most forceful language of his assurance is reserved for melancholy's *resistance* to being "helped":

Inveterate Melancholy, howsoever it may seeme to be a continuate, inexorable disease, hard to bee cured, accompanying them to their graves most part, as *Montanus* observes, yet many times it may be helped, even that which is most violent, or at least, according to the same Author, *it may be mitigated and much eased. Nil desperandum.* It may be hard to cure, but not impossible, for him that is most grievously affected, if he be but willing to be helped.[40]

Willis declares that when melancholy is "suddenly excited, from a solitary evident cause," it may sometimes "cease of its own accord, or with a little help," cease relatively quickly.[41] "The Cure very difficultly, and not under a long time succeeds," however, when the illness is well-established.[42] Overcoming despair is not equivalent to curing melancholy, especially a long-settled melancholy such as Samson's.

If Milton does not represent Samson as a cured melancholic, then why represent him as a melancholic at all? If he is not cured by the play's end, must we interpret his destruction of the Philistines as an act of self-slaughter induced by melancholic desperation? It is easy to forget that there *is* a representational choice to be made, for Samson's melancholy seems too "natural" to require investigation. How, we may wonder, could a man who has lost his sight, his freedom, and his ability to serve his country with his God-given strength *not* be melancholy? We may even feel that in Samson's pain we glimpse what Milton may actually have felt in the last years of his life.[43] Yet melancholy's primary role in *Samson Agonistes* is a structural one. It motivates Samson's inability to act, which ensures the duration of the play. Milton's prefatory note to the play calls attention to classical precedent. But the influence of "*Æshulus, Sophocles, and Euripides*" does not preclude the influence of Kyd and Shakespeare on Samson's plight.[44] Elizabethan revenge tragedy has as one of its chief conventions the hero's delay in seeking vengeance. In *Hamlet* and *Samson Agonistes*, if not *The Spanish Tragedy*, the subtle energies of waiting, composed of doubt, second-guessing, and the paralyzing perception of interpretive ambiguity, are more compelling than the violent clarity of the final action. The hero's melancholic state focuses attention on his thinking processes, on how correctly he interprets (the Ghost, in *Hamlet*; the Holy Ghost, in *Samson Agonistes*). Readings which argue for Samson's ultimate restoration to health, and indeed those which assert his climactic violation of the moral code, see his waiting as a means to the greater end (whether seen as good or bad), not as the play's central action. *Is there a greater end than waiting?*

"When I consider…" suggests not. If "[t]hey also serve who only stand and waite," then waiting to serve God *is* serving God. As Anna Nardo comments: "awaiting the fullness of God's time is equivalent to waiting on God as a servant."[45] Patience so comprehensively overcomes the speaker's "fondly" self-important impatience that it may seem irrelevant to ask: "How long must the waiting go on?" Yet the sonnet hints at an answer. The breathless hurry, the intense activity, of those who "speed / And post o're Land and Ocean without rest" (ll. 12–13) colors the last line, whispering that momentous events are imminent, that the waiting may not be long. The powerful consolation offered by the sonnet derives in part from this effect.

Samson Agonistes offers no such consolation. "There I am wont to sit" (l. 4): Samson's opening direction to an anonymous helper indicates a longstanding habit of dreary waiting. There is no hint that justice, vengeance, or revelation approaches. Does that invalidate waiting as a way of serving God? Is not waiting in utter ignorance of "the day and the hour of Christ's coming" the condition of living in the fallen world?[46] It was a condition undoubtedly made clear to many by the Restoration, a sort of anti-Revelation. Significantly, a faint, distorted echo of "When I consider…" may be heard in *Samson Agonistes* at the moment that Samson decides to *cease* waiting:

> [*Sam.*] But who constrains me to the temple of *Dagon*,
> Not dragging? The *Philistian* Lords command.
> Commands are no constraints. If I obey them,
> I do it freely; venturing to displease
> God for the fear of Man, and Man prefer,
> Set God behind: which in his jealousie
> Shall never, unrepented, find forgiveness.
> Yet that he may dispense with me or thee
> Present in Temples at Idolatrous Rites
> For some important cause, thou needst not doubt.
> *Chor.* How thou wilt here come off surmounts my reach.
> *Sam.* Be of good courage, I begin to feel
> Some rouzing motions in me which dispose
> To something extraordinary my thoughts.   (*SA* 1370–83)

The ghostly presence of "When I consider…" behind Samson's speech may implicitly criticize Samson's decision not to wait. Like the speaker in the sonnet, Samson claims at first to know better than God how God

would or would not command him to serve. In the sonnet Patience intervenes to prevent that murmur, inducing the volta halfway through line 8.
In the passage just quoted, Samson interrupts his own first thoughts, pre-
maturely inducing the volta at the beginning of line 1377. In response
to the speaker's impatience, Patience explains that waiting is serving. In
response to the Chorus's anxiety, Samson hints at, but does not fully
articulate, his reason for ceasing to wait: "Some rouzing motions" is so
neutral as to be opaque.[47]

"The end... will be sudden," Milton declares of the Second Coming
in *De Doctrina Christiana*, and it will be "full of light."[48] Samson's end is
indeed sudden, but it is hardly full of light. "When I consider..." reveals
the value of waiting; "But who constrains me..." declines to reveal the
value of waiting no longer. Nonetheless, there is no overt condemnation of
Samson's decision in *Samson Agonistes*. The play itself withholds judgment,
though scholars have not.

To have waited or not to have waited: that critical debate focuses
on Samson's *final* act demonstrates how powerfully typological reading shapes our understanding of *Samson Agonistes* – typological reading,
that is, which asks if Samson is a glorious or a deeply flawed type of
Christ. Does his death demonstrate Christlike self-sacrifice, or does it
rather reveal how far short the type falls of the antitype? Typology's
sway has been vehemently rejected or embraced, but always in terms of
Samson's relationship to Christ. Thirty years ago Stanley Fish famously
renounced typology as the basis of a critical methodology for the poem,
which evoked from Joseph Wittreich the observation that "while distanc-
ing himself from typological readings of *Samson Agonistes*, Fish achieves
no distance at all from typologically determined [i.e., positive] interpretations of the Samson story."[49] Wittreich himself reinstates typology's
interpretive centrality and finds that it leads to a darker view of Samson's last act: "it [is] necessary that we entertain Samson's final action
as a negative, as a foolhardy embracing of self-destruction, while he is
engaged in the slaying of others."[50]

Ostensibly opposed in their methodology, the two readings agree in
concentrating on Samson's final act because they assume he must be
seen in relationship to Christ. But the play's insistent emphasis on the
centrality of waiting suggests that typology's focus in the play is not on
those who sacrifice themselves on the altar of judgment but on those who
wait in the painful darkness of unknowing for judgment to be revealed.
That, of course, is Samson's condition. He waits, blind and suffering, for
justice, for revelation, and, like all those who died "not having received

the promises," for the Messiah.[51] He thereby becomes the type of those born afterward who wait, in darkness, for Judgment, for apocalypse, for the coming of the Lamb. His melancholy is crucial to this representational strategy.

Samson, Judge of Israel, is a teller of riddles. On earth riddles and judgment reside together, and we are left with the necessity of inter-pretation. Only at the Second Coming, so the last book of the Bible promises, do judgment and revelation coincide. *Samson Agonistes* reflects on what the lack of such coinciding means for choosing to act or not to act. The echo of Milton's sonnet suggests it would probably have been better for Samson to choose the latter, but the play does not con-demn him for not waiting. In its representation of Samson's final ac-tion, the play is not merely open to interpretation; Samson's melancholy resolves interpretive uncertainty into perfect ambiguity. The "rouzing motions" that lead him to act may stem from suicidal despair, but they may stem from *enthusiasmos*. Melancholy allows, indeed sets the seal on, both possibilities.

Under melancholy's influence Samson is imprisoned by his own in-wardness, morbidly aware of his darkened consciousness. The play just hints that acute awareness of one's thought processes ("the great mat-ter in his mind") may also be the ground of inspiration. Formerly, in its grandeur, able to "explain" the mystery of creativity, the inspired trans-formation of unknowing to vision, melancholy under the new political and medical regime of the Restoration is reduced to making windy illu-sions. In polemical opposition to the prevailing opinion of his day, Milton fashions a Restoration tragedy for Samson the riddler which insists on the necessity of living with mystery, chief among them "the day and hour of Christ's coming."[52] Reading Samson as a type of the believer wait-ing for Revelation allows interpretive ambiguity to assume its rightful place not only in a reading of the play but also as the condition for all those who wait "in the middest."[53] Waiting, even until death from over-work at a mill, is probably better than rushing ahead to help God with his judgments, probably better than anticipating apocalypse. But only probably, for "rouzing motions" *may* be of God. To read Samson as a type of the self-sacrificial Christ (besides seeming to justify "incidental" slaughter) risks overriding the careful equivocation of the play. It also risks construing an author who is always supremely confident in his in-terpreting of divine inspiration and his voicing of God's judgment. It is to miss what *Samson Agonistes* extraordinarily allows us, the glimpse of a Milton who acknowledges that to claim certain revelation is, perhaps, to mistake – though to disclaim the *possibility* of revelation is certainly to mistake.

It is appropriate, then, that the Chorus's final image of Samson has something of the riddle about it. Unlike Satan, who is essentially untransformed by the explosive touch of Ithuriel's spear or indeed by the flames of hell, Samson is not a *failed* phoenix. Nor, however, can we read Samson-as-phoenix as an unproblematic figure of regeneration:

> So vertue giv'n for lost,
> Deprest, and overthrown, as seem'd,
> Like that self-begott'n bird
> In the *Arabian* woods embost,
> That no second knows nor third,
> And lay e're while a Holocaust,
> From out her ashie womb now teem'd,
> Revives, reflourishes, then vigorous most
> When most unactive deem'd,
> And though her body die, her fame survives,
> A secular bird ages of lives.   (*SA* 1697–1707)

Even images of resurrection and eternal life are subject to time's depredations: animal analogies, like every other mode of construing the natural world, were transformed over the course of the epistemological revolution of the seventeenth century. It is impossible to know when belief in the existence of a self-regenerating bird ceased, if such a belief ever flourished. But in an age when scientific natural history was developing apace, the growing certainty about the nonexistence of the phoenix began to matter. The Chorus's representation "knows" that the creature's ontological status has changed. In the passage just quoted, the body of the phoenix dies, but fame, rather than a new body, is born from it. This phoenix is "self-begott'n," but it is not "self-begetting." The poem thus validates and undermines the Chorus's moment of ecstatic vision: Samson is a phoenix, but a phoenix whose rising from the world's ashes can no longer be confidently predicted.

NOTES

1. Citations of Milton's poetry are from *The Riverside Milton*, ed. Roy Flannagan (Boston, 1998).
2. John Guillory, *Poetic Authority: Spenser, Milton, and Literary History* (New York, 1983), p. 170.
3. Although critical disagreement over the date of composition for *Samson Agonistes* remains unresolved, the weight of scholarly opinion tends toward a late date. My reading of the poem as being opposed to new Restoration

conceptions of melancholy makes this likely. For a recent and carefully measured summary of the arguments in favor of the poem's Restoration context, see Sharon Achinstein's chapter on *Samson Agonistes* in Thomas Corns (ed.), *A Companion to Milton* (Oxford, 2001), p. 412.

4. The phrase is from the prophetic section that concludes *Of Reformation* (1641), in which Milton sets out his belief in his poetic inspiration in the context of imminent apocalypse (*CP* 1: 616).

5. Henry More, *Enthusiasmus Triumphatus* (London, 1656), p. 2.

6. J. A. Simpson and E. D. S. Weiner (eds.), *Oxford English Dictionary* (2nd edn., Oxford, 1989), s.v. enthusiasm, sense 1.a.

7. See Aristotle, *Rhetoric*, III, 7; *Poetics* 17; and Plato, *Ion*, *Symposium*, and *Phaedrus*. For a detailed history of the classical and Renaissance tradition, see Michael Heyd, *"Be Sober and Reasonable": The Critique of Enthusiasm in the Seventeenth and Early Eighteenth Centuries* (Leiden, New York, and Köln, 1995), pp. 44–64.

8. Basil Clarke, *Mental Disorder in Early Modern Britain: Exploratory Studies* (Cardiff, 1975), traces with particular clarity the complex and ancient roots of Renaissance humoral theory in its relation to melancholy and other mental illness (pp. 16–23).

9. Robert Burton, *The Anatomy of Melancholy*, ed. Thomas C. Faulkner et al., 5 vols. to date (Oxford, 1989–), III:386–88 [III.4.1.3.].

10. Ibid., III:388 [III.4.1.3.].

11. Treatises on hypochondriacal melancholy were written between 1665 and 1672 by, among others, William Drage, Andre Du Laurens, Henry Stubbe, Thomas Willis, and Gideon Harvey.

12. See Burton, *The Anatomy of Melancholy*, I:374 [I.2.5.2.].

13. The term "hypochondria" has a complex history. By the mid-eighteenth century, "hypochondria" and "hypochondriasis" had begun to denote a neurotic obsession with bodily health and nonexistent or exaggerated ailments. Stanley Jackson describes this last stage as "the gradual separation of hypochondriasis from melancholia until the former was usually a syndrome of physical complaints and a non-psychotic depressed state." See *Melancholia and Depression from Hippocratic Times to Modern Times* (New Haven and London, 1986), p. 130. John F. Sena, "Melancholic Madness and the Puritans," *Harvard Theological Review* 66 (1973), pp. 293–309, provides a succinct account of changing medical (and political) attitudes toward hypochondriacal melancholy in the seventeenth and eighteenth centuries.

14. Burton, *The Anatomy of Melancholy*, I:378 [I.2.5.4.].

15. Sena, "Melancholic Madness," p. 296. By the eighteenth century, "the vapours" had become a synonym for hypochondria.

16. More, *Enthusiasmus Triumphatus*, p. 17. Temperamental melancholy was associated with black bile; melancholic disease, or "melancholy adust," resulted from the burning (or heating) or putrefying of humors, which caused black bile to become "adust" and produce fumes which harmed the brain.

17. Among those adopting More's approach were Joseph Glanvill, *A Loyal Tear Dropt on the Vault of Our Late Martyred Sovereign* (London, 1667), *The Way of Happiness* (London, 1670), and *Philosophia Pia* (London, 1671); Henry Hallywell, *An Account of Familism* (London, 1673); and George Rust, *A Discourse of the Use of Reason*, trans. Henry Hallywell (London, 1683). In *Wisdom Justified of Her Children, from the Ignorance and Calumny of H. Hallywell, in ... 'An Account of Familism'* ([London], 1673), William Penn responds to the charge that enthusiasm stems from hypochondriacal melancholy.

18. Glanvill, *A Loyal Tear*, pp. 27–28.

19. Ibid., p. 29.

20. Rust, *A Discourse of the Use of Reason*, pp. 32–33.

21. Raymond Waddington, "Melancholy Against Melancholy: *Samson Agonistes* as Renaissance Tragedy," in Joseph Wittreich (ed.), *Calm of Mind: Tercentenary Essays on* Paradise Regained *and* Samson Agonistes *in Honor of John S. Diekhoff* (Cleveland and London, 1971).

22. Thomas Willis, *De Anima Brutorum* (London, 1672), trans. Samuel Pordage as *Two Discourses Concerning the Soul of Brutes* [London, 1683] (Gainesville, 1971), p. 188.

23. Burton, *The Anatomy of Melancholy*, I:172 [I.2.1.1.].

24. Willis, *Two Discourses*, p. 192.

25. Ibid., pp. 188–91. Burton provides a useful definition of spirit: "a most subtile vapour, which is expressed from the *Blood*, & the instrument of the soule, to performe all his actions; a common type or *medium*, betwixt the body and the soule" (*The Anatomy of Melancholy*, I:141 [I.1.2.2.]).

26. Willis, *Two Discourses*, p. 188.

27. Ibid., p. 188. See Burton, *The Anatomy of Melancholy* I:162 [I.1.3.1.].

28. Willis, *Two Discourses*, p. 188.

29. Ibid., p. 193.

30. Ibid., p. 188.

31. "Il Penseroso" (l. 12). Milton's withholding of names as a poetic strategy – though not as a result of a changed cultural-discursive context – is discussed by John Leonard in *Naming in Paradise: Milton and the Language of Adam and Eve* (Oxford, 1990), pp. 86–146.

32. Waddington, "Melancholy Against Melancholy," p. 263, citing Raymond Klibansky, Erwin Panofsky, and Fritz Saxl, *Saturn and Melancholy: Studies in the History of Natural Philosophy, Religion and Art* (London, 1964), p. 302, n. 75, who describe a German engraving of 1644 representing melancholy "as a sleeping woman with head propped on hand, into whose brain a bat-winged demon is blowing delusions by means of bellows, the delusions being symbolised by swarming insects." The image also has relevance for the passage in *Paradise Lost*, Book 4, with which this essay began.

33. Edward Topsell, *The History of Four-Footed Beasts and Serpents and Insects*, 3 vols. [1658] (New York, 1967), III:756.

34. William Shakespeare, *Macbeth* III.ii.36, 35, in *The Riverside Shakespeare*, ed. G. Blakemore Evans et al. (Boston, 1974).

35. Burton, *Anatomy of Melancholy* I:389 (I.3.1.2.).
36. D. C. Allen, *The Harmonious Vision: Studies in Milton's Poetry*, enlarged edn. (1954; Baltimore and London, 1970), pp. 71–94. John Carey's introduction to *Samson Agonistes* in *Milton: Complete Shorter Poems* (2nd edn., London, 1997) provides a full bibliography of scholarship arguing for and against the regenerationist view (pp. 350–52).
37. Scholars such as Joseph Wittreich who oppose regenerationist readings of *Samson Agonistes* relegate the apocalyptic tone of his last act to Milton's representation of the delusional state. Hence, perhaps unwittingly, they echo More and Willis.
38. Those scholars who argue for Samson's relatively swift cure do not, of course, imply that it is easy. Waddington, refining Allen's approach, argues for Samson's two-steps-forward, one-step-back, progression. "In each encounter," he states, "there has been a cyclical pattern as Samson resists the destructive image with which he is presented, rises to a height of new illumination and resolution, then in reaction falls back into a depressed state" ("Melancholy Against Melancholy," p. 277). Nonetheless, the overall movement Waddington traces is toward restored health.
39. A. C. Hamilton et al. (eds.), *The Spenser Encyclopedia* (Toronto, 1990), p. 214.
40. Burton, *The Anatomy of Melancholy* II:1 (II.1.1.1.).
41. Willis, *Two Discourses*, p. 193.
42. Ibid., p. 193.
43. Milton's subjectivity in relation to *Samson Agonistes* has received important and sophisticated treatment in John Shawcross, *John Milton: The Self and the World* (Lexington, 1993), pp. 227–31; Ashraf Rushdy, *The Empty Garden: The Subject of Late Milton* (Pittsburgh and London, 1992), pp. 329–31, 397–99; and William Kerrigan, *The Sacred Complex: On the Psychogenesis of* Paradise Lost (Cambridge, Mass., and London, 1983), pp. 204–05.
44. See John F. Andrews, " 'Dearly Bought Revenge': *Samson Agonistes, Hamlet*, and Elizabethan Revenge Tragedy," *Milton Studies* 13 (1979), pp. 81–107.
45. Anna K. Nardo, *Milton's Sonnets and the Ideal Community* (Lincoln and London, 1979), p. 150.
46. "Only the Father knows the day and the hour of Christ's coming" (*CP* vi: 615).
47. The corresponding phrase in the "Argument," "perswaded inwardly that this was from God," similarly withholds judgment.
48. *CP* vi: 615, 618.
49. Joseph Wittreich, *Interpreting* Samson Agonistes (Princeton, 1986), p. 225, and Stanley Fish, "Question and Answer in *Samson Agonistes*," *Critical Quarterly* 2 (1969), pp. 237–64.
50. Wittreich, *Interpreting* Samson Agonistes, p. 231.
51. Hebrews 11:13.
52. *CP* vi: 615.
53. The phrase is Spenser's translation of *in medias res* in the letter to Raleigh explaining his intention in writing *The Faerie Queene*.

Afterword: "The time is come"

David Loewenstein

Milton's great poems offer multiple, divergent, and indeed sometimes conflicting visions of the apocalypse and the millennium. Many of the apocalyptic and millenarian responses to them have been richly explored from a range of critical perspectives in the preceding chapters of this book. Moreover, a number of chapters (for example, those by Barbara Lewalski, Stella Revard, Sarah Hutton, and Ken Simpson) convincingly show that while Milton may have remained officially silent after 1660, he never rejected radical millenarianism in the late poems, as previous scholars claimed (see the introduction to this book by Juliet Cummins). Recent historians, in any case, have challenged the view that English millenarianism was a shortlived and monolithic phenomenon (with a single view of the millennium) which first appeared in the tumultuous 1640s and 1650s, and have confirmed that millenarianism continued to flourish after the Restoration in both radical and more orthodox manifestations.[1] The millenarianism of Milton's late poems discussed in this book provides further evidence for this claim. In this short afterword I wish to suggest that the divergent and conflicting visions of the ends of time and Christ's kingdom are not, however, always reconciled in Milton's great poems. Rather, the multiple visions of the apocalypse and the millennium express the radical religious poet's conflicted and divergent responses to the religious politics of Restoration England.

The vision of the last days in *Paradise Lost* can register a sense of exultation, such as in the millennial passage which immediately follows the Father giving power to the Son (elevated by merit more than birthright) in Book 3. There the millennium is presented as a kind of triumphant providential masque: from the ashes of the burning world shall "spring":

> New heaven and Earth, wherein the just shall dwell
> And after all their tribulations long

> See golden days, fruitful of golden deeds,
> With joy and love triumphing, and fair truth.[2]
>
> (3.334–38)

This triumphant millennial vision imaginatively expresses Milton's radical politics, as even the "regal sceptre" – symbol of God's power and monarchy – will then be laid aside (3.340–41). Indeed, Milton's passage, with its promise that "the just" will see "golden days" after "all their tribulations long," has a polemical edge to it. It offers a countermillennial vision to the eschatological vision presented in the flood of royalist poems and tracts hailing Charles II as the messianic king whose miraculous return was to herald a restored golden age, a triumphant new era which would shed all the bitterness of the old; during the mid-1660s such millennial fervor reached new heights as the momentous year 1666 approached.[3]

Moreover, the ending of the War in Heaven in *Paradise Lost* can be seen as an apocalyptic fantasy of political and religious triumph which has its own polemical edge to it. There the Son of God, expressing the wrath of the Father and riding in his sublime apocalyptic chariot, astonishes the rebel angels and is victorious over them.[4] Despite fighting a "righteous cause" (6.804), God's loyal angels – or faithful "saints" as they are called in this holy warfare – have been humiliated and are "wearied" (6.695) after two days of cataclysmic battle. On the third day of the war, the warlike Son emerges as a terrifying figure – "His count'nance too severe to be beheld / And full of wrath bent on his enemies" (6.825–26) – as his holy anger is given visionary expression. Visions of holy anger, warfare, and triumph can be found, after the Restoration, in the apocalyptic writings and scriptural interpretations of Sir Henry Vane, the prominent godly republican admired by Milton: the Lord "shall Muster up his Heavenly Troops and take to himself his great Power, in which he shall begin to reign, by the executing of his Wrath and divine Vengeance upon his Enemies."[5] In the War in Heaven in *Paradise Lost*, it is the Son himself who embodies that apocalyptic wrath and power – and the subsequent glorious victory. Riding triumphant in his chariot after the expulsion of the rebel forces, the Son is met by "all his saints" (6.882): with its resonances of zealous Puritan warfare, this holy war ends in the triumph of the saints with the Son of God as "victorious king" (6.886). In the context of the dark days of the Restoration, this apocalyptic victory over the "godless" (6.811) enables Milton to dramatize a scenario in which the triumph of the saints, achieved by the fiery wrath of the Son, can be imagined with great potency. Yet this apocalyptic scenario is one of multiple, sometimes conflicting, visions of the apocalypse and millennium in the great poems.

In Book 12 of *Paradise Lost*, before Milton registers his vision of "New heavens, new earth" (12.549), the depiction of the "tribulations long" suffered by the "just" is unusually keen during the grim account of tragic postapostolic history. Whereas the millennial vision there finally offers some sense of dramatic release from the tribulations of human history, it cannot erase them, for Milton gives considerable narrative weight (from lines 507 to 539) to the harrowing prophecy of an ungodly world where those faithful few who follow "the Spirit within" suffer "heavy persecution." Without evoking particular contemporary radical groups or individual dissenters under siege, this final prophecy of "sharp tribulation" (11.63) nevertheless evokes the religious and political crisis of Restoration England when militant Anglicanism clashed with the religion of the Spirit:

> Whence heavy persecution shall arise
> On all who in the worship persevere
> Of spirit and truth; the rest, far greater part,
> Will deem in outward rites and specious forms
> Religion satisfied; truth shall retire
> Bestuck with slanderous darts . . .   (12.531–36)

The tension is acute between this account of truth retiring in the midst of "a world perverse" (11.701) and the vision of the millennium which immediately follows – "New heavens, new earth, ages of endless date / Founded in righteousness and peace and love / To bring forth fruits, joy and eternal bliss" (12.549–51) – with its emphasis on a purged and refined creation.[6] As in *Lycidas*, where conflicting emotional responses are juxtaposed and allowed to coexist (intense feelings of loss, doubt, and angry apocalyptic protest along with a vision of triumph), so here, near the end of *Paradise Lost*, Milton juxtaposes the poem's bleakest account of postlapsarian history with a vision of the millennium and its promise of "joy and eternal bliss." The postapostolic historical narrative in *Paradise Lost* expresses the poet's powerfully conflicted responses – including expressions of defeat, withdrawal, polemical defiance, and the need for millennial renewal – to a "perverted" Restoration world where "works of faith / Rarely be found" (12.547, 536–37).

Milton's 1671 volume is notably open-ended in its inclusion of both apocalyptic and millenarian visions. It is important to see how Milton's last major spiritual poems – one whose story is rooted in the violent world of the Old Testament and the other which reimagines the spiritual battle between Jesus and Satan in the wilderness of the New Testament – enabled the visionary poet to register divergent responses to the political and spiritual crisis of the Restoration. Milton's drama ends on a note of apocalyptic vengeance and destruction; its companion poem, his brief epic, is more closely aligned, at moments, with visions of the millennium. *Samson Agonistes* is not a millennial drama in the sense of offering a vision of the millennium – of "New heavens, new earth" (*PL* 12.549) – after the devastating apocalyptic destruction of its ending. Milton explicitly signals the importance of *Samson*'s apocalypticism by citing in its introduction David Pareus's immense commentary on the Book of Revelation, a commentary which depicts the Apocalypse as "a *Propheticall Drama*, show, or representation"; as tragic ("the forme of this Prophesie is truely Tragicall"); and as highly relevant to the present ("this Booke . . . containe[s] very profitable and necessary Doctrines, especially for this last age"), including, as Milton would have devised, that of Restoration England, a world of "idol-worship" "Where outward force constrain[ed]" (*SA* 1365, 1369) the consciences of the persecuted godly.[7] The apocalyptic interpretation of Pareus, however, did not offer a millenarian prophecy based on Revelation; but neither, in its own way, does the "*Propheticall Drama*" of *Samson Agonistes*.[8]

Samson Agonistes is an apocalyptic drama whose representation of apocalypse is particularly terrifying. Moved by "Some rousing motions" – the Spirit acting within him – Samson scorns, as Milton does in his polemical prose, the "well-feasted priest . . . soonest fired / With zeal" (1382, 1419–20) as the blind Hebrew is led off to the idolatrous Philistine temple.[9] Within the Philistine temple Samson tugs the "two massy pillars / With horrible convulsion to and fro" so that the structure collapses "with burst of thunder" (1648–49, 1651) and wipes out the Philistine aristocracy. Manoa describes a "hideous noise" (1509) and the frightened Messenger at the end reports on the "horrid spectacle" (1542) of destruction which God's power has manifested through Samson's sudden and overwhelming act: it has desolated "a hostile city" (1561), turning it and the idolatrous temple of worship into a "place of horror" (1550). The God of *Samson Agonistes* is a God of terror and dread – the Semichorus refer to him as "our living dread" (1673).[10] He contributes, moreover, to the horrid apocalyptic spectacle and catastrophe: among the Philistines "Drunk with idolatry, drunk with wine," "he a spirit of frenzy sent" (1670, 1675), while Samson also performs in the apocalyptic drama something of his "own accord" (1643). Milton believed that hating "the enemies of God or the church" was nothing less than a "religious duty" and that "we are not forbidden to take or wish to take vengeance upon the enemies of the church"; the apocalyptic ending of *Samson Agonistes* enacts – one last time in the poet's career – that vision in a terrifying manner.[11] To be sure, that vision of apocalyptic vengeance is complicated in the tragic drama by Milton's powerful depiction of Samson's anguish, self-reproach, despair, and rage as he labors in his mind and body.

A spiritual poem about the faithful waiting for "due time," *Paradise Regained* does, however, give millenarian themes – especially the conflict between the kingdom of Christ and glorious worldly monarchies – new resonance and urgency in the Restoration when the radical godly were "brought lower than ever, and [were] in greater danger...than ever."[12] The Conventicle Act of 1670, issued the year before Milton published his 1671 volume and banning groups of people meeting for religious worship outside Church of England services, was perhaps the most vicious of the new penal laws against dissenters; its penalties (including heavy fines), its empowerment of a solitary justice to convict on confession, and its invitation to would-be informants to spy on nonconformists aimed to provide "further and more speedy remedie against the growing and dangerous practices of seditious sectaries and other disloyal persons."[13] Radical nonconformists, especially groups such as the Quakers and Baptists, were put on the defensive as they faced national waves of persecution.[14]

In this context the anguished speeches of the perplexed faithful in *Paradise Regained* take on new and urgent meaning. Thus the humble followers of John the Baptist and two disciples of Jesus, Andrew and Simon, express their perplexity as they appeal to the "God of Israel" for deliverance at the beginning of Book 2:

> Send thy Messiah forth, the time is come;
> Behold the kings of the earth how they oppress
> Thy chosen, to what highth their power unjust
> They have exalted, and behind them cast
> All fear of thee, arise and vindicate
> Thy glory, free thy people from their yoke,
> But let us wait.   (2.43–49)

"The time is come": the yearning for God's Messiah among the dissenting godly and suffering saints could still be keenly expressed in the midst of the hard trials and hostile wilderness which they associated with the world of Restoration England. The prominent radical Puritan Henry

Vane persisted in his faith in the advent of the millennium and the destruction of Antichrist, and thus he seemed dangerous to Charles II and his advisors.[15] Imprisoned and facing execution in 1662, Vane would not relinquish his vision of "the thousand years Reign of Christ on Earth" when Satan's earthly reign would end and there would be "no more beastly Government."[16]

Despite being "fully tried / Through all temptation" (1.4–5), the solitary, inward-looking Jesus of *Paradise Regained* remains "unmoved" (3.386, 4.109) as he asserts that his time "is not yet come" (3.397); in this imaginative portrait of Jesus, who is led by a "strong motion" into the wilderness (1.290ff) and who patiently perseveres through trials and temptations, Milton has created a model for unseduced, unshaken radical Puritan saints in the uncertain world of Restoration England.[17] Jesus, who prefers overcoming the forces of Antichrist by "winning words" (1.222), may eschew achieving revolutionary ends by violent means ("the stubborn only to subdue" [1.226]), but he defiantly envisions a time in the future when he will indeed fulfill his future millennial role and end Satan's earthly reign:

> Know therefore when my season comes to sit
> On David's throne, it shall be like a tree
> Spreading and overshadowing all the earth,
> Or as a stone that shall to pieces dash
> All monarchies besides throughout the world,
> And of my kingdom there shall be no end.
>
> (4.146–51)

In her contribution to this book, Stella Revard rightly considers this passage, with its language and images derived from prophecies in the book of Daniel, as an expression of Milton's ongoing millenarianism after the Restoration.[18] So it was, we might add, for the unrepentant radical millennialist Henry Vane: the great metal image smashed in Nebuchadnezzar's dream (Dan. 2:31–35) was "the prophetical Image of worldly Monarchy," Vane wrote, as he depicted "the thousand years Reign of Christ to spring up, in that Kingdome of his that shall never end."[19] Milton's potent vision of Jesus' "everlasting kingdom" (3.199), though that kingdom might not come soon (as Barbara Lewalski and Stella Revard remind us),[20] would thus nonetheless have resonated for persecuted radical dissenters who, faced with severe persecution and political uncertainty, still had not given up on Christ's reign and a kingdom set up by God "which shall never be destroyed" and which "shall break in pieces and consume" all worldly kingdoms (Dan. 2:44).

"I shall reign past thy preventing" (4.492), the Son of God tells his adversary after remaining unshaken in "the vexed wilderness" (4.416) by Satan's terrifying storm of apocalyptic dimensions in which "tallest pines, / ... and sturdiest oaks / Bowed their stiff necks, loaden with stormy blasts" (4.416–18). In his account of the besieged Quakers during the early 1670s, Milton's student and friend Thomas Ellwood describes several "storm[s] of persecution" raised by Satan: the dark period of the 1670 Conventicle Act was a particularly "stormy time," Ellwood recalls, since "[t]he clouds had been long gathering and threatening a tempest."[21] As Milton's spiritually inward Jesus himself recognizes about his messianic career, he must endure "many a hard assay" – including "injuries, insults, / Contempts, and scorns, and snares, and violence" – before he can attain "the promised kingdom" (1.264–65, 3.190–91) and victory at the Last Day: and that he could do so "neither ... disheartened or dismayed" (1.268) – remaining "unappalled" in the midst of "a dismal night" (4.425, 452) – offered a powerful scriptural model for radical dissenters under a state of siege during the Restoration.[22]

The fact that Milton published *Samson Agonistes* with *Paradise Regained* suggests the poet's desire to depict, within this one volume, a double-edged response to the crisis of the Restoration. The vision of spectacular apocalyptic destruction in *Samson Agonistes* is juxtaposed with the millenarian vision offered in *Paradise Regained*. Because they coexist, they express alternative visionary responses; there is no need, I believe, to see one response as negating the other. These visions enabled the poet to articulate divergent or alternative eschatological responses, yet ones which are not necessarily incompatible: the comparison of Jesus to Daniel's "stone that shall to pieces dash / All monarchies besides throughout the world" recalls the Miltonic Samson as a mighty apocalyptic force dashing to pieces the temple of Dagon. No doubt the vision of apocalyptic vengeance retained great potency for the radical religious poet during the dark days of the Restoration; but so would those moments of millennial vision in *Paradise Regained* when the prophecy of Christ's everlasting kingdom and of dashing worldly monarchies to pieces would have resonated with the visions of radical dissenters. During the Restoration Anglicans still feared that the nexus of republicanism and dissent threatened the foundations of the traditional church and state.[23] The poems of Milton's 1671 volume, with their combination of apocalyptic and millennial visions, enabled the poet to imagine, in a double-edged way, how those foundations might yet be dashed to pieces.

NOTES

1. See, for example, William M. Lamont, *Richard Baxter and the Millennium* (Totowa, N.J., 1979); Bryan W. Ball, *A Great Expectation: Eschatological Thought in English Protestantism to 1660* (Leiden, 1975); Frank E. Manuel, *The Religion of Isaac Newton* (Oxford, 1974); Richard L. Greaves, *Enemies under His Feet: Radicals and Nonconformists in Britain, 1664–1677* (Stanford, 1990), p. 4; David S. Katz and Richard H. Popkin, *Messianic Revolution: Radical Religious Politics to the End of the Second Millennium* (New York, 1999), chapters 3 and 4; and Richard W. Cogley, "Seventeenth-Century English Millenarianism," *Religion* 17 (1987), pp. 379–96. For the association of Restoration millenarianism with the crown and established church, see B. S. Capp, "The Political Dimension of Apocalyptic Thought," in C. A. Patrides and Joseph Wittreich (eds.), *The Apocalypse in English Renaissance Thought and Literature: Patterns, Antecedents and Repercussions* (Manchester, 1984), p. 117.

2. Milton's poems are quoted from *Complete Shorter Poems*, ed. John Carey (2nd edn., London, 1997), and *Paradise Lost*, ed. Alastair Fowler (2nd edn., London, 1998).

3. See Michael McKeon, *Politics and Poetry in Restoration England* (Cambridge, Mass., 1975), especially chapter 8, with a wealth of examples illustrating royalist eschatology; and Capp, "The Political Dimension," p. 117.

4. For its visionary dimensions, see Michael Lieb, "Milton's 'Chariot of Paternal Deitie' as Reformation Conceit," *Journal of Religion* 65 (1985), pp. 359–77.

5. *An Epistle General, to the Mystical Body of Christ on Earth, The Church Universal in Babylon*, ([London], 1662), p. 56.

6. For an account of this millennial transformation and purging in terms of material transmutation in the poem, see chapter 9 in this book by Juliet Cummins; see also Lewalski, "Milton and the Millennium," p. 22.

7. David Pareus, *A Commentary upon the Divine Revelation of the Apostle and Evangelist John*, trans. Elias Arnold (Amsterdam, 1644), pp. 20, 26, 15.

8. See Pareus, *A Commentary*, title page, and pp. 506–11 (disputing the millenarianism of Thomas Brightman's exposition of Revelation), 514ff. For Pareus opposing a millennial vision, see Paul Christianson, *Reformers and Babylon: English Apocalyptic Visions From the Reformation to the Eve of the Civil War* (Toronto, 1978), p. 106; Ball, *A Great Expectation*, p. 160.

9. For the gluttony of prelates feeding fat upon the foolish people, see, for example, *CP* I: 792, III: 241. For preaching "thir own bellies" and the affected zeal of their pulpits, see, for example, *CP* V: 449.

10. Michael Lieb, " 'Our Living Dread': The God of *Samson Agonistes*," *Milton Studies* 33 (1996), pp. 3–25.

11. *On Christian Doctrine*, *CP* VI: 743, 755. For apocalyptic themes in the drama, see also Barbara K. Lewalski, "*Samson Agonistes* and the 'Tragedy' of the Apocalypse," *PMLA* 85 (1970), pp. 1050–62.

12. I quote from Isaac Penington the Younger's *Concerning Persecution* (1661), in *The Works of the Long-Mournful and Sorely Distressed Isaac Penington* (London, 1681), Part I, p. 344. For Milton's respect for Penington, see Thomas Ellwood, *The History of the Life of Thomas Ellwood*, ed. C. G. Crump (London, 1900), p. 89.

13. J. P. Kenyon (ed.), *The Stuart Constitution: Documents and Commentary* (2nd edn., Cambridge, 1986), p. 356; Anthony Fletcher, "The Enforcement of the Conventicle Acts, 1664–1679," in W. J. Sheils (ed.), *Persecution and Toleration, Studies in Church History* 21, (Oxford), pp. 236, 239, 246; Greaves, *Enemies under His Feet*, pp. 154–55. See also Ellwood, *The Life of Thomas Ellwood*, pp. 168–71, and Ken Simpson's chapter in this book.

14. As Ellwood observes, "the brunt of the storm fell most sharply on the people called Quakers." See *The Life of Thomas Ellwood*, p. 170.

15. George Sikes, *The Life and Death of Sir Henry Vane, Knight* (London, 1662), and Violet A. Rowe, *Sir Henry Vane the Younger: A Study in Political and Administrative History* (London, 1970).

16. Henry Vane, *The Face of the Times* ([London], 1662), p. 71.

17. See my book *Representing Revolution in Milton and His Contemporaries: Religion, Politics, and Polemics in Radical Puritanism* (Cambridge, 2001), chapter 8.

18. See pp. 67–68.

19. Vane, *The Face of the Times*, pp. 68, 73.

20. See pp. 22 and 70, and *De Doctrina Christiana*: "Christ will be slow to come" (*CP* VI: 618). See also John Shawcross's account of Milton and an imminent millennium in chapter 6 in this book, and Ken Simpson's chapter, p. 209.

21. Ellwood, *The Life of Thomas Ellwood*, pp. 186, 169.

22. For the poem's implications for dissenters during the Restoration, see also Laura Knoppers, *Historicizing Milton: Spectacle, Power, and Poetry in Restoration England* (Athens, Ga., 1994), chapter 5, especially p. 141; my study *Representing Revolution*, chapter 8; and Ken Simpson's chapter in this book.

23. For Anglican insecurity and fears, see Fletcher, "The Enforcement of the Conventicle Acts"; Jonathan Scott, *England's Troubles: Seventeenth-Century English Political Instability in European Context* (Cambridge, 2000), pp. 393–94, 425–27. For the vitality of radical and nonconformist opposition to the restored Stuart regime, see also Greaves, *Enemies under His Feet*.

Index